Silke Ellenbeck

A Soul Fc

Volume 1: From R

188

A Historical Biographical Novel of Princess Alice of Greece,
née Battenberg,
Mother of Prince Philip, Duke of Edinburgh

DeBehr

Publisher: @Verlag DeBehr, Radeberg
www.debehr.de
First edition: 2025
ISBN: 9783987274497

Foreword

As a historian and author, I have been researching the history of the German aristocracy and its connections through marriage to European imperial and royal houses for more than twenty-five years. In my research, particularly on the last tsarist family around Tsar Nicholas II and his wife Tsarina Alexandra, née Princess of Hesse and by Rhine, I have always been struck by the fates of individual princes and princesses. The Russian tsar's family cultivated family ties to Hesse through the marriage of princesses, and over the decades these ties were strengthened.

As the research for my biography of Grand Duchess Maria Nikolaevna, third daughter of the last Tsar of Russia, which was published in 2015, required me to take a close look at the House of Hesse, I came across the fate of Princess Alice of Battenberg, later Princess of Greece and mother of Prince Philip of Edinburgh, who in turn would later become Prince Consort to Queen Elizabeth II of England.

Alice was born in England in 1885 as the great-granddaughter of Queen Victoria. She was deaf from birth and, thanks to the efforts of her family, learned to lip-read in several languages and to speak at a level adapted to her disability. Through her marriage to Prince Andrew of Greece in 1903, she became a member of the Greek royal family.

With the beginning of the First World War and the subsequent collapse of the political influence of the aristocracy due to the collapse of the monarchies in Europe, her perfect world, her family and not least her aristocratic standard of living also fell apart. Due to the political unrest in Greece, Alice and her family had to leave the country. They tried to make a fresh start in exile in Paris, but life in exile took its toll on the princess's mental health and she was forced into a sanatorium at the instigation of her husband and mother. She was treated by Dr. Sigmund Freud and Dr. Ernst Simmel, among others.

Her youngest child Prince Philip and his sisters were deliberately not present at the violent removal of their mother, and this separation marked the end of Alice's intact family. Throughout her life, the relationship between mother, son and sisters was strained as a result.

Added to this were marital problems, which led to a separation between Alice and her husband. Nevertheless, the princess tried to build her own life again, returned to Greece after her mental recovery and became involved in the resistance against the Nazi occupation by saving a Jewish family from deportation.

Later in life, she converted to the Orthodox faith and became a nun in a specially founded order. Helping other people who were in need, whatever the

circumstances of their lives, became a need and a goal in her life.
It was only in the last years of her life that she became close to her son again, so that she spent the rest of her life near his family in England.
In this biography, I would like to pay tribute to this impressive personality and give a voice to a princess who has gone largely unnoticed by history. In order to express her point of view more clearly, I have chosen a personal narrative style.
But let's let Alice herself have her say ...

The author, June 2025

"Man was created for this purpose alone: To teach that whoever destroys a single soul destroys the whole world. And whoever saves a single soul saves the whole world ..."
(Jerusalem Talmud, Excerpt: Sanhedrin, 23a-b)

"For Alice...to an uncommon woman."

A Soul Forged in Silence

Silke Ellenbeck

The new Hessian line of the Battenbergs - my father's family

From 1830 until his death in 1848, Grand Duke Ludwig II of Hesse and by Rhine ruled the Grand Duchy, which until then had had no particular political significance. The first student unrest and uprisings, the fluid transition between *the Vormärz* and attempted revolution, only began in the year of his death and the foundation of a united empire, the end of the German *petty statehood*, was still a long way off.

Ludwig was married to Princess Wilhelmine of Baden. She bore her husband seven children, one of whom died shortly after birth, but the couple's marriage was anything but happy. Wilhelmine used her husband's financial means to have a retreat built for herself on the Heiligenberg so that she could escape the court.

The two sons, Hereditary Grand Duke Ludwig, to whom his father handed over the reins of government before his death when the first unrest broke out in the country because he did not feel up to it, and Prince Karl were almost certainly descendants of the Grand Duke. The deceased daughter was also his biological child.

However, the children born after him, his daughter Princess Elisabeth, born in 1821, Prince Alexander, born in 1823, and Princess Marie, who was born in 1824, were actually the result of his wife's liaison with the Grand Duke's chief equerry August Ludwig von Senarclens-Grancy. At first it was only a rumor, but this can be confirmed by the fact that the Grand Duke did not have any intimate contact with his wife in those years and she kept her lover close to her retreat so that he was always close by. The Grand Duke recognized the children as his own, but rumours swirled in the Grand Duchy as to what had happened to the children throughout their lives.

In 1826, Wilhelmine had to cope with the death of her daughter Elisabeth from scarlet fever and had a mausoleum built for her on Rosenhöhe instead of having her buried in the grand ducal crypt in the town church in Darmstadt in accordance with tradition. She thus established, no doubt unintentionally, the future burial place of the family of Hesse and by Rhine, even though the Rosenhöhe had previously been a popular summer residence for the family and was now converted into a cemetery, much to the displeasure of the Grand Duke. The Grand Duchess finally followed her young daughter in 1836 after contracting typhoid fever.

In 1839, the Russian Tsarevich Alexander Nikolayevich, who later became Tsar Alexander II of Russia, went on the hunt for a bride in Europe. He first tried to court Queen Victoria of England, whose uncle King Leopold of

Belgium was already trying to arrange a marriage between her and Prince Albert of Saxe-Coburg and Gotha. His persistence in this matter was to end in the marriage of Albert and Victoria.
When the Tsarevich traveled on to Hesse to pay a visit to his relatives, as Luise, a sister of Grand Duchess Wilhelmine, had been the wife of Tsar Alexander I of Russia as Tsarina Elisabeth, he met Princess Marie, who was just fourteen years old. He fell in love with her at first sight. Their love could not be clouded by the fact that Marie's illegitimate origins were an open secret. As she was in very fragile health at the time, the couple were only able to get engaged in 1840, with the wedding following in 1841.
Prince Alexander of Hesse accompanied his sister when she moved to St. Petersburg. His presence was not to do the young bride any good, as she immediately fell ill due to the cold climate, recovered only with difficulty and did not really feel welcome at the great Tsar's court, as her mother-in-law, a Princess of Prussia by birth, openly flaunted her contempt for the small and, in her view, insignificant Grand Duchy of Hesse. In addition, rumors about the questionable descent of the Hessian princess and her brother had reached the European aristocratic courts and the situation threatened to escalate in St. Petersburg. Alexander intervened, noting that he and his sister bore the name of their father, the Grand Duke, with pride and that no one could prove otherwise. The Russian court was a prestigious one among the European courts at the time - ostentatious, with strict labels, French court language and, how could it be otherwise, amidst this splendor of grand, festive balls and pomp, also a breeding ground for rumors and intrigue.
Although Alexander received important posts in the Russian military from his brother-in-law, it was above all his passion for excessive alcohol consumption, debauched parties, gambling and beautiful women that influenced his life. He fell in love with his brother-in-law's sister, the Grand Duchess Olga, known as *Olly*, and yet he knew that she was promised to the son of the King of Württemberg. Olly, for her part, therefore did not return his advances.
When uprisings broke out in the Caucasus in 1845, led by the Muslim fanatic Shamyl, Alexander volunteered to put down the uprisings with the troops sent. In doing so, he showed great courage and earned much recognition, as every soldier knew that prisoners on both sides were only taken in order to torture them in a cruel manner and then return their lifeless, violated bodies to the enemy. But Alexander proved successful. During the retreat of the defeated rebels, he captured a copy of the Koran, which turned out to be that of Shamyl . It was his 'booty', which he was able to present to the tsar. He returned the favor with the highest military honors. Thanks to his military education in Hesse, Alexander enjoyed fighting and was skilled with the sword, the pistol and on horseback.

He was also to prove his worth in the Crimean War between 1853 and 1856.

Alexander told his brother-in-law that it was worth a lot for a soldier to often look into the face of death, because that was the only way to earn the right to wear a uniform.
But even though he proved himself in the military, he suffered from a broken heart and continued to indulge in an excessively extravagant lifestyle. He was sent back to Darmstadt to give him some distance from this lifestyle.
Princess Louise of Mecklenburg-Schwerin was offered to him as a bride. *Vivi*, as she was called, seemed to be a good match, but Alexander refused to marry her and traveled back to Russia, where his brother-in-law read him the riot act, causing him to change his lifestyle in 1848. He cut down on his womanizing, rarely drank and gave up gambling.
He eventually fell in love with Countess Sophie Shuvaloff and made advances to her, which she reciprocated, but her mother was very skeptical about the relationship, as she knew Alexander's previous busy life like everyone else at court. The thought that he might break her daughter's heart moved her to take a step that would involuntarily establish the new line of the House of Hesse, the Battenbergs.
At a ball in January 1848, Countess Sophie's mother sent a message to the prince saying that if he danced the next mazurka with her daughter, she would take her home immediately. She chose a lady-in-waiting of the prince's sister, Julie von Hauke, to deliver the message. As Julie stood in front of the prince to deliver the countess's harsh words, he immediately took hold of the young woman and danced the next dance with her, to the utter surprise of the countess and her daughter. This dance marked the beginning of their love, although Julie initially fell head over heels in love with the prince, who then only hesitantly sought her company. He had lost his heart to the countess's daughter, and both soon used Julie as the bearer of their love letters; she also organized secret meetings between the two. Sophie's parents soon became aware of this and decided to send their daughter to relatives for a while, so Marie asked her brother to make it clear to the young woman that everything was over so that she would not grieve too much for him in the distance and could put the affair behind her. Alexander sensed the true sender of this request, the tsar, and so he complied, which was a very difficult step for him to take. The tsar then asked him to finally marry in order to find peace. He recommended the Grand Duchess Catherine Michaelovna, his niece.
As with most princes of the Hessian line, the period in which they sowed their wild oats was very long, but afterwards they themselves longed for a haven of peace in their lives.
Alexander finally took notice of Julie, even though she was so different from

the women at court. She was not particularly beautiful, not one of those French-looking, pompously dressed ladies, she had black hair, brown eyes and was only 157 cm tall. Nevertheless, she was intelligent, educated and cordial, so that the two soon began to meet in secret and write love letters to each other. If the tsar had found out about the affair with a lady-in-waiting of his daughter-in-law, the future tsarina, everything would have been stopped immediately on the highest orders.
One day, however, Tsar Nicholas I took a shortcut on his way to the rabbit warren in the Winter Palace and came across the couple in love. It was said that his anger at this discovery lasted for many days. He immediately ordered the relationship to end and Julie had to leave the court. Neither was to see each other again, but Alexander was just as heartbroken as Julie and asked to be released from all military obligations for an indefinite period. The Tsar agreed and Alexander immediately traveled back to Hesse.
The year 1848 was quite a striking one in Europe, as another revolution had broken out in France, in the course of which the imperial family had to leave the country, the Foreign Minister Metternich had been overthrown in Vienna and the offshoots of the March Revolution there soon reached Berlin and the other states of the German Confederation, as well as Hesse, where a bourgeois desire for reform had long been smouldering anyway. This political unrest placed an additional burden on Alexander, as his father died soon afterwards and his brother was already ruling the Grand Duchy as co-regent. The new Grand Duke Louis III had seemed to his father to be more suited to quelling the unrest, but from Alexander's point of view his brother was by no means a capable man. So in 1850 he traveled to Paris and then to London to seek distraction. Both cities seemed more cosmopolitan and modern to him, but he could not forget Julie.

During his stay in London, Prince Alexander visited the editorial offices of The *Times* and its printing plant with its huge machinery. After talking to the editors, he was particularly impressed by how freely the daily newspaper was allowed to report on the British royal family. The everyday private life of the Queen, her husband and her family was often a topic in the newspaper, which surprised Alexander not a little. Such a thing would have been unthinkable in Russia. At the same time, however, it brought them closer to the people, for example how private parties, birthdays or holidays were celebrated. Everyone in England was able to gain an insight into the Queen's life. It had such a great effect on the prince's future life plans that he now wanted to continue his life in England.
When Alexander returned to Russia in 1851, he had made up his mind and Julie was immediately ready to follow him wherever he went. However, Julie

was not in keeping with his status and the Tsar did not approve of the relationship, nor did Alexander's brother in Hesse. The Grand Duke wrote a letter to his brother in which he warned him not to enter into such an inappropriate liaison. But Julie was so full of joy that she could not contain herself. The news of her relationship with the prince spread like wildfire around the court. The Tsar demanded a clarifying conversation with Alexander when he asked for Julie's hand in marriage, told him to come to his senses and threatened to strip him of all military titles and decorations. At the age of just twenty, the tsar had appointed him a major-general and opened up all military opportunities to him, and yet Alexander refused to give in. In a romantic way, he professed his love for Julie, they became engaged and at the beginning of October 1851, after weeks of arguments with the Tsar, who wanted to expel him from court, Alexander and Julie fled to Warsaw at night in a carriage. There they enjoyed their days together and continued their journey to Wroclaw at the end of October. Alexander married her quietly and without telling her relatives. There were no more friends, no more titles, no more home, all ties were severed, there was only them as a couple - finally united. In the early days, they were now *personae non gratae*, both at the Hessian and the Tsar's court. Alexander had been dishonorably discharged from the army, both had been banished from Russia by the Tsar and Alexander had tarnished the good name of the House of Hesse for his brother.
The reason for all this lay in Julie's origins. She was born Julia von Hauke in Warsaw in 1825. Her great-grandfather came from Mainz, also lived in Wetzlar for a time and had been appointed secretary to Count Brühl of Saxony in Dresden, then to Poland. When he returned to Germany in his old age, one son remained in Poland. His great-grandfather and grandfather had already held important military posts. Hans Moritz Hauke was a professional soldier and rose to become Minister of War of *Congress Poland* when Poland was incorporated into the states of Russia and Prussia. He fought in Napoleon's army and also in the army of the Duchy of Warsaw, including in Austria.
In 1826, he and two of his brothers were awarded the hereditary Polish title *of von for* their military merits. To give his name an aristocratic ring, Hans Moritz changed his actual surname *Hawke to von Hauke*. Tsar Nicholas I appointed him All-Russian Minister of War in 1829 and elevated him to the rank of Count.
In 1830, there were uprisings in Warsaw and von Hauke saw it as his duty to rush to the aid of the Governor General, Grand Duke Konstantin. Von Hauke rode alongside the carriage of his wife and two daughters from his official residence in the so-called *Saxon Palace* to *Belvedere* Palace, the residence of the Grand Duke, where he encountered revolting cadets, whom he ordered to return to their barracks. The cadets opened fire as von Hauke gave them a

sermon. He was hit by nineteen bullets and died on the spot. Julie and her sister Sophie Salomea witnessed the murder of their father, both traumatized by the incident, as was their mother, who died of heart failure in 1831.
The two daughters now became wards of the tsar. Their brothers were not as loyal to the tsar as their father and two of them soon emigrated to the USA, two died as soldiers and one sister was already married.
From then on, Julia was only called Julie, as she wrote her letters in the French court language and signed them with the French form of her name. She became lady-in-waiting to Alexander's sister and was only twenty-three years old when she met him. She spoke fluent German without an accent, was very well read and could also converse eloquently in Russian, Polish and French. But she was an orphan who saw Alexander as her social savior. And her flaw lay in the fact that she was the daughter of a newly ennobled count and the marriage was therefore a *morganatic* or *left-hand marriage*, as the bride was of a lower rank than her husband.
When they finally tied the knot, Julie was already five months pregnant with their daughter Marie Karoline. Without money, the couple's future looked more than bleak.
Julie needed a name so that she could gain prestige among the European nobility, as the young couple were downright terrorized by relatives and other royal houses with bitterly angry letters due to their improper marriage.
Alexander felt compelled to ask his brother to confer a title befitting his status on his wife and he finally agreed after learning of the letters that had just reached the couple from England. He awarded Julie the title of *Countess of Battenberg*, which was no longer in use at the time. Battenberg was the former title of a dynasty of counts that had already died out in 1310, and was also the name of a small town in Hesse, after which the dynasty named itself.
In 1858, the Grand Duke elevated Julie to the rank of *Princess of Battenberg*. Alexander was thus also transformed from a Prince of Hesse and by Rhine into a Prince of Battenberg and a new line of the House of Hesse was established. The only fly in the ointment was the fact that this line and its descendants had no claim to the throne of Hesse.
This love story of my father's parents was always a romantic myth in our family and always reminded me of a dramatic romance novel, but here the fiction became reality.
In February 1852, little Princess Marie Karoline was born in Strasbourg. Alexander and Julie first retired to a small hotel in Geneva, then rented a villa in Strasbourg. Alexander was given a military post as colonel of a brigade in 1853, as the Austrian imperial family was somewhat lenient with such faux pas in matters of love. Archduke Johann, the emperor's uncle, had entered into a relationship with the daughter of a postmaster. The problems of an

improper marriage were therefore well known.
The emperor transferred Alexander to Graz, where he could live with his family away from the gossip of the Viennese court. The emperor's uncle also lived there, so there were two *black sheep* in the town.
My father Ludwig Alexander was born in Graz in 1854.
However, as my grandfather was not Austrian and still held a prestigious position in the military, he always had problems with other Austrian soldiers and officers. So he had himself transferred to Italy for a short time. His second son, my uncle Alexander Joseph, called *Sandro*, was born in Verona, followed by his brother Heinrich Moritz in Milan in 1858. They were followed by the birth of the youngest and last son, Prince Franz Joseph, *called Franzjos*, whose godfather became the Emperor of Austria. Due to the fact that certain first names were always repeated in aristocratic families, and to ensure that people could be distinguished from one another, nicknames were usually essential. My father and his brother Heinrich grew up with Italian nannies who called them *Alessandro* and *Enrico*. Over the years, this became *Sandro* and *Liko*. These nicknames stuck in our family.
In the fall of 1861, the new Tsar Alexander II of Russia offered Grandfather a pension for his previous services to the Russian military, perhaps also following the intervention of his wife Marie, Alexander's sister.
In 1862, the family moved to Darmstadt with their entire household and servants after Alexander resigned from his service with the Austrian Emperor.
From then on, the family's permanent residence was the *Alexander Palace* in Darmstadt, built by Alexander, and summers were spent at *Heiligenberg Palace*, just south of Darmstadt.
From this point on, Julie and Alexander settled down. They had property, a good income and were able to pass the time by going to the theater, ballet and opera. While Julie enjoyed her now more prestigious life in Darmstadt, enjoyed attending balls and needed some distance from everything she had experienced, her husband passed the time painting, collecting coins, reading or spending time with the children.

Julie, the grandmother, had seen and experienced so much in her previous life that these difficult times had perhaps also made her a little tough. She spent very little time with her children and her daughter Marie Karoline, who would one day write down and publish her memoirs, characterized her mother as not exactly a tender, loving woman, which was often a topic of conversation between her and her brothers. She had finally found recognition, which she now wanted to savor accordingly. She was therefore only too happy to take part in social engagements. During the summer months at Heiligenberg Castle in Jugenheim, the children soon felt most at home, as this was where they

celebrated large family gatherings, balls, concerts and enjoyed the charming countryside.
My father was eight years old when his family returned to Darmstadt. He was a tall boy, friendly, well-mannered and loved to dress up in a Russian costume for festivities - a blue silk shirt with long sleeves, shorts made of the same fabric, a silver belt and a hat with peacock feathers, topped off with red boots. Even at this young age, he wore this costume like a uniform.

Little Ludwig idolized his father for his military career.
The children spoke German with each other, but the grandmother only spoke French with them. It was an essential part of the children's upbringing that they learned several languages. At the age of eight, my father already spoke German, Russian, Italian and a little French - by the age of four, he had already read and written something in German.
In the summer of 1863, my grandparents were still unwelcome at the Russian court, but my grandfather had never broken off written contact with his sister, who was now Tsarina, and so the Russian relatives arrived at Heiligenberg for the first time for a visit. The children all got on very well, as they were all the same age. However, my father later recalled how stiffly some things had to be arranged during the Russian visits. Lunch was served punctually at thirteen o'clock and the children were only allowed to join us for dessert. They had to eat the first courses separately from the adults. Until the afternoon, the ladies sat together and drank coffee, while the men enjoyed themselves playing games in the garden, such as boules. If there was no hunting scheduled at sixteen o'clock, they would take carriages to the *New Palace* in Darmstadt or to *Wolfsgarten*, the summer residence of the grand ducal family. There they enjoyed tea, coffee and cake, returned to Heiligenberg in the evening and dinner was served at around twenty o'clock. The evenings were spent playing cards or listening to music on the piano. My father and his siblings, however, had already been served a light supper and dined with their nannies - they only heard the music, if at all, from their beds. My father once joked that the Russian relatives arrived with half the imperial palace, because a large number of servants also had to arrive and be accommodated, so Papa's family moved into the back part of the palace with tutors and servants and the Romanovs occupied the entire front part. Even though the finest wines and the best food were served and there was a strict time protocol, the relatives were not supposed to feel at home as if they were on an official state visit, but rather in an all-round organized cosiness, if you want to put it so profanely.
On her first visit to Darmstadt in 1863, the Tsarina was already suffering from tuberculosis and traveled to Bad Kissingen for a cure in 1864, to Bad Schwalbach and then to her old home. When her first-born son, Tsarevich Nicholas,

known as *Nixa*, died of meningitis in 1865 and her husband began an affair from which children were also to be born, the Tsarina's suffering worsened and she was only able to rest during visits to Darmstadt, as the Tsar was in St. Petersburg in the meantime, as he could not leave the affairs of state to himself.
Grandmother's relatives only visited her sporadically in Heiligenberg, including her brother Alexander, who came to Hesse once. However, the family ties on her side were not very close.

On July 1, 1862, Prince Ludwig of Hesse and by Rhine, a nephew of Grandpapa's brother, the Grand Duke, married the English Princess Alice, a daughter of Queen Victoria, in England. The young princess now moved into Darmstadt and was very well looked after by Grandpapa and Grandmama, as she suffered from the Queen's guilty conscience because she had gone to Germany. The English queen was a widow and now believed that her children had to look after her more. Alice suffered from constantly receiving letters of reproach and life advice, but my grandparents understood this and took care of her grief. As they soon visited each other regularly and Alice and Ludwig were welcome guests at the Battenbergs', my military-minded father met Alice's brothers when they visited Hesse, Prince Alfred and Prince Edward, the Prince of Wales and future heir to the throne. Prince Alfred loved the *Royal Navy* and enthused so much about life at sea that my father was soon hooked. As he was studying in Bonn, he often came to Darmstadt and his stories fascinated my father.
During a visit from Prince Alfred, he finally asked him if he could join *the Royal Navy* as a foreign prince, when he was just thirteen years old. My father was a very welcome guest of Princess Alice at the time, and it is perhaps fair to say that she took a fancy to the young man as a companion. She encouraged my father in his endeavors, as she believed it would strengthen the ties between England and Germany. Her brother Alfred also supported the idea, but my father's parents were not so keen - he was the first-born son and the military tradition in Hesse was not based on a career at sea. But my father was determined to become an officer in the English Navy and he pushed his parents until they finally gave in.
It has to be said that there was no all-German Navy at that time; it was only founded in 1870. But after the *German-German War* of 1866, in which Prussia and the German Confederation under the leadership of Austria and its allies had faced each other and Hesse was unable to withstand the Prussian armies as they marched through the country, it would never have occurred to any Hessian to join a Prussian Navy. Both Grandpapa and Alice's husband, Prince Ludwig, had fought against the Prussians and now had to accept

defeat.
Nevertheless, my father did not lose respect for his grandfather, in fact he appreciated his military commitment to his country, but he still had his goal in mind. He could have joined the Austrian navy, but he wanted to join the Navy with the best reputation, the biggest - and that was the English Navy.
Prince Alfred took my father under his wing when he was given command of the frigate *Galatea*. But it wasn't easy for him there.
Grandpapa gave his son another twenty-four hours shortly after his fourteenth birthday to reconsider his decision, and when he realized that he would have to accept his wish with a heavy heart, he telegraphed to Queen Victoria in Osborne, England, asking her permission for Papa to join the British Navy. Grandfather was particularly pained by the fact that his son wanted to go to a foreign country when he was still so young.
At the age of fourteen, the age of entry had already been reached. It was the last chance to start training as a cadet on the *Britannia*. So Princess Alice appealed to her mother to raise the age limit for my father by six months and soon a teacher called Mr. Everett from Magdalen College, Oxford, traveled to Darmstadt to prepare Papa for the entrance examination at Portsmouth Naval College in December. My father had to study algebra, Euclidean geometry, Latin and essay writing in English. The summer of 1868 was very warm, the Russian relatives were present, the Tsarina had brought all her children with her, and while the merry band traveled to Wolfsgarten for picnics and gatherings, my father had to stay at home to study, which was often very difficult for him. Prince Alfred had planned to *take* him on a trip around the world on the *Galatea*, but this seemed totally unwise, and it didn't fit in with the time frame, even though Papa had been looking forward to it.
On September 25, it was time to say goodbye. Papa traveled to England with his grandfather and the teacher for further exam preparation. His mother was distraught because Grandma feared that her son might drown. She had never been to England and so it seemed as far away as Australia.
My father was placed in an institute in Alverstoke, between Gosport and Portsmouth, where he was to continue preparing for the exams. The principal of the school, a certain Dr. Burney, let my father stay with him and his family, because due to his special status it was not thought that he wanted to spend much time with the other boys. Dr. Burney took care of him, but soon my father suffered from homesickness. He didn't like the English food and felt lonely, so his mother advised him to play soccer and eat with the other boys from time to time to make friends. She was not aware that her son had a special status among them and that she did not integrate him because of this fact. She had only heard that soccer was a very popular sport in England and that people liked to play it in their free time. Her grandfather went to see him, but

my father was supposed to learn, that was the most important thing now. And when Dr. Burney took him and twenty other boys preparing for exams to watch a flagship of the British fleet in Portsmouth Harbour in early December, Papa was so impressed that it reaffirmed his desire.

Dr. Burney took him to the best tailors to have uniforms made, all on the recommendation of Queen Victoria, and my father had to be photographed in them, because the Queen was soon extremely impressed by his ambition.

On December 14, my father passed all his exams with flying colors and was allowed to return to Heiligenberg for Christmas as a cadet of Her Royal Majesty. On his return in the New Year, he was to begin his service on the *Bristol.*

My father wore his uniform with pride every day, on every occasion, and when the Prince of Wales, Edward, offered him the opportunity to go with him as his personal *aide-de-campe* on a Mediterranean voyage planned as a vacation for members of the English royal family, Papa felt honored and accepted immediately. But it was to be a very boring voyage for him. He still had no practical knowledge, was shunned by the experienced sailors and officers and the whole thing was purely an excursion. Papa was to regret his decision shortly after the voyage began, because every evening he served more as company for the ladies present and their entourage than learning anything.

However, Papa was not deterred by this experience and soon trained on other ships. He was promoted to sub-lieutenant on April 7, 1874. The next year he traveled to India with the Prince of Wales on the *Serapis* and on May 18, 1876 he finally became a lieutenant. His career in the *Royal Navy* was successful and he worked towards soon having his own ship under his command.

The Grand Ducal Family of Hesse and by Rhine - my mother's family

Mama's parents were the aforementioned Prince Ludwig of Hesse and by Rhine and the English Princess Alice, daughter of Queen Victoria of England. My great-grandfather was the younger brother of Grand Duke Ludwig III of Hesse and by Rhine, Prince Karl.

Although the Grand Duke had married Princess Mathilde Karoline, a daughter of King Ludwig I of Bavaria, in 1833, the marriage had remained childless and Mathilde had died at the age of forty-eight in 1862. As the Grand Duke had entered into an irregular marriage with the ballet dancer Anna Magdalena Appel in 1868, to whom he conferred the title of *Freifrau von Hochstätten*, descendants from this union would not have been entitled to inherit, which would have interrupted his direct line of succession. However, this second marriage also remained childless and shortly after the wedding the Grand Duke withdrew from public life. He spent the last years of his life until his death in 1877 at Braunshardt Castle, a rococo palace and country estate near the southern Hessian town of Weiterstadt. He decreed that his nephew, my grandfather Ludwig, should become the new Grand Duke after his death. And so Grandfather unexpectedly came to rule over the Grand Duchy as Grand Duke Ludwig IV of Hesse and by Rhine.

The first period of their marriage, until Grandfather became Grand Duke, was not easy for the couple. Although Grandmother Alice had brought a good dowry from England into the marriage, they built their own home, the *New Palace* in Darmstadt, on whose grounds the *botanical gardens* had once stood. The park was therefore beautifully designed in reminiscence of this. The princess was a very helpful woman and so they donated a lot of the money they had to the needy. The couple can therefore be described as charitable in the first years of their marriage, but not wealthy for the same reason. Queen Victoria's husband, Prince Consort Albert, had died of typhoid fever in 1861 at the age of just forty-two and Alice had devotedly cared for her father mostly on her own. Her mother had been unable to do so. Moreover, the Queen did not have the patience to deal with the sick. The eldest daughter, the Princess Royal Victoria, had been married to Crown Prince Frederick of Prussia, the future German Emperor Frederick III, since 1858. Alice therefore saw it as her duty, as the eldest living daughter, to care for her father and, after his death, for her mother. Her mother suffered terribly from the loss of her beloved husband and so it pained her greatly when Alice married. She insisted that her daughter visit her in England as often as possible, but such trips were expensive and therefore not possible as often as the Queen

demanded. My mother, Princess Victoria, was born at Windsor Castle on the fifth of April 1863, as the Queen had insisted that her daughter should give birth in England. As head of the family, she also decreed that every girl born into the family should bear her first name. So Mama was the first grandchild to be born in the Queen's house.
The grandfather, Prince Louis, was also present in England to witness the birth of his first grandson. The Queen was not particularly fond of small children, but this had only applied to her own when they were toddlers. Now, however, she warmly welcomed every new addition to the family. If she had always had something to complain about or find fault with her own children, this changed after the death of her husband. However, her youngest daughter, Princess Beatrice, whom she affectionately called *Baby*, had a special status. She had only been four and a half years old when her father died, and the Queen projected all her love onto her youngest daughter, a love that the other eight siblings perhaps longed for or had longed for at one time or another. She did the same with her grandchildren. They were also allowed to be relatively uninhibited in her presence.

The only downer for the Queen was my mother's christening on April 27 in Windsor, as it had to be held according to the Lutheran rite, for which a German pastor, the court preacher Bender, traveled especially. But the fact that she was allowed to hold the child during the ceremony quickly put her mind at ease.

On the first of November 1864, Mama's sister, Princess Elisabeth, was born. She was born in Darmstadt and Queen Victoria was annoyed by the fact that her daughter breastfed and cared for each of her children herself, which was unusual at the time. It annoyed the Queen so much that she promptly named a breeding cow in her stables after her daughter.
The third daughter, Princess Irene, was born in July 1866, Prince and later Hereditary Grand Duke Ernst Ludwig in November 1868, Prince Friedrich, who was called *Frittie*, in October 1870, Princess Alix in June 1872 and Princess Marie, who was called *May* because she gave her first cry in May 1874, followed as the last child.
The seven children grew up in an English-influenced atmosphere, something Princess Alice attached great importance to. She also took over the initial upbringing of her grandchildren, which was also influenced by her own English upbringing. The food was spartan, yet adequate, but there was no extravagant cuisine. Mama later remarked how much she hated the constant serving of rice cakes and baked apples, as these had always been available in her childhood.

Grandma was a very warm-hearted and kind woman who loved her children more than anything. There was never a bad word said about her. Grandfather was also a family man and enjoyed playing with his children, but when he became Grand Duke he was rarely available for them, so they really enjoyed their time with him.

Every summer, they traveled to England to spend time with the Queen and her English relatives - either at *Balmoral* Castle in Scotland, *Osborne* on the Isle of Wight or *Windsor Castle* in Berkshire. As already mentioned, the strict rules that the Queen had applied to her children did not apply to her grandchildren. They therefore enjoyed their summer retreat in a very relaxed atmosphere.

Mama also often talked about the nannies and governesses who looked after her and her siblings.

The first one was Mary Anne Orchard from England, who came into the children's lives in 1867. *Orchie*, as the children soon affectionately called her, was perfect, because although she introduced a strict schedule for the children's daily lives, she also encouraged them to play all kinds of fun games. When their mother was reading or writing letters in her room, the girls were allowed to put on her discarded clothes and play *dress-up* under Orchie's guidance. She soon became the head governess and was sometimes very strict in her punishments for misdemeanors or nonsense, but planned each day so that the children could always spend a lot of time with their mother. Orchie was to remain in the family until her death in 1906 at the age of seventy-six. When Mama's sister Alix married the Russian Tsarevich, Orchie went with her to Russia and was her companion as well as helping and guiding her in the upbringing of the children.

In Darmstadt, Orchie had a German nanny called Katherine, who was called *little Katrinchen*, and a Miss Emma Bailie from England. But there were also nannies who didn't fit into the family.

A nanny called Fräulein von Eckenstein from a noble Prussian family taught the children the song *Die Wacht am Rhein*. However, after Hesse lost the war against Prussia, people in Darmstadt thought nothing of singing songs of praise to them when Prussia won the *Franco-Prussian* War of 1870/71.

Another girl called Kitz suffered constantly from migraines. My mother remembered a game in which she and her siblings played English knights loudly. The poor girl was sitting on a bench with a damp cloth on her neck, her head in her hands and moaning about the pain, which wasn't helped by the noise. It was suggested to her that she might like to work as a governess for a smaller group of children.

An English governess by the name of Hasters was always fibbing, a Miss

Graves took such a liking to my mother that she was only ever concerned about her welfare. Soon she didn't want to let my mother out of her embrace, hugging and kissing her so intimately that Grandmother Alice dismissed her from the service without further ado. It later turned out that she had been institutionalized due to a diagnosed persecution complex.

Miss Margaret Hardcastle Jackson, who was called *Madgie*, felt very much at home with the Hessian Grand Duke's family and proved to be an extremely competent person. She had given up her previous position after the lady there had converted to the Catholic faith. Consistently a conservative Protestant, she nevertheless taught children charity, responsibility and honesty. She more than hated gossip and did not tolerate malice towards one another, yet she was warm and would stay with the family until all the children were grown up. Even as young women, when they were already married and had moved out, the girls in particular kept in touch with Orchie and Madgie by letter or met Orchie, when they visited their sister Alix in Russia.

From time to time in the early years of my mother's life, money was tight in the family, and governesses were sometimes given temporary leave. Tutors were also hired early on to teach the children to read and write. My mother was taught by a Mr. Geyer. It was only small lessons day by day, but by the age of seven she could already read in German and English. She soon picked up every children's book that was available. Her love of reading was to continue unabated in her later life. Grandmother Alice got her books and readily supported her enthusiasm, as she also enjoyed reading a lot herself.

My mother shared a room with her sister Elisabeth, called *Ella*, but did not share her passion for dolls, but loved to climb trees in the park or play or even tussle with her brothers. Little *Frittie* needed special care when romping around, however, because he suffered from *hemophilia*, the bleeding disorder that grandmother Alice fortunately only passed on to one son from her mother. But she knew all too well about this treacherous disease, as her younger brother Leopold also suffered from it. When Frittie was eighteen months old, the first bruises and hemorrhages were noticed. When he cut his ear once, the bleeding could only be stopped after three days by applying firm bandages soaked in iron to the wound. Of course, the treatment caused even more pain and the otherwise lively little boy could hardly be held in bed or carried around because he could not be soothed from the pain.

My mother and her siblings learned to take special care of their sick brother. Grandma taught her children all to have compassion for the suffering and fate of others, and so during the *Franco-Prussian War* she also visited the wounded in the hospitals and soup kitchens for the poor, with her two older daughters always following her.

In March 1873, Grandmother Alice traveled alone to Italy to visit churches,

cathedrals and art galleries in Rome, Florence and Naples. She returned to Darmstadt at the beginning of May, refreshed but also somewhat exhausted from her trip. She stayed in bed for a long time in the mornings, read a lot or played the piano. The children were allowed to visit her in her rooms at this time before their governesses looked after them or lessons began.
On the morning of the twenty-ninth of May, Grandma got up, played Chopin on the piano and then went back to her bedroom. Ernst Ludwig, who was nicknamed *Ernie*, and his younger brother Frittie ran into the room. The governess had briefly lost sight of both boys. They ran to the large windows, as they could wave to each other when one was standing in one room and the other in the other with the windows slightly open. Ernie wanted to wave to his brother from the bedroom, but Frittie was nowhere to be seen, and when Grandma called for him, he didn't answer. She ran into the next room, saw him standing at the window and was sure that everything was all right. The boys waved to each other, Ernie came to his mother afterwards, but Frittie didn't show himself. Grandma thought he was teasing her and went back into the other room, but the boy had disappeared. Full of fear, she ran to the window. She had unconsciously played Chopin's *Funeral March* on the piano because she loved Chopin so much. Now it seemed like a bad omen to her, because Frittie had fallen out of the window, directly onto the steps of the stone staircase below. An elderly maid carefully picked up the boy and handed him to his mother, who had hurried down in her nightgown. He was carried into the house, but no doctor in the world was able to help the little boy. His head injuries and the bleeding in his brain were so severe that the child never regained consciousness. Frittie died in the arms of his desperate mother.
My mother was ten years old at the time and would never forget this terrible event. It was the first terrible loss to hit the family.

When Grandpapa became Grand Duke of Hesse and by Rhine in 1877, the family's financial situation also changed. Whereas they had previously spent their summer holidays in England, at the hunting lodge Kranichstein near Darmstadt, in Blankenberge on the coast in Belgium, they were now able to travel to a more upmarket French seaside resort.
The Battenbergs and the Mamas family met often, as Julie von Battenberg had a great interest in so-called amateur dramas and Alice and her children also enjoyed watching them. In addition, many well-known German writers, musicians and composers often came to Darmstadt, as Grandma Alice, in her enthusiasm for literature and music, also invited them. She even played the piano with Brahms once.
Mama had not inherited her talent for playing the piano, she was very good

at math and science, but loved literature, theater and opera. Concerts and other cultural performances were usually enjoyed with the Battenbergs. Mama remembered my father's uniform, the *Royal Navy uniform*, which he wore with pride when he visited home.
Both families were very close, even when Grandfather was not yet Grand Duke. They enjoyed evenings together when family members performed dramatic plays together.
The strict English upbringing had an effect on the children's personalities. They were hard-working and ambitious and did not demand special treatment or extra attention. They had to get up early in the morning and go to bed early at night. Mama once told me how they had to get up shortly after six o'clock every day, both in winter and summer. The first lessons started at seven in the morning. Two hours later, Ella and Mama had breakfast with her mother and father, if he had time. They had porridge, sausages and cold meat such as cold cuts. After that, they had to go outside for an hour, regardless of the weather, either riding out or going for walks in the park. In the morning they had a small breakfast with milk, fruit and cookies. Then it was back to home schooling until 2 p.m., followed by lunch with their parents and all their brothers and sisters. There was never any chocolate, no sweets, just a little sugar in the tea. Grandma Alice demanded a certain simplicity in her children's lives, a certain modesty. And even in England, when the Queen wanted to spoil her grandchildren, she could only slip them a sweet in secret.

The next very hard blow hit the family in 1878. At the beginning of November that year, my mother read *Alice in Wonderland* to her younger siblings. She had a slight sore throat, but they didn't attach much importance to this little thing in winter. They thought she was coming down with a cold and that warm caMamaile tea would help. But when Mama went to bed in the evening, she developed a fever, which rose within a very short time. She soon suffered from severe neck pain and could hardly breathe. A doctor was immediately called to the castle. He immediately recognized the symptoms of diphtheria. Mama had to be separated from Ella immediately and moved to another room. Ella moved in with Irene. But when she showed the same symptoms just one day later, Grandma decided it was best to take Ella out of the castle altogether and sent her to her paternal grandmother, Princess Elisabeth of Hesse and by Rhine, who lived in Seeheim Castle in Seeheim-Jugenheim near Darmstadt. Ella was the only one to escape the fatal illness that was now gradually taking hold of the family.
The very next day, six-year-old Alix, who was called *Alicky* or *Sunny* because of her cheerful nature, also fell ill. Then Ernie and finally little May was in bed with a high temperature and breathing problems. Orchie came to

Although my mother had been used to this correspondence with her grandmother since childhood, the conditions under which the letters were written had changed.
Nevertheless, the Queen also did something for the family: by always inviting her grandchildren to visit her, she tried to ease their grief. The other grandmother, Princess Elisabeth, and other relatives and friends were also involved.

The Queen sent her son Leopold to Darmstadt, who was ten years older than my mother. As a hemophiliac, the Queen had always paid special attention to him. There was actually no special career path for him in the royal house, as he was unable to hold a military post due to his illness. In addition, he already had severe knee problems after several attacks of the disease. He got on very well with Grandfather Ludwig, enjoyed spending time with the children and was a great help to my mother, as he also proved to be a very good listener to any grief. He and little Alicky in particular soon had a very close relationship and he adored his niece. My mother's otherwise cheerful sister had become a quiet, introverted child as a result of the losses. Nevertheless, her uncle often managed to bring her out of her grief.
Leopold was to marry Princess Helene zu Waldeck-Pyrmont in 1882. They had two children, and he named his daughter Alice after his sister. Unfortunately, he died in 1884 as a result of a knee injury he sustained after falling from a horse, but my mother would be eternally grateful for his support.
Mama was very disciplined as a result of her upbringing and, even at the age of fifteen, she had the maturity to face up to everything. As Grand Duke, her father also had military obligations and was rarely at home. From her point of view, however, he did not seem to be up to the burden of looking after the children all by himself, especially when it came to their care and upbringing. Grandfather was grieving himself, seeking distraction, immersing himself in his duties. Unconsciously, he burdened my mother with them. But when the Queen wrote to her, asking her to walk in her mother's shoes, to be selfless, loving and kind, to always follow her advice because it was necessary for her, my mother later said that this prescribed sense of duty sometimes almost crushed her. She was not like her mother, but she was supposed to become like her, as the queen raised her dead daughter to the status of an angel in her memory, although there is no question that her grandmother always had an oversized heart for people in need and always went to great lengths for her charitable obligations.
Mama later confessed that she wasn't particularly self-confident back then. She was often afraid that people wouldn't like her, that her clothes weren't appropriate or that she wasn't pretty.

The queen also sent her daughters Louise and Helena to Darmstadt so that they would have a good influence on the girls. Helena, who was called *Lenchen*, was married to Prince Christian of Schleswig-Holstein-Sonderburg-Augustenburg. Louise, who had married the Marquess of Lorne John Douglas Sutherland Campbell, looked very much like her sister Alice and probably also had some of Grandmother's traits.
Crown Princess Victoria of Prussia, the Queen's eldest daughter, traveled to Darmstadt once a year before Alice's death, but now only rarely, as she also had commitments in Berlin, and her grandfather found the Prussians too militaristic and did not share his interest in art. Victoria was already too influenced by the Prussian spirit and her son, the future Kaiser Wilhelm II, studied in Bonn. He was twenty and four years older than my mother, a heavy smoker and seduced her into smoking at the age of sixteen. She was never to give it up again. In this respect, my mother showed a certain self-confidence.
In England, smoking was strictly forbidden by the Queen. Anyone who wanted to smoke fled to a room and smoked in secret. But Mama didn't want to pretend and always smoked in public whenever and wherever she wanted - even in the presence of the Queen. The Queen looked after her because she loved my mother. She had been present at her birth and tried to support her, so once, when the mosquitoes were bothering her too much during tea, she asked her to light a cigarette to drive them away. The queen herself also took a puff, but found the taste disgusting. Throughout her life, her granddaughter had a special status.

Ties of love are forged

In the spring of 1880, the Queen traveled to Mama and Ella's confirmation and was saddened to see her daughter's sarcophagus and those of Frittie and May for the first time. She then lingered in her daughter's bedroom, where everything had been left as it was at the Grand Duke's instigation. She had treated her husband's room in the same way all those years and even had fresh shaving lotion brought to him every morning and laundry laid out.
At the age of seventeen, my mother had blossomed into a beauty with only one flaw. She talked too much and too loudly, something she would keep all her life. Her mother had also loved to talk, and every topic of conversation could be picked apart down to the smallest detail. The Queen's daughters, Louise and Beatrice, could also talk for hours. There were only three people who could stop Mum talking - the Queen, in her later life my father, who would ask her sternly but with polite firmness to shut up for once, or my brother Dickie, by simply not answering or doing something else while she was talking.
My mother was considered a *tomboy* in the family. That was the name given to a lively girl, a tomboy who behaved like a boy. And even as a young woman, Mum still lived up to it when she rode a horse at a wild gallop, which the Queen considered unfeminine and inappropriate. She was also irritated when Mama mentioned in her letters to her that she had been hunting with her grandfather and had also shot at animals. For the queen, this was not very ladylike behavior. Ladies usually detested hunting and stayed away from it. She commented that only *fast ladies*, i.e. light girls, behaved like this to impress men by appearing tough and masculine.

At the beginning of 1883, Queen Victoria tried to find suitable marriage candidates for Ella and Mama. Although she always protested against this, the Queen was a passionate *matchmaker*, as they call it in English. It seemed like her life's work to always find a suitable partner for every female relative. Unfortunately, her *attempts at matchmaking* were rarely successful, which usually hurt her greatly. She saw herself as the head of the family, who naturally had such responsibilities.
So she slipped in a remark about a possible connection between Ella and Hereditary Grand Duke Friedrich von Baden, the son of Grand Duke Friedrich I von Baden, in a letter dated January 1, 1883, referring to the many good things she had heard about him. Mama was supposed to make this suggestion to her sister in passing, but she did not. The Queen advised that Ella should marry in about two years' time, but not to anyone from Russia, because she

thought that Russian nobles lived too ostentatiously, flaunted their wealth too much and that the tsars were tyrants and enemies of a parliamentary monarchy. For her, this also applied to the French court, the Prussians were too stiff and too concerned with ceremonial and protocol at court, and the Guelphs in Hanover were also too lavish. She and her late husband had wanted the English court to be more like a household of the upper English bourgeoisie in order to show a certain closeness to the people. It can be argued that this did not have a positive effect on her reputation among the British population.
Nevertheless, she made it clear to my mother that it was also in her daughter Alice's interest if the girls married as she wished. Grandmother Alice had already made contact with Grand Duchess Luise von Baden, as she had also been in favor of Ella marrying the hereditary Grand Duke during her lifetime. The future Emperor Wilhelm II of Prussia had also fallen in love with Ella during his visits to Darmstadt, but she had no feelings for him and did not want to marry Baden. Grandfather Ludwig told his two eldest daughters that they should choose their own spouses, as he did not believe in arranged marriages.
Empress Augusta of Prussia, who also wanted to see her grandson Friedrich married to Ella, arranged a ball to which she invited Ella and Mama. She wanted to announce her grandson's engagement to Ella there, but was disappointed to find that Ella did not agree, so she cut the two young women off in public. They were both literally dead to her. This weighed heavily on my mother and her sister for a while.
Ella was already in love with the Russian Grand Duke Sergey Alexandrovich Romanov, the fifth son of Tsar Alexander II of Russia and brother of Tsar Alexander III. Sergey had often visited Darmstadt with his mother, Tsarina Marie, and they had become close at family gatherings. Sergey had a bad reputation, as he was regarded as an eccentric due to his gruff manner and imperious demeanor. And even though Queen Victoria protested against the marriage, Ella married Sergey out of love. On the third of June 1884, the couple said "I do" in the chapel of the Winter Palace in St. Petersburg. And it was at this wedding that twelve-year-old Alicky, Mama's youngest sister, met Tsarevich Nicholas Alexandrovich of Russia, who was sixteen years old at the time. Both immediately had more than friendly feelings for each other, but they had to wait a few more years.
Mama had a brief flirtation with the Grand Duke Michael Nikolayevich of Russia, but by then her heart was already spoken for, even if she didn't realize it immediately. She had always been impressed when her cousin Ludwig Alexander von Battenberg visited Hesse, and remembered the great impression his *Royal Navy uniform* had made on her when he met her at a family reunion in 1870. He was sixteen at the time, she was only seven, but over the years

and with each subsequent meeting, her feelings for him had grown.
In the summer of 1878, the Grand Ducal family visited England and Mama remembered this summer particularly well, as it was the last one for them all as a family with her mother and May. And she remembered a visit to Buckingham Palace where her Uncle Edward, the Prince of Wales, gave a garden party at Marlborough House. My father was a lieutenant at the time and soon had to go on duty on the *Inconstant*. Those were days when he and Mama saw a lot of each other. She was very impressed by how gallant he was and his elegant and cheerful manner.
When she and Ella wanted to go on a boat trip on the lake by the palace, Orchie was afraid that something might happen to them, so he hired my father to look after them. After all, who seemed better suited to the job than a real sailor?
In the winter of 1882, Mama and Papa met again in Darmstadt. For him, Mama had blossomed - a young, fresh, lively person who sometimes spoke her mind and had a lot of wit. Papa delighted her with his stories of foreign places he had seen on his travels, and suddenly they both realized that they had feelings for each other. Mama said that all of a sudden the moon seemed bigger and more beautiful than before, the cold of winter had disappeared and she felt happier than she had in a long time.
Papa was amazed at what the little tomboy had become, he had already had a few love affairs, but this one was different. He fell head over heels in love with my mother.
This winter, they danced together at all the balls, and before they knew it, the whole court suspected that they were getting married.
Queen Victoria invited Ella and Mama to Balmoral, Mama wanted to cancel - for the first time. And Ella went to Grandfather and said that if her sister canceled the visit, the reason would be an engagement to Ludwig von Battenberg. It was just a humorous prophecy, but in June 1883 my parents got engaged and it was officially announced on the first of July.
Grandfather was initially against the two of them marrying, because he thought my father was only after the dowry, as he was not very wealthy himself. Although he received a good salary for his service in the *Navy*, he didn't have a home of his own, only his parents' home when he was in Darmstadt. Mama fought for her love and so Grandpa finally gave in because he wanted to see his daughter happy.
For Ella, her choice of a Russian Grand Duke meant a shake-up in her relationship with the Queen in England, for she made it unmistakably clear in a letter to my mother that if Ella, as she had expressed it, wanted to spend more time with her relatives, even despite her new home in Russia, she would not be able to travel to England with Sergey. In the letter of September twenty-

first, 1883, the Queen made it very clear that Ella should not expect to spend time with her in England if her husband was traveling with her, because the Queen could not have a Russian Grand Duke around her for a long time. The Russians were unscrupulous and Ella would be seduced into a life that was not good for her. For these reasons, it was impossible for her to endure such a visit.
But it was different for Mama and Papa, she emphasized, because Papa was in her service and always had a home with her.
The Queen was caught up in her desire to marry Ella to the Hereditary Grand Duke of Baden, and because she thwarted this wish and also married a Russian she hated, Mama repeatedly received letters, as did Ella, in which she expressed her displeasure and tried to make her future husband look bad with rumors she had allegedly heard about Sergey. She later had to admit that Ella really loved Sergey and that he adored his wife, and the Queen wished her well, but her resentment was always present.
She was also worried that the modest Ella might become too spoiled and vain because of all the pomp, jewels and palaces that surpassed the Queen's wealth. Mama reassured her that Ella did not value these things, that only her happiness counted for her, and this was to prove true in later life.
She wanted to be at her mother's wedding, but feared for her health and, more seriously, that of one of her dogs. But these were just normal problems brought on by her age and her love for her dogs.
On the twenty-eighth of March 1884, Uncle Leopold also passed away and this also touched Mama very much, as her uncle had been very supportive of her after her mother's death.
Grandfather had taken refuge in an affair with the née Comtesse Alexandrine von Hutten-Czapska. She was thirty years old in 1884, grandfather was seventeen years older and she was certainly not a suitable match. Mama and her siblings wanted to see their father happy, but the lady took her mother's place and a scandal was brewing in Darmstadt. The Comtesse, actually Madame de Kolemine, had been married to the Imperial Russian Legation Secretary Alexander de Kolemine at the Darmstadt court and had divorced him for Grandfather. This was of course also unacceptable.

On the day of Mama's wedding, Grandfather married his beloved in the evening and elevated her to the rank of *Countess of Romrod*. Grandfather's minister of state acted as registrar for the quick wedding ceremony.
However, following the intervention of his relatives and children, he had the marriage annulled that same year, on the ninth of July. The countess, whose feelings had been hurt, caused a scandal in the European press by selling her story and the *injustice* she had suffered for a profit, even though she had been

given the title and a settlement.
Queen Victoria had traveled to Darmstadt especially for Mama's wedding, had already been outraged by the exuberance with which her son-in-law had greeted her at the train station in Darmstadt, as she found it inappropriate for a widower, and now she was extremely outraged by her son-in-law's behavior. She set all her relatives in motion to put pressure on Grandfather. After the immediate interventions, Countess Alexandrine fled hastily to Moscow, naturally with Grandfather's love letters in her luggage and the blackmail letters from her relatives.
The countess remarried shortly afterwards, but her settlement continued to be paid. It is fair to say that she profited from the marriage.
For Mama, this cast a very unfortunate shadow over the most beautiful day of her life and the start of her honeymoon in Heiligenberg.

Papa's parents had been very fond of the connection to Mama from the very beginning. For Grandmother Julie, this established a good and solid bond between the Battenbergs and the Grand Ducal House, the Heiligenberg and the *New Palace*. Grandmother Julie initially regretted very much that at nineteen Mama was considered too young to marry and that she was burdened with thinking primarily of her father and younger siblings. The Battenbergs were proud of their son; it was incomprehensible to them that they thought a marriage with him was unacceptable because he would be at sea too often.
Mama didn't want to break out of her home when she married, but she also didn't feel responsible for correcting her siblings' every mistake. When her brother Ernie neglected his studies, no longer followed his lessons and developed a weakness for sweets, as Miss Jackson reported to the Queen in writing, Mama had to correct this. But now she handed this task over to her younger sister Irene.
Mama later said that she had never had anything against her father having a new relationship, and that she didn't care about the lady's status as long as she was a sensible person who treated her father well. She was aware of how much grandfather was suffering from the loss of his wife, but he should have waited until all three eldest daughters were out of the house.
Grandmother Victoria's words, which she gave her before the wedding night, were later echoed in the family. Whenever a young bride in the family was worried about the first night alone with the groom and her deflowering, the Queen would give her this advice: "Close your eyes and think of England!"

A new union was forged at Mama's wedding. The Queen's youngest daughter, Princess Beatrice, who had been chosen by her mother as a companion for life, as was customary for the youngest daughter at the time, fell in love with

Papa's brother, Prince Henry Moritz. They married on the twenty-third of July 1885 at Osborne House on the Isle of Wight. Beatrice had pleaded with her mother for eight months, begging her to be allowed to marry, until the Queen finally agreed when she realized that the two were very much in love with each other.

Mama and Papa spent a week in Heiligenberg and enjoyed their honeymoon. My mother knew the castle from her childhood and from visits, and she immediately felt at home with the family, but after these short days, Papa had to return to England. On September 14, 1883, he was transferred to the royal yacht *Victoria and Albert* and had to return to his duties on the ship. However, as the yacht was being overhauled, he was still able to spend time with his mother.

Papa had rented a property with a large garden, called *Sennicotts*, near Chichester on the south coast of England, close to Portsmouth. This meant he could reach the port quickly, but also be with my mother often. Mama and Papa only spent three weeks there at first, then they had to travel back to Germany and from there with the family to Ella's wedding in Russia.
When they arrived in Darmstadt, they were immediately confronted with their grandfather's poor state of mind, who had fallen into depression since his unexpected marriage and the scandal surrounding it. The Queen had invited him to England to hunt, which he had always loved, but now he was not very happy at the thought of it. It was a gesture of reconciliation from the Queen, but Grandpa was so depressed that nothing could really cheer him up. Papa, Mama, Ella and Irene tried to cheer him up in every possible way, but it didn't seem to work.
Since the marriage had been annulled, everyone in his wide-ranging family had forgiven him.
In Russia, Papa found himself temporarily overwhelmed by the situation, as he was considered a defector. He had committed himself to Russia's enemy, the English. By now he had English citizenship, it was his home and on top of that he was in the *Royal Navy*. England was preventing Russia from expanding in the Middle East and Asia because it had sent ships to the Dardanelles to stop the Russian troops, and Papa of all people had served on one of these ships. This man, of all people, now became Sergey's brother-in-law and had married a sister of his bride. The Russian relatives clearly made Papa feel bitter about this, but he was happy to ignore it.
It had been a long journey to Russia. Grandpa, Ella, the bride, Irene, Ernie, Alix and Mama with Papa had taken three days and two nights by train. It opened up completely new impressions for all of them and Mama still raved

about this first trip to Russia years later, because the vast landscapes had impressed her so much. Mama was also fascinated by Sergey's grand palace, where Ella now lived in St. Petersburg. She and her husband were also able to spend the summers on the extensive Illinskoye estate outside Moscow.
The only condition for the marriage from her grandfather's side had been that Ella could keep her religion and did not have to change from Lutheran Protestantism to Russian Orthodoxy. Sergey had agreed to this, and the supposedly so enterprising husband was quite different from what everyone believed from the rumors. He was charming, adored Ella and was very friendly and exuberant.
As guests from England and Denmark were attending the wedding, the English yacht *Osborne* arrived in the port of St. Petersburg a few days earlier. Papa wore his uniform throughout his stay and, of course, at the wedding.
At the banquet, however, Papa was not allowed to sit next to Mama, but was placed between the other officers on the yacht. Although this was an affront to him, Papa took it in his stride and chatted happily with the officers. Later, however, he said he was glad to live in England, a free country where such harassment was not the order of the day.
Mama wrote to the Queen after the wedding in St. Petersburg, but didn't tell her any details about the wedding, the pomp or anything like that, and also avoided mentioning the faux pas so as not to upset her unnecessarily. She simply wrote to her that it had been beautiful.
My mother had other things on her mind, because shortly after her return to England she discovered that she was pregnant.

My childhood and teenage years, 1885 to 1903

As Mama was in good spirits, she spent the fall of 1884 in a rather relaxed manner. She followed the Queen's advice not to ride, took long walks with a little dog that Aunt Louise had given her, or rode in a small carriage through the countryside around Chichester. From time to time she visited friends, read a lot and also did some light gardening.
In September, she met Grandfather briefly in London, who was passing through on his way to Balmoral, where the Queen had invited him to hunt again. She did not want to expose herself to the rigors of a trip to Scotland, preferring to stay at Sennicotts to spend time with Papa, who was taking part in a torpedo training course.
The Queen was naturally very excited, awaited the new life with great joy and asked Mama to give birth to the child at her home in Windsor. With nine children, the Queen had a great deal of experience of pregnancies, births and child-rearing, so she wrote to Mama in her letters with instructions as to which wet nurse she should choose, which nanny would be suitable and offered her every support.
At the beginning of February 1885, Papa and Mama traveled to Windsor to await the birth of the child together with the Queen.
On the night of February twenty-fifth, Mama was already lying in the *Tapestry Room*. It is one of the most beautiful rooms in Windsor with wonderful stucco decorations on the ceiling, precious paintings and wallpaper on the walls. Of course, Mama had no view of it in labor, but it was the room where she herself saw the light of day.
The Queen and Papa were by Mama's side all day until I finally saw the light of day at twenty past five in the afternoon. I was a bit small, but the Queen commented shortly afterwards that I was a very pretty baby. Mama and Papa were naturally very proud.
In accordance with the Queen's wish to pass on her first name to every girl born into the family, I was given the name *Victoria Alice Elizabeth Julie Marie*, but my first name was to be *Alice*.
Mama told me that the Queen was very happy when she was allowed to rub me dry in a cloth after I was born, gently rubbing my little arms, just as she had done with her when my mother was born. She was an old lady, born in a different time, and so there was always a drop of bitterness in her joy when she thought of deceased friends or her favorite dog *Noble*. She would then let her grief run its course in long lines, waxing eloquent about how he had chased Stöckchen, which did not abate when she later wrote to me to enquire about my well-being.

chairman of the Admiralty immediately backed Papa. He had full confidence in his excellent abilities, he confessed publicly, and it was not a question of favoring a German prince in the English navy, but of employing a capable officer as was appropriate.
My father showed courage and commitment, impressing his enviers, because he was not above shoveling coal himself on the *Dreadnought'*. In a letter, he told Mama how he ate his meals standing up with the other working men, sleeping only an hour on deck before continuing to shovel with them in the scorching sun and sweltering heat of the day. The ship was loaded with coal in Smyrna, later Izmir, on the Turkish Aegean coast, which took three days. No job was too hard for my father and his critics soon realized that.
In the summers we always went to Darmstadt, usually accompanied by Papa. In the summer of 1887, however, my mother fell ill with typhoid fever and so I was left in the care of my grandparents Battenberg in Darmstadt. Due to their small budget, my parents couldn't afford a large staff to accompany us at all times, so there weren't many nannies for me. However, this was an advantage, as my mother, father or relatives always looked after me themselves. In the latter case, I could then be taken in by the nannies they had. They simply took me under their wing as another child.

Due to his job, Papa spent his time alternating between England and the Mediterranean, so it made sense for Mama to visit Uncle Alfred and his family in Malta. Duke Alfred of Saxe-Coburg and Gotha was stationed there as a naval officer. His family had a second residence on the island due to his professional activities and his youngest daughter Beatrice was two years old at the time. She was the youngest child in the family and was called *Baby Bee*. Uncle Affie's wife Marie had a very unhappy marriage to her husband, but this was also due to the fact that she had enjoyed a very pampered youth as a born Grand Duchess of Russia and daughter of Tsar Alexander II. After the death of her first daughter, she was the only one left and the tsar always fulfilled her every wish. As a result, she always caused a stir in English society, as she always saw herself as the Grand Duchess and daughter of a tsar above other women in the family. Malta thus offered her a pleasant refuge.
We traveled to Malta for the first time in October 1887, partly so that Mama could recover from her typhoid illness in the warm climate.
Marie was not exactly overprotective, which Mama noticed immediately, because she preferred to hand the children over to the nannies and when she looked after them herself, she was very strict with them. Mealtimes were also very stressful, because the children were not supposed to fill their bellies, but eat in an elegantly restrained manner. I was a very good eater, which manifested itself in my later life in that I often ate far too much and felt sick

afterwards, but I just liked it. So at dinner, my mother would usually make me bread with lots of butter on it, which I loved. But little *Baby Bee* was quite precocious and had already been brought up in such a way that gluttony was not tolerated. So she loudly remarked that I ate butter with bread instead of bread with butter. Mama wasn't embarrassed at all, but rather found the little girl's behavior inappropriate. However, Aunt Marie approved, as she also liked to loudly criticize the misbehaviour of others. During a game later, I tried to bite *Baby Bee* because she was constantly teasing me in an unpleasant way.

My mother didn't really want to extend the vacation unnecessarily, as she was afraid that if I made a mistake and hurt the little one, I wouldn't be forgiven. But when Papa was by her side, everything seemed easier. We were to stay there until April 1888.

Malta was an island full of life. There were many processions and festivities such as the carnival in Valetta, the capital. Affie lived in a very large estate with all the wealth. He was the commander-in-chief of the ships in the area and lived quite a posh life with his family in San Antonio. We moved into a small house in Valetta and rented a small apartment next door, which was my home. Mama insisted that I had my own little kingdom, which I could later share with a nanny. A Miss Joey Rolleston came from England to look after me from then on. She was very kind and understanding.

Sometimes I was allowed to ride out with the Affie children on the ponies that had been brought over from England especially for them. The eldest son Alfred, *Young Affie*, was thirteen years old in 1887, his sister Marie twelve, Victoria Melita eleven, she was called *Ducky* because of her somewhat strange voice, and Alexandra, who was called *Sandra*, was nine years old. The last of the bunch was the aforementioned *Baby Bee*.

The year 1887 was also a special one for the Queen of England, as she celebrated her fiftieth anniversary on the throne, the *Golden Jubilee*. The festivities lasted from May to June. The service in *Westminster Abbey* on June twenty-first was the ceremonial highlight. After more than fifty monarchs and princes from Europe and delegations from overseas had already arrived, the Queen's relatives paid homage after the service. First all the sons, sons-in-law and grandsons had to step forward to kiss her hand, then all the daughters, daughters-in-law and granddaughters. It must have been very moving, as my mother once told me.

Only the Russian royal family was not invited to the celebrations and the joy was somewhat overshadowed for everyone by the news that Crown Prince Frederick of Prussia had fallen ill with throat cancer. The Queen was very worried about her son-in-law and sent one of her best doctors to Berlin.

Mama was happy to be able to take part in the celebrations. She was only able to recover quickly thanks to Papa's good care, as she always emphasized.
As part of the celebrations, the Queen presented me with a small medal that had been specially made to mark her golden jubilee on the throne, and I held my treasure very tightly in my hand, proud of the gift.

In December, my parents were looking forward to the upcoming Christmas in Malta, because it was going to be a big celebration, you would go from ship to ship for the presents and English dishes such as plum pudding would be served.

The year 1888 brought major changes for Prussia. On the ninth of March, Kaiser Wilhelm I died at the age of ninety-one. His son succeeded him to the throne as Emperor Frederick III, making Victoria, the Queen's daughter, Empress of the German Empire. However, her husband's throat cancer had a very poor prognosis and so his short reign was marked by unspeakable suffering. He died on the fifteenth of June of that year at the age of just fifty-seven. This year was later known as the "Year of the Three Emperors", as his son became emperor upon his death
Wilhelm II of Prussia came to power. In mourning for her beloved husband, the Empress Dowager, who from then on only called herself *Empress Frederick*, retired to Kronberg Castle in the Taunus Mountains, where she was to spend the rest of her life.
Everyone in the family regretted Friedrich's death.
The Queen had visited her son-in-law and daughter once again in Berlin, but her grief was correspondingly great, especially because she considered her grandson Wilhelm too young to take over the reins of government at the age of twenty-nine. She shared her grief with Mama in her letters and still always asked about me.
At the age of three, I finally started to form a few words, but all that came out was babbling, which was so incomprehensible that my mother tried very hard to improve my pronunciation, but she couldn't do it. She tried to come to terms with my conspicuously slow speech development at first, as I was only three years old. Nevertheless, it worried her.

On the twenty-fourth of May that year, Aunt Irene and Uncle Heinrich were married in the chapel of Charlottenburg Palace. We traveled to the wedding, but the mood was slightly somber because Emperor Frederick III, Uncle Heinrich's father, was so seriously ill.

Shortly after the Kaiser's death, we spent the summer in Darmstadt again and

Papa's father was not in good shape. He was suffering from severe back pain, could hardly walk and had lost a lot of weight. Papa was able to take a longer break from the navy, but didn't want to worry his father. The doctors told him that his father was dying because he was suffering from kidney cancer. Mama, of course, supported my father in every way and shared his grief, just as she tried to comfort Grandma Julie. Nevertheless, despite his severe suffering, everything was to remain the same for Grandpa. Everyday life should not be changed or limited to him, as everyone thought he would then have to spend his last weeks in great fear.
So we traveled back to Malta in the winter to be with Papa, who had resumed his duties. There, my parents received the news that Grandpa had died on the fifteenth of December. Grandma Julie had cared for him devotedly and was deeply shocked by his passing. Mama therefore thought she needed a distraction. She stayed in Darmstadt after her father-in-law's funeral so that she could keep her father`s company.

My mother also believed that a longer stay in Darmstadt would be good for me, as I could play with my cousin Edda, who was only a year older than me. Aunt Marie Karoline had also come to comfort her mother in her time of grief.
But even when I played with Edda, it didn't improve my language skills.
Shortly after my fourth birthday, my grandmother suspected that I might be deaf, because although I was a bright and lively little girl, I made up words myself and had a very incomprehensible pronunciation. My relatives had got used to it and tried to understand what I meant, but it was impossible for outsiders to understand me.
Grandma thought that perhaps my ears had been damaged by the trips at sea. The strong wind might have damaged my ear canals. She finally decided to take me to a doctor who specialized in my symptoms to examine me thoroughly. He discovered that I had been born with a defect. The Eustachian tubes in my head were thickened. This would always be a problem that I would have to learn to live with.
Mama immediately started practicing with me so that I could lip-read people's words, which was very difficult. Both German and English were spoken in our family. But Mama was tireless, she wanted me to be able to follow conversations, so she also asked all relatives to treat me like any other person, like someone without a disability. She was afraid that a special position would not help me in my later life, but would only marginalize me. I don't know if she ever blamed herself for my disability, even though it wasn't anyone's fault. She will certainly have been affected as a mother, but at the same time she was so committed to supporting and helping me that I was always grateful

to her.
It's not easy when you can't hear other people. Sometimes I still felt left out later on, because it was difficult for me to follow the conversations when lots of people were sitting at a table talking. When someone laughed, I sometimes feared that they were laughing at me.
However, I later delighted my family by explaining to them the real words of the actors in the silent movies when we watched films on the Cinematograph. I remember one movie that was about a declaration of love between a man and a woman. The text was about love, but in reality the man was talking about how he couldn't pay the rent for his small apartment and was afraid he would end up on the street. Everyone found that very funny.
Through my mother's strict teaching I also learned to speak, albeit in my own way, and I communicated with gestures, learning sign language, as this became popular in the nineteenth century.
Teaching deaf children to speak, to become so-called *oralists*, was only taken up at the beginning of the twentieth century. In a way, my mother was a pioneer in this.
My mother was pregnant again in 1889 and the baby was due to be born in July. So when we returned to England in the summer, we spent a few days with the Queen.
She also wanted to get an idea of my progress. So when we visited her, it was customary to kiss her hand in greeting. The Queen was not particularly lenient with young children when it came to etiquette, so she was indignant if a great-grandchild or grandchild did not want to kiss her hand in greeting. When I refused, she gently slapped my hand and called me a naughty child. But much to her astonishment, I returned her slap, slapped the back of her hand and called her a cheeky grandmother. Of course, I immediately had to be removed from Grandma's sight by Mama, who was very embarrassed.
I had been speaking very beautifully since May 1889, Mama said, and after the situation she regretted having raved about it to the Queen.

On July thirteenth, my sister Louise was born in Heiligenberg in Hesse. Grandmother Julie was delighted that my mother wanted to give birth near her, so Grandmother could look after her and the baby in the early days. The Queen had always encouraged my mother to have another child so that I would have a playmate.
Louise was born a few weeks prematurely after Mama was shaken a little too much on a carriage ride to Felsberg. From Mama's point of view, she was nothing like herself, lacking any resemblance. Louise's nose was too big for her, the baby was too small overall, more like a *miserable little worm*, as she put it, and so my little sister was nicknamed *Shrimp*, a name that was to be

attached to her throughout her youth.
She was baptized in Heiligenberg on the ninth of August and I always remembered fondly how I noticed that the pastor didn't wash Louise's head properly, which caused some small laughs during the ceremony.
Aunt Irene had given birth to little Waldemar on the twentieth of March that year. She was now living with her husband on the Hemmelmark estate near Kiel, as her uncle was employed by the Prussian Navy. Unfortunately, it soon turned out that little Waldemar suffered from hemophilia. It was a great shock for Aunt Irene when she was told, as she knew about the dangers of this disease through her little brother Frittie and Uncle Leopold. As a carrier, any other son born could also inherit the disease from her. And it also meant that she had to keep a constant eye on her son so that he did not injure himself. Her second son Sigismund, born in 1896, was supposed to be healthy, but her third son, Heinrich, born in 1900, inherited the disease. He died at the age of four as a result of a fall. Aunt Irene was forever blaming herself for this, as she had briefly left the little boy alone. He had climbed onto a chair at the table and tipped over with it, falling on his head. Although a healthy child would only have ended up with a small bruise, Heinrich died from internal bleeding.
Mama and her sisters all knew about the disease, but each hoped not to pass it on to their sons. Mama was certainly always afraid when she was pregnant, but she was not supposed to pass on the disease.

Papa had been ordered to serve on the '*Scout*' on October 3, 1889 and was in command of the ship.
When my grandfather died, my father, as the eldest son, inherited Heiligenberg Castle. Grandmother Julie had the right to live there for life, but we finally had a real home of our own that my parents didn't have to pay rent for. That's why we naturally spent more time in Darmstadt.
Mama wanted to spend the winter in Malta again, and as Louise was still too small, it was decided to spare her the long journey and leave me and my sister in the care of our grandmother Julie for five long months, whom I liked very much, but I still missed my parents very much.
The Queen found it more than strange that Mama could leave such a small child alone for such a long time, but my mother assured her that we were in good hands, because Aunt Alix, Uncle Ernie and Grandpa Ludwig were still there, and Louise was so weak that she had to find her feet in this world first. My mother was a very loving woman, but she really wanted to accompany Papa to Malta so that she could be with him.
The queen thought a lot of Julie as she was very well educated and I was undisputedly her favorite. She had also had to endure two very great losses.

Firstly, the death of her husband and then the break-up with her son Sandro, whom she was never to see again. Aunt Marie Karoline found her mother locked up in a snail shell, sad and bitter, but we children quickly cheered her up. Grandmother Julie spoke four languages, read Dante in Italian and Shakespeare in English.
When the Queen later met Sandro's wife, the former opera singer Johanna Loisinger, she was very impressed by the woman's kindness, but when she mentioned this to Grandmother in a letter, it hurt her all the more. She knew the pain and sorrow of a morganatic marriage, had tried to advise her son against it and in the end had caused the break with him.
Grandma spoiled me in every way, perhaps also because of my disability. Like Mama, she was very committed to helping me and supporting me in my learning.
When Mama finally returned on April 8, 1890, I didn't leave her side for days, I had missed her so much. The first thing she noticed about me was my growth and that I had become a little thinner. The early childhood curves had fused together.
The next separation was imminent in September, when Mama visited Uncle Sergey in Russia together with Grandpa Ludwig, Ernie and Alix, Aunt Ella and spent a few weeks with them on their Ilinskoye estate.
As Aunt Alix was now eighteen years old, Queen Victoria wanted to prove herself again as a matchmaker in matters of love and suggested to her mother that she make her grandson, Prince Albert Victor, the first-born son of Uncle Bertie, palatable to her sister as a marriage candidate. He was eight years older than Alix and was called *Eddy* in the family. When Alix visited England, he seemed to be very attracted to her and was probably also a little enamored of her. But Aunt Alix had been writing letters to Tsarevich Nicholas of Russia for a long time and from their first meeting, he too hoped that he might one day marry her. For the Queen, it was an abomination to lose a second granddaughter to the Russian tsarist dynasty, and Aunt Alix did not want to exchange her Protestant faith for the Russian Orthodox faith. Converting was out of the question for her due to her deep religious convictions, but as the future tsarina she would have had to do so. Tsar Alexander III and his wife Tsarina Marie, who was a born Princess of Denmark, also had their objections to a marriage. Alix was not a princess from a royal house, but *only* the daughter of a grand duke and from a relatively insignificant grand duchy at that. What's more, she was German. The Tsarina actually hated the Germans, as her father, King Christian IX of Denmark, had been forced to cede the Duchy of Schleswig to Prussia during the *German-Danish War* of 1864. All in all, Alix was not a good match for her. Her shyness also made her unsuitable to be tsarina and, moreover, she did not speak French, which was

the court language at the Russian tsar's court. Aunt Alicky suffered terribly because she loved Nicky, as we all called him, very much, but the pressure on her was immense.
She shared her grief with Mama and her other sisters, with Ella in particular telling her to listen to her heart. Alicky knew very well that she never wanted to marry Eddy, which in turn hurt the Queen very much, as she once again felt that her wishes had been rejected. Mama was urged in letters from the Queen to mediate, but she herself had married for love and wanted to see her little sister happy herself. Grandfather Ludwig felt the same way. He had not been a happy man for a long time, constantly worn down by great grief for his wife, the *faux pas* with his marriage not befitting his station and finally sinking into depression. He was rarely seen smiling. Even the hunting vacations in England, to which the Queen liked to invite him, brought him only brief joy.
Mama was back from Russia in October and I had to say goodbye to my beloved nanny Mary Jones, who had been sent to us by the Queen but wanted to retire for personal reasons. She was replaced by Ellen Hughes, a very friendly and dedicated woman.
As Louise was developing well in the meantime, we spent the winter of 1890 in Malta again and the next one a year later, because on the thirty-first of December 1891, Papa was promoted to captain. Of course, my mother was very proud of him.

Miss Hughes taught me in Malta under Mama's guidance and by the end of 1889 I could already read fluently in German, which was also thanks to Grandmother Julie, who always studied diligently with me during Mama's absence.
I started to write my first words in English and had one lesson a day.

As a child, I didn't know why my parents were often in such a bad financial position in the early days of their marriage, even though my father received a good salary in the *Royal Navy*. Years later I was to learn that in 1880, before he married my mother, he had had a secret affair with the actress Lillie Langtry, who had also been Uncle Bertie's mistress. Lillie unfortunately became pregnant by Papa and gave birth to a daughter named Jeanne-Marie on March 8, 1881. The girl grew up mostly on the island of Jersey with foster parents and her mother was her *aunt*. It would have been a huge scandal at the time, as Lillie was still married at the time of her affair with Papa. It was agreed to keep everything secret. But my father still paid child support for their daughter, even after we, his own children, were born. Jeanne-Marie only found out about her mother and her relationship with her father when she was an adult

contacts with both sexes. It was therefore understandable that both Aunt Alix and a Princess of Orleans, whose hand he asked for, never wanted to marry him due to his well-known lifestyle.
However, as the Queen was not particularly aware of his excesses, she persuaded him to become engaged to Princess Maria von Teck in December 1891. The wedding was to take place in February 1892.
Curiously, his brother George, who was now crown prince, soon courted his brother's fiancée.

Mourning reigned in Darmstadt after the death of Grandfather Ludwig. His funeral took place on the seventeenth of March, all stores were closed and long, black mourning banners hung from private homes. He was laid to rest next to Grandmother Alice in the mausoleum.
But my family couldn't get out of their grief. Maximilian, the fourteen-year-old son of my aunt Marie Karoline, died just twelve days after his grandfather's death. *Maxi* had been mentally handicapped because he had been given too little oxygen at birth. My aunt had always described her son as a little angel, but she saw his death as redemption for the boy, who was destined for a life with little hope due to his severe disability. Despite all this, it was a great loss for her.
With Grandfather Ludwig's death, Uncle Ernie was now the new Grand Duke of Hesse and by Rhine. He was only twenty-three years old and, in the eyes of many, too young for the job. In April, the Queen traveled to Darmstadt and presented him with his father's *Order of the Garter*, the Order of the Garter, which for members of the English royal family was a kind of honorary membership of the Order of *St. George*. As a foreign monarch, Grandfather had once been presented with it by the Queen. It was a great honor for Uncle Ernie, whom the Queen now urged to find a wife as soon as possible, referring to Victoria Melita, with whom Ernie had already got on so well at Balmoral. She saw it as a great task to bring the two together, and although this was to be crowned with success, it was also to prove her wrong once and for all shortly afterwards. With this union, she finally renounced *matchmaking* in the last years of her life.

But back to the summer of 1892, which still meant court mourning for Darmstadt, which according to the protocol always lasted a year when a ruler passed away. I noticed very little of this mourning. I missed my grandfather, saw the sad faces of my mother, my aunts and uncles, that of grandmother Julie, who was also very saddened by the death of little Maxi, and yet I had other worries. My milk teeth had to be removed by a dentist in Frankfurt am Main. However, my nanny Sophie Hahn later remarked that I had been very

brave and hadn't cried.
We were surprised by a very shocking experience in July of this year. Aunt Beatrice and Uncle Liko were visiting us in Heiligenberg from England. They had brought their son Alexander, called *Drino*, with them. He was six years old and was supposed to be a playmate for me and my sister Louise. Aunt Beatrice and Uncle Liko didn't have it easy. First they had had to fight for their marriage for many months because the queen wanted to keep the aunt as the youngest of her children as her companion, then the marriage had only been possible if both agreed to stay with the queen at all times, in other words, to live with her. The uncle had little money, no opportunity to rise in the Prussian military and the union with the aunt was not quite befitting. So they accepted the evil of being at the Queen's constant disposal as company, although they also had to put up with her interfering in their children's upbringing, their lifestyle and, in fact, the couple's entire life. The couple were happy to escape her influence for a while.
The summer was very hot, there was a veritable flood of mosquitoes and poor Aunt Beatrice was soon completely bitten up. Together with her chambermaid, she tried to attract and catch the mosquitoes at night in her bedroom with a lighted candle. In principle, this was an effective method, but the two women were so committed that they brushed the candle against an insect net attached to the bed. They opened the window and in an instant the aunt's entire bedroom was ablaze. The two ladies fled outside, but the fire engulfed the roof of the pavilion above with the old bell tower and clock tower. When our nanny Sophie Hahn was startled out of her sleep by the screams and cries of her aunt and her chambermaid, she immediately ran to my mother and we were hurriedly dressed. My mother ordered us to quickly throw some valuables that were within reach into a basket.
Drino, Louise and I were placed in a safe spot away from the inferno and gazed in amazement at the flames. Auntie, of course, was also a point of our attention as she ran around completely headless in her nightgown with only Mama's cape over her shoulders, crying for her pearls and jewelry. It was sad, of course, because the aunt really didn't have much, but no one could save anything from the fire.
The fire department came from Jugenheim. The chambermaid feared that she too was only wearing a nightgown, despite the summer heat of the night, and Mama made sure that Drino trembled with fear when she told him that the firemen were there. He interpreted this as men coming out of the fire burning to scare everyone. He was immediately in tears. He hadn't seen firemen in his short life and this was his personal perception of them, especially since Mama mispronounced it.
As there was no wind, the fire was extinguished by five o'clock in the

morning, but the damage was massive.
The next morning, her aunt sat in the chaos of her bedroom, of which only ashes remained. She mourned the loss of emeralds that had been broken, pearls that had crumbled like chalk, and many of her most beautiful clothes had also been destroyed by the flames. It was all the worse for her that she now had to speak to the fire insurance people, her head covered by a hat, because her wig had also been burnt.
All the excitement was getting on Mama's nerves. She was four months pregnant and feared losing the baby.
My mother told my father about all the events in writing, but he couldn't leave his current command on the '*Andromache*' and he also knew about my mother's strength.
She stayed in Heiligenberg until the winter.
One Sunday, November 6, 1892, Grandmother Julie was on her way to church when her old servant ran up to her and told her that a prince had arrived at the *Altes Palais*. Grandmother was indignant because she found it outrageous that a visitor had come to Mama's house, unannounced, when she was preparing for the birth of her child. It made her angry and she gave verbal expression to this until her servant finally intervened, but Ernie and Alix came to her and explained that it was about the baby. Of course, her anger immediately subsided and she immediately turned back so that she could greet the new citizen of the world.
George, or *Georgie* as we soon called him, was immediately everyone's favorite. The birth had been easy for Mama, the baby was healthy and a real bundle of joy. Louise in particular was fascinated by our little brother, seeing him as something like a doll that had to be looked after. She was to remain very close to him in later life.
Of course I was also happy about my brother and for the Queen it was the thirteenth great-grandchild, which also made her very proud.
On November twenty-third Papa was promoted to *Naval Adviser to Inspector General of Fortifications*. This was a very important post in the *Royal Navy* and meant that he was now responsible for peacetime and wartime matters as Secretary to the War Office. This involved the defense systems of the ships. Papa got an office with the *Horseguards*, a military equestrian unit in Whitehall, and rented a house in Pimlico. Both were in a district in the *City of Westminister* in London.
My mother traveled to him in March 1893 and we children stayed in Darmstadt until May, when we moved back to England. Until the summer of 1894, we traveled with Mum to the Queen's residences again and were in very close contact with her, which pleased her greatly.
Before that happened, however, my mother insisted that we take a three-

month break as a normal small family. My parents rented a small house in Sandgate near Folkestone. The house was near the sea and it was a wonderful time there, with us children often playing on the beach.
As I was now seven years old, I was given proper lessons by a tutor called Miss Robson. She had already been the governess of Princess Margaret of Connaught in India and came highly recommended. Margaret was the daughter of Uncle Arthur, a son of the Queen, who served in India as a general and commander-in-chief of the army in Bombay.

I really missed a new little friend I had made in England. In the spring of 1893, the English diplomat Sir George Buchanan had come to Darmstadt with his family to work as a so-called *chargé d'affaires*, i.e. to represent the English embassy in Darmstadt. When he visited us on the Heiligenberg for the first time with his daughter Meriel, we girls immediately took a liking to each other. There was a little wooden house where we children used to play. Meriel and I soon spent a lot of time there together, playing housewives by sweeping out the cottage with little brooms, making tea or trying to bake scones. A governess was always there to help us with the latter and keep an eye on us. Meriel was a year older than me. After a short time, her admiration for me grew to such an extent that she wanted to copy me in almost everything. Like me, she soon no longer wanted to wear a ribbon in her hair, but a barrette, and she kept telling me that I had beautiful brown eyes. She once confessed to me that she liked my slightly faraway look the most. Sometimes it seemed like I was dreaming when I didn't listen or notice when someone was talking to me. I could hardly wait for Meriel to come and play and the separation was very bad for me.
As her father worked as a diplomat in many countries, such as Italy, the Netherlands, Luxembourg and others, her family was constantly traveling. She was unable to settle down and regretted this very much. Because every time she made friends, her father was transferred. In 1910, her father became ambassador to Russia. Meriel later wrote a book about her time as the daughter of an ambassador, paying particular attention to her time in Russia. She also wrote novels, but these were not a great success. It was only when she included her own memories of the Tsar's family during the turmoil of the Russian Revolution in her written memoirs that she was able to celebrate success.

The wedding of Princess Mary of Teck to Prince George, Duke of York, took place on the sixth of July 1893. As mentioned, Mary had been engaged to his younger brother Albert Victor, but after his death she was made to like George and agreed to marry him. They became engaged in May. With the death of his elder brother, Uncle Bertie's son George would later become king. This was another reason why he was a good match for Mary, whom everyone called *May*. She was actually still mourning the loss of her first fiancé, but her parents were probably also putting a lot of pressure on her. Her mother Mary was privately known at court as *Fat Mary* because of her corpulence, and her parents both lived very exclusively, residing in very posh hotels in France, among other places, and had large debts despite a good royal allowance. Marrying her daughter into a wealthy house only had advantages for her too.

I was invited to be one of the bridesmaids at Mary's side. Mama, like me, was very proud of this honor.
However, we only found out after the wedding that Princess Alice of Albany, the daughter of the late Uncle Leopold, had been chosen first. Alice was eleven years old, very happy and had already received an invitation. She was staying with her mother, Aunt Helene and her brother with relatives in Arolsen at the beginning of the summer, as her aunt was a Princess of Waldeck-Pyrmont by birth. During this vacation, poor little Alice received the news that a different decision had been made and she was uninvited without further ado. The queen had recommended me as one of the ten bridesmaids and the simple reason for Alice's disinvitation was that they thought I was prettier.
Alice of Albany knew that. She was very offended that May von Teck had decided against her, and she was never to forgive me for it, although I was not to blame.
She was a pretty blonde girl who looked like the spitting image of her father. Perhaps I would have spoken to my mother about it as a child if I had been told everything, because when my mother found out, she wasn't exactly happy about the situation. And Aunt Helene later let her know how well she remembered this injustice to her daughter even after a long time.
The wedding took place in the *Chapel Royal* at *St. James Palace* in London. I wore a beautiful satin dress with a little pink and red rose on the shoulder and little bows on my shoes. It was a beautiful ceremony, but I didn't really like big parties like that because I had a hard time making out what anyone was saying or if they were talking to me amongst all the people. Perhaps it was because I was deaf that I always felt more comfortable in smaller groups than in large parties.
Of course, Alice from Albany had to assure me later on how much she enjoyed such big family celebrations, making it immediately clear how much I had offended her, even though I was the least to blame.
The Queen invited Mama and us children to spend ten days with her in Windsor after the wedding. During these days, she obliged me to attend dance lessons, one of which she attended with a critical eye. As I couldn't hear, I had

to feel the music, which was very difficult. But as the man leads the woman, the queen said it would be fine and I should just be careful not to step on my dance partner's feet. I remarked that it could be that the partner in question had no sense of rhythm, in which case we would make a very strange couple on the dance floor. When a big orchestra was playing, I could feel the vibrations, but when someone was just playing the piano, I couldn't hear anything. For the Queen, however, dance lessons were as much a part of a young lady's education as learning other etiquette.

Interestingly, rumor had it that among the bridesmaids were three young ladies who would have been only too happy to swap places with Mary for George as her husband and thus the future King of England. One of these ladies was Sandra and it was an open secret that everyone knew about.

My parents had heard that there was a possibility of an operation for my hearing impairment, so in the summer my mother took me to an ear specialist in London who had a very good reputation. She and Papa were very worried as I wasn't making any progress and was now eight years old. Some hearing-impaired people improve as they develop from childhood to adulthood if, like me, their *Eustachian tubes* are thickened. Sometimes there was a slight reduction in swelling and I was then able to perceive sounds. Of course, never like a person without a hearing impairment, but at least quiet and muffled. Like all parents of a disabled child, they clung to any hope, however small, but after an intensive examination, the doctor was unable to tell my mother that there was any chance of her hearing improving. An operation was not an option for me. However, he noted that sometimes removing the tonsils could help.

That summer, during our stay at Buckingham Palace, I had to have my tonsils surgically removed by the Queen's doctor, Sir James Reid. As Louise often had a cold and suffered from a sore throat, she also had the operation.

Unfortunately, the operation didn't improve my disability and I had a hard time recovering from the procedure. So we traveled back to Sandgate a few days after the operation so that we girls could lose our paleness and fatigue in the fresh sea air.

This was followed by a short stay with Grandma Julie in Darmstadt and at the end of July we moved into our house in London. It had a lovely garden where we could play, and when the weather was nice we went for walks in nearby Battersea Park, which was only a quarter of an hour's walk from the house. Uncle Bertie, who visited us once, thought the house was very nicely furnished, but the neighborhood was very *middle-class* - i.e. *cheap* - and told Mum that only poor musicians lived there. It's worth mentioning that the uncle had no idea about our low income, i.e. Papa's, which he had to use to feed us all. It wasn't enough for a lavish lifestyle of luxury. My mother found the neighborhood *middle-class* and pleasant. She didn't need a palace to be happy.

The Queen didn't like it at all when she found out how we children were playing in a public park, because London wasn't exactly a clean city, as she put it. So she gave Mama a key to the garden at Buckingham Palace. But we also got dirty in the soot-blackened bushes there. The dirt and dust also came to London through the surrounding factories. The wind carried it through the city, spreading the fine layer over everything. Where the middle class lived, the burghers, the streets were relatively clean, apart from the horse droppings from the carriages, but in the working class areas the living conditions were characterized by stench and waste, and of course it was not nice for the Queen to hear that we were romping around in the bushes and playing like street urchins.

Christmas in 1893 was something very special for us children, because for the first time we were allowed to celebrate with the Queen and relatives at Osborne House on the Isle of Wight.

The children's rooms were located directly above the queen's living quarters. There was a room full of beds where all the children could sleep together, a huge playroom filled with the most wonderful toys that many a child could only dream of, classrooms, one of which was for the little ones, one for the children over six. Aunt Beatrice's children usually had lessons in both.

There was a Swiss-style cottage in the grounds where we children could play. Grandfather Albert, the Queen's husband, once had this built for his children. It had a pantry, a small kitchen, a dining room and was furnished like a real house. The Queen's children, especially the girls, had once learned housekeeping, cooking and baking here in a playful way. Albert had always wanted his children, even if they were of royal blood, to get to know a down-to-earth life.

There was also a museum where everyone in the family had brought something from a faraway country. It was filled with very interesting things from all over the world. We children could marvel at the artifacts for hours.

For the boys, there was a small original fort to play in with miniature cannons that could be operated properly, and we were allowed to admire the queen's so-called *bathing machine*. It was a square with a wooden frame that she could use to get into the water when it was warm, and was protected from view so that no one could catch a glimpse of her in her bathing costume and bathing cap.

This Christmas was a very gloomy one for the queen. Her lameness had increased, she was finding it increasingly difficult to walk and her eyes were

also getting weaker.
Papa's brother Sandro had also died on the seventeenth of November. I had mentioned that the Queen had met Sandro's wife and was in contact with Grandmother Julie, who was not to see her son again after his morganatic marriage.
The news of Uncle Sandro's death took us all by surprise, as his wife had said that he had died suddenly. Papa and his brothers hadn't had any real contact with him either. As it turned out later, his uncle had had appendicitis and, as the surgical options were not yet fully developed at the time, he developed peritonitis after the operation and died shortly after the operation.
Johanna, Uncle Sandro's wife, made no attempt to integrate herself into the family, even after his death. Possibly because she could not forgive grandmother Julie for her opposition to her son's morganatic marriage. So the widow moved to Vienna with her children Assen and Zwetana. However, as the uncle was Prince of Bulgaria for several years, he was given a state funeral in Sofia. However, no one from our family attended.

The Queen traditionally celebrated Christmas on Christmas Eve. As her husband had been German, from the House of Saxe-Coburg and Gotha, and she herself also had German roots, the German tradition was adhered to. Among other things, the Queen and her family had introduced the Christmas tree as a custom in England. The bourgeois families and other aristocrats had then followed the royal family in this tradition; one could also say that it had become fashionable to have a Christmas tree.
The Christmas service took place at eleven o'clock in the afternoon and at eighteen o'clock in the evening the candles were lit on the beautifully decorated tree and the presents were distributed.

On the second of January, 1894, the Queen was present when Drino, Ena and I were drilled in a playful manner by a constable. He was employed *at Parkhurst*, one of England's most famous prisons on the Isle of Wight. It was also known as *Parkhurst Barracks*. Alongside *Albany Barracks*, which was located in Newport, just outside the island, the prison was considered one of the most notorious. Both prisons were heavily guarded and escape was almost impossible. Many criminals were also sent from *Parkhurst* to the colonies in New Zealand and Australia in the mid-nineteenth century.
I can't remember why he played with us, but it was an interesting experience. The days on the island were otherwise filled with tea parties, and as we children were all together, there was never a dull Mamaent. There was always someone to play with.
I also celebrated my ninth birthday with the Queen and I was given a lovely

party. The Queen thought I was now old enough to accompany Mama and her on afternoon carriage rides to West Cowes and Newport. These rides were to become a special event for me when the Queen visited from then on, as she let me know how much she enjoyed it when I was there. She once said freely that she loved me and my siblings as much as our parents.
From Osborne we then traveled to Uncle George and Aunt May in Sandringham. We stayed there for a weekend. You can say without a doubt that there was even more on offer there than at the Queen's. There was a very large tea party, the uncle showed us the stables, the dog kennels, his pheasantry, and before we left, a large feast was held in our honor with many guests, for which 400 partridges were shot beforehand.
Shortly afterwards, we learned of a terrible accident that had caused the Queen great concern. Ena, Aunt Beatrice's seven-year-old daughter, had fallen off her pony while riding and got caught under its hooves. The pony stumbled and fell on top of her. For days, it was feared that little Ena might have suffered serious brain damage, but when she finally woke up from her unconsciousness, it soon became clear that she had suffered nothing apart from bruises, cuts and a concussion. But of course we were all very worried about her. Ena had become a dear playmate to me and it would have been terrible if she had been disabled after the accident. As I was familiar with this from Maxi von Erbach-Schönberg and knew about such a serious disability, I was very relieved when she recovered.
Before Easter, we moved from London to Elm Grove in *Walton-on-Thames*. The town is in the county of *Surrey* in the south-east of England. The Thames flowed close to the town and we were allowed to take a small rented boat up the river from time to time. Our new home, on the other hand, was far more spacious than the one in London, the furniture was rather antique but still comfortable and there was a small garden. The town had a population of around twenty-two thousand. So life there was much more tranquil than in the big city of London.

At the end of 1893, Uncle Ernie and Ducky of Saxe-Coburg and Gotha became engaged. It had been the Queen's express wish that the two should marry, and Ducky's mother, Duchess Marie, had also been very keen on a union. Both were artistically inclined, cheerful people and had their birthdays on the twenty-fifth of November. Moreover, they had got on so well together at meetings in England that the Queen had literally urged the now twenty-five-year-old Ernie to marry Ducky. The Duchess had already married off her eldest daughter Marie well. She married Crown Prince Ferdinand of Romania and would one day become queen, and she also thought the future title of Grand Duchess was a very good idea for Ducky.

Ducky was only seventeen years old, but a real beauty with curly, dark hair and a tall build. She had suffered greatly from her shyness as a child, was rather introverted and only signed photographs of herself "*The ugly child*". The Duchess and the Duke had rarely been available for the children, often governesses and governesses, who were very strict, replaced the parental roles, and Ducky was often as much bullied by them as by her mother, so that she would overcome her shyness. Even her sister Marie often remarked on how much the poor child was being put through. Perhaps Ducky saw marriage as a way of escaping the confines of her parents' home and her mother's strictness, but to outsiders, Ernie and she really did seem to be very much in love. On April nineteenth, 1894, they married at Ehrenburg Castle in Coburg in Bavaria, where his parents had lived.
For Aunt Alix, Uncle Ernie's marriage meant that the close bond between her and him, which had united them since the death of their mother and father, was loosening. She no longer needed to feel responsible for her brother, and when she heard that Tsarevich Nicholas was arriving from Russia for the wedding, she asked to speak to him. If the Queen in England had hoped that Alix's desire to marry Nicky had perhaps been extinguished by the change of religion and the other circumstances, she was mistaken. They still loved each other, had kept in close correspondence over the years and their love had grown steadily with each family reunion. Now, when they met in Coburg, Nicky promised her that she would not have to give up her religion, she would have to convert, but he would never reproach her if she kept the Lutheran faith for herself. It was of secondary importance to him, because he told her he couldn't imagine life without her. To everyone's surprise, they got engaged on the twentieth of April in Coburg. For Mama, her sister's happiness was all that mattered and she did everything she could to convince the Queen, who then offered Alix the opportunity to travel to England to meet with the Bishop of Ripon, Dr. Boyd Carpenter, who would explain the similarities between the Russian Orthodox and Lutheran faiths. In doing so, she showed that she now accepted her granddaughter's decision and had to let her go. If it was her dearest wish to go to Russia and become tsarina one day, she would not stand in the way of her happiness.
So we celebrated two big parties in Coburg and I was delighted to see Uncle Ernie and Aunt Alix happy.

Aunt Alix traveled a few days after her engagement, first to Uncle Ernie and Aunt Ducky in Darmstadt, then to the Queen in Windsor, accompanied by Gretchen von Fabrice, her lady-in-waiting. Margarethe, who was called Gretchen, had been her faithful companion and a close confidante since Aunt

Alix was sixteen. Gretchen was very religious, just like Alix, and was supposed to guide her to find her place in life, as she was a few years older, but she had one disadvantage - like Alix, she was very shy and rather reserved. She also blushed quickly in company when there were too many people around her. But perhaps this was also a reason why the two women got on so well, and Gretchen would stay close to Alix forever.
They both visited us in our new home in Walton at the end of April. I loved Aunt Alix very much because she was such a kind and open-hearted person. She knew how to be compassionate to everyone, which also ensured that she never judged anyone for a disability or other weakness. Everything she did or said showed an honesty and warmth that often impressed me.
Uncle Nicky came to visit us in mid-June, accompanied by his old valet, and he was just as warm and open with us as Alix. I thought they were a wonderful couple, you could really feel how much they were in love. Even when it rained heavily for a few days, they went for a walk together under an umbrella, laughing in the rain. It was a little break for them both. Uncle Nicky invited Louise and me to join him and Alix for some carriage rides around Walton. He was to regret this invitation somewhat, as we both often jumped up in the carriage to show them something. The jolting got to him a little, but he took it with humor.
Uncle Franzjos also visited us for a few days and Mama said that the house was getting very crowded with so many people and we would probably have to move to the garden soon. She loved family gatherings. It wasn't meant in a bad way, but more as a joke.
I remember rowing with Uncle Fanzjos on the Thames and he turned out to be a really bad rower. So they gave me a rope and put me ashore to keep the boat on course, but going against the current was very difficult as Uncle Fanzjos and I were not really in sync in our efforts. I tried to go faster, the uncle swung the oars and they kept touching the embankment and the shore. For the others in the boat, it was a really difficult rowing trip, because everyone was afraid of falling into the water.
One day after Uncle Franzjo's departure, two royal carriages and a liveried horseman arrived to take us all to Windsor for a visit at the Queen's invitation. The residents of the surrounding houses stood on the sidewalks and were amazed at the spectacle.
In August 1894, we traveled to Darmstadt. Papa's father was reburied in the newly built mausoleum on the Heiligenberg and it was very sad to see Grandmother Julie walking behind the coffin crying.
On October sixteenth, Papa was given a new command on the '*Cambrian*' and was separated from us again. We would only see him again in Malta in the winter and be able to spend more time with him.

In the meantime, Russian Tsar Alexander III's health was deteriorating. In 1888, the imperial train derailed near Borki in the Caucasus due to an unknown cause. The Tsar, a tall, strong man, had raised the roof of the train so that his family could get to safety. It was assumed that this superhuman effort had caused damage to his internal organs.

He had been suffering from severe kidney inflammation, nephritis, for some time and the doctors were powerless. The family had retreated to Livadia in the Crimea, the summer resort on the Black Sea, because they hoped that the warm climate there might help him. Uncle Nicky telegraphed Aunt Alix that his father was dying and she traveled there immediately to support him and her future in-laws. Mama accompanied her sister for part of the journey from Darmstadt until Aunt Ella met them both on the way and traveled on with Alix.

But the tsar died on the first of November. He was buried in St. Petersburg and Uncle Nicky became the new Tsar of Russia. His father had only just turned forty-nine. His death came as a complete surprise to everyone. On November twenty-sixth, Aunt Alix and Uncle Nicky married in a small circle in the chapel of the Winter Palace in St. Petersburg. However, due to the year of mourning, the coronation had to wait. A big celebration was planned for this.

For the Queen in England, the wedding meant the end of any hopes that her grandchild Alicky might still change her mind. She had supported her somewhat, but inwardly, as she wrote in letters to Mama, she still had a quiet hope that the wedding would not take place. She liked Uncle Nicky, but feared that she would hardly see her granddaughter again, if at all, and said freely that she had lost her to the Russians.

In the fall of 1894, we had already received the happy news from Darmstadt that Aunt Ducky was pregnant, and the baby was due in March of the following year. The Queen was naturally delighted to have a new great-grandchild, but she insisted, as so often with births in our family, on choosing a good gynecologist. When Uncle Willy, the son of Empress Friedrich, was born, there had been errors, which meant that one of his arms was underdeveloped. The Queen also blamed Maxi von Erbach's disability on a mistake made by the doctors at his birth. Ducky's mother only asked for a Russian wet nurse for the baby. The Queen was willing to grant her this, but she always had the best and most knowledgeable doctors on hand, so her advice could be relied upon.

On March eleventh, 1895, little Princess Elisabeth was born in Darmstadt. I was very happy about the birth of my little cousin. She was baptized in Darmstadt on the twenty-fourth of March, with all of us in attendance. Aunt Ella, Ducky's sister and Crown Princess Marie of Romania had also come, as they

had been chosen to be the baby's godparents. The Queen of England and Aunt Alix were also godparents, but neither of them were able to come. The Queen did not feel well, the journey was too strenuous for her and Aunt Alix was pregnant.
From the day she was born, little Elisabeth was her father's everything. Uncle Ernie loved his little girl and took great care of her. She was blessed with a dark mop of hair and wonderful brown eyes, but there was always a sadness in them, even in later years, which we did not interpret as a bad omen at the time. Aunt Ducky loved her child too, of course, but you got the feeling that she didn't adore him as much as her husband did.
In the run-up to the birth, a minor dispute had broken out between Ducky's mother and the Queen because the Duchess Marie ultimately wanted to trust a German gynecologist rather than an English one. Offended, the Queen wrote to her mother, as her efforts were obviously unwelcome.

In the summer of 1895 we were in Heiligenberg and enjoyed the time with our relatives very much, I was especially happy to be with Grandmother Julie. It came as a great shock to me when she died unexpectedly on September nineteenth at the age of sixty-nine. We had wanted to celebrate her milestone birthday in November. It wasn't the first bereavement I had been confronted with in our family, but it hit me hard because I had lost a very loving grandmother and close confidante. Of course, the loss of his mother also weighed heavily on Papa, as it did on our entire family.
It was terrible for Mama to see how much I suffered. I often couldn't stop crying for my beloved grandmother, and when she told the Queen, she was equally devastated. She had kept in very good correspondence with Grandmother Julie for years and spoke very highly of her. She understood my grief all the more.
I said goodbye to my grandmother, who had been laid out in the castle's conservatory. And it was very painful to see her so still in her coffin, with all the beautiful flowers that we draped around her. My brother Georgie cheered us up a bit, because he said that although she loved flowers, she loved fruit all the more, especially pears. So he ran off, came back with a pear and put it next to her. Nobody was angry because he was right. Grandma had said more than once how important fruit was for your health. It just seemed more logical to my little brother that she would be better off with a pear in heaven.
Nevertheless, Louise and Georgie didn't miss her as much as I did, at least that's how I felt. Her death made me very grumpy and introverted for a while.
In the fall, we traveled to Aunt Irene and Uncle Heinrich in Hemmelmark, where we could swim in the sea, go fishing on a lake or sail on the sea in my uncle's yacht '*Esperance*'. It was a nice change of pace and these visits were

soon to become a regular occurrence, but it brought me little distraction. Mama immediately feared that I might fall behind in my development. I wasn't quite eleven yet, but I had grown so much that most people who met me and didn't know me thought I was fourteen. And it was even worse for my mother that I was so withdrawn. She just had to give me some time and a few weeks later I opened up again. I showed myself to be sensible again and amazed my mother with my transformation into a thoroughly *tame* child. It's worth mentioning again that my mother was a great talker, which also extended to arguments. If she had something to complain about, she could discuss it down to the smallest detail. So if you were naughty in her eyes, she didn't scold you, she analyzed the misbehavior to the extreme, so that you actually lost the desire to be naughty.
On the fifteenth of November, Aunt Alix gave birth to little Grand Duchess Olga in the Tsar's palace Tsarskoye Selo in St. Petersburg.
The Queen naturally became one of her godmothers. Although she was again made to feel that her advice and suggestions regarding an English gynecologist were not heeded before she gave birth. Aunt Alicky chose a German doctor who had been recommended to her.
We then spent the winter back in Malta and Papa was happy to be with us, because after not being at sea for a while, but more in the office, he was almost sad to be taking command again, at least that's what he hinted at once. Of course he loved the sea, his job, but also his little family. He and his mother were very reluctant to be separated for long periods of time, although they wrote letters to each other, of course, but it was nothing like living together.

In 1895, it was discovered that in the Ashanti region of Ghana, which was a colony of Great Britain, local people were being captured and sold as slaves. Attempts were made to forbid the tribal chief Prempeh, who was regarded as king there, from engaging in such a cruel form of trade. However, Prempeh refused to give up this very lucrative source of income. The Queen was forced to send a military expedition under Sir Francis Scott, a British Major General, to confront Prempeh by force. Uncle Liko was tired of sitting around in England, if you like. He wanted to fight for his native England and prove to the Queen that there was a militarist in him too. Although she found his decision honorable, she didn't want to let him go at first. He had a family and she knew how much her daughter, Aunt Beatrice, would suffer if he left, as they had never spent a single day apart. There was also, of course, the fear that he might lose his life in the war that was now brewing on the Gold Coast. But Uncle Liko persisted and so the queen finally gave in. Of course, she also felt honored that he had the courage to sacrifice his life for the crown.

When his regiment left on the seventh of December 1895 and a military band played *Auld Lang Syne*, Aunt Beatrice's eyes filled with tears.
However, Uncle Liko was only supposed to study the topography of the country on the journey and, as he wrote to his aunt, was glad to have survived the strong swell on the Bay of Biscay. When he arrived in Africa, he went with the main group of the expedition to the capital Kumasi.
On January 4, 1896, they crossed the Pra River and shortly afterwards the first soldiers showed symptoms of a severe fever. Only a little later, on the tenth of January, when they reached the town of Kwisu, Uncle Liko also contracted the disease. The doctors quickly diagnosed malaria. Uncle was brave and did not want to travel home because he did not want any special treatment, but he was taken on board the *HMS Blonde* to take him back to England. But as soon as the ship passed the coast of Sierra Leone, his uncle was in such a bad way that he died shortly afterwards. It was the twentieth of January, and when Aunt Beatrice received the news, she collapsed. They put Uncle Liko's body in rum and took him back to England for his funeral, which I found very strange when I was told about it as a child.
My father also found it difficult to get over the death of his brother, as he had just had to bury his mother, and seeing his aunt in her grief was just as painful for all of us. She had her children and, now that she was alone again, as a widow she spent more time with the queen, her mother. She became her companion and secretary again, as she had been in the years before her marriage, and focused her life on her mother.

On the fourteenth of May 1896, Uncle Nicky and Aunt Alix were crowned in Moscow. We traveled there, of course, and my father was very proud that he was allowed to ride in the parade in honor of the Tsar and Tsarina. He also received a much warmer welcome in Russia this time, just like Alix's and Nicky's brother-in-law, as a guest of honor. The Battenbergs were welcome again after many years, my father remarked with a smile.
Aunt Irene would also have liked to attend the celebrations, but she was about to give birth to her second child, Prince Sigismund.

I had discovered a strange side to Mama during the coronation celebrations in Moscow. She suddenly seemed to become superstitious, because she thought she sensed something dark in all the joy, a kind of strange premonition that something bad might happen. She called it a fatal shadow peeking around the corner. At first it was just little things that made her tremble inside. First there was a mysterious fire that broke out in Uncle Sergey and Aunt Ella's private chapel the morning before the coronation. The chapel was located in *Usovo*, a solid brick house on the banks of the Moskva River, where

we stayed during our stay. What was special about the house was that it had a technical innovation that was unusual for the time - central heating. Uncle Sergey, who was already wearing his uniform for the festivities, discovered the fire, set off the fire alarm and rushed into our rooms to save our clothes. Just thirty minutes later, the fire would have been completely out of control and there would have been nothing anyone could do because everyone would have been at the celebrations. But it was a mystery why the fire had broken out, as it was later discovered that the central heating was not faulty.
During the ball in the Moscow Kremlin, Mama wandered around, as she had always been curious about what went on in such large buildings. In a small adjoining room, she saw some men standing and talking. Some wore a uniform, some a tailcoat, two or three wore simple peasant clothes. Mama asked who these men were and was told that they were descendants of men who had all saved the life of a tsar since the Romanovs were in power. It was a very old tradition to invite these descendants to the coronation of a new tsar. Mama was reminded of the assassinations of the tsars, the last one only thirteen years ago. Back then, Tsar Alexander II, Nicky's grandfather, had been so badly wounded in the legs by an assassin's grenade that he died in the palace just an hour later, and Uncle Nicky, who was just twelve years old and had come back from ice-skating, could never forget the sight of his dying grandfather. The terrible event had ensured that he had no interest in ever becoming tsar, as everyone knew, because he had told them about it. In the same breath, Mum remembered Uncle Nicky saying that he was afraid of becoming tsar because then no one would be honest with him.
The assassinations and the subservience to the ruler of Russia gave Mama pause for thought, but another terrible event darkened the shadows on her soul even more.
Four days after the coronation, a large public festival was to take place on the Khodynka Field near Moscow, where troops from the Moscow garrison would normally parade. The field was criss-crossed by trenches, which later proved to be an important factor in the disaster.
At ten o'clock in the morning, four hundred thousand bags of gifts were to be distributed to the people there. These bags contained sweets and an enamel mug that had been specially made and decorated for the coronation. There were also one hundred and fifty buffets for the people with snacks and fifteen pavilions with theater and music groups. And as a special feature, the Tsar himself was to appear with the Tsarina at two o'clock in the afternoon. However, no one expected the rush of people who had already gathered on the field the night before the festival. Although it was a moonlit night, the first people fell into the ditches and injured themselves slightly. More and more people arrived, and before the sun had risen, there were already half a million

people who had also come on foot from the Moscow region to take part in the festival and receive the gifts. The security forces soon realized that they could no longer cope with the crowds. At six o'clock in the morning, a rumor spread through the crowd that the first presents were about to be distributed. Like animals, people rushed to the buffets that had been set up. There were many poor people among them who were looking forward to the presents - children, adults, old people. As the first fell into a ninety meter long and three meter deep ditch, those who followed simply pushed on, fell on top of them or climbed and crawled over them. On that day, 1,389 people died and a further 1,300 were injured, some of them seriously.

For Uncle Nicky and Aunt Alix, as well as for us and everyone else, this was a terrible misfortune. Throughout the day, Uncle and Aunt visited the injured in the hospitals and Uncle Nicky immediately decreed that each family of a casualty should receive one thousand roubles from his private fortune, and that he would also pay for each funeral.

But that evening there was a ball for the French legation, and since France was Russia's only real military ally, Uncle Sergey insisted that the ball not be canceled, and Uncle Nicky and Aunt Alix had to be there. Both had refused in view of the tragedy, but finally they agreed. Uncle Nicky was always to be reproached for this during his reign. He had danced in the face of the many dead, they said.

Of course they were looking for someone responsible for the accident, but Uncle Nicky, who had the incident investigated, could not have Uncle Sergey publicly accused. He had commissioned him to organize the party, but Uncle Sergey was part of the family and was Aunt Ella's husband. It was also feared that the Russian monarchy could lose authority if family members were brought to trial. The Moscow chief constable Alexander Alexandrovich Vlasovsky was therefore called to account, but the people were reluctant to accept this and nicknamed Uncle Sergey *Prince Khodynsky* - after the tragedy on Khodynka Field.

When my Aunt Alix was later described as an unfeeling, cold-hearted woman who only thought about her pleasure when she attended the ball, I have to disagree. Because only we saw the tears in her eyes. Mama and Aunt Ella tried to comfort her and encouraged her to go to the ball, but she was very reluctant to go, as was Uncle Nicky, because the tragedy hit them both very hard.

For my mother, however, this accumulation of incidents and the misfortune on the Khodynka field was a bad omen and unfortunately her premonition was not to prove her wrong.

The Queen in England was also horrified when she learned of the tragedy and was even more outraged that the ball had been attended. For her, too, it cast a dark shadow over Uncle Nicky's reign.

After the celebrations, we traveled on to Ilinskoye to visit Uncle Sergey and Aunt Ella. Ilinskoye was about sixty-three kilometers outside of Moscow. The estate covered over nine and a half square kilometers and was located on the left bank of the Moskva River; Uncle Sergey had inherited it from his mother.
In addition to a palace in St. Petersburg, the couple also owned a villa near Peterhof, the summer residence of the Tsar's family on the Gulf of Finland.
Ilinskoye was a dream. Aunt Alix traveled there with us, and although she and Aunt Ella were now richer than my mother could ever have imagined, she did not envy them. For her, they were still her sisters and their personalities remained the same, just as their status did not change in the years that followed, even though it was far higher than my mother's.
We spent our days in Ilinskoye quite relaxed, went swimming, fishing, enjoyed our free time with games and small dance events in the evening.
Uncle Sergey and Aunt Ella often looked after the children of Grand Duke Paul Alexandrovich, Uncle Sergey's brother. His wife, Grand Duchess Alexandra, a Princess of Greece by birth, who was called *Aline* in the family, had died in 1891. Aline was a very petite and often pale person who was often ill. Her daughter Maria was born in 1890. The following year, when she was seven months pregnant, she tried to board a boat while visiting Aunt Ella in Ilinskoye and fell onto its edge. Nothing much seemed to happen to her at first, but the next day she collapsed at a ball in the evening and suffered severe abdominal pain. Shortly afterwards, she gave birth to her son Dmitri, but fell into a coma after the birth, from which she was never to wake up. Six days later, she died in Ilinskoye in the presence of her aunt Ella and her husband. At her funeral in St. Petersburg, her husband wanted to throw himself into the grave because he mourned her so much. And it was also hard for Aunt Ella to bear, as she had got on very well with Aline. What's more, the accident had happened at her house of all places. No one blamed her, because she was not to blame, but from then on she saw it as her duty to look after her children. Grand Duke Paul also felt unable to do so in his grief for his beloved wife.
In 1895, the Grand Duke had begun an affair with a married woman, Olga von Pistohlkors. She had four children, the youngest daughter having only been born in 1890. At a ball at court, Olga wore jewels that had once belonged to the Grand Duke's mother, whom the Dowager Tsar Marie recognized. The Grand Duke had given them to Olga as a gift, but now she was expelled from the ball, making the affair public and turning it into a scandal.
In December 1896, Olga gave birth to Grand Duke Paul's son Vladimir. However, it was not until 1902 that she was allowed to divorce her husband, on

the premise that she would never marry the Grand Duke. But shortly after the divorce, the couple fled to Italy and married morganatically. For Uncle Nicky, this was an unforgivable faux pas and the Grand Duke and his wife were banished from Russia. As the two children Maria and Dmitri had been brought up by Aunt Ella and Uncle Sergey as their own children for many years, Uncle Nicky then gave his uncle the godparenthood for them. Aunt Ella in particular was to be absorbed in this task, as she felt sorry for the children because their biological father showed little interest in them. And as Aunt Ella could never have children of her own, she treated them as her own. Back in 1896, when we were in Ilinskoye, we met the two children, who were still small at the time.

On the fifteenth of June, Papa had to leave us and travel to St. Petersburg. As he still held his post in the Ministry of Defense and the Queen thought highly of him, she arranged for him to meet the Russian Prime Minister, Prince Lobanoff-Rostofsky, in St. Petersburg to discuss some political and military problems, through the mediation of the English Prime Minister, Lord Salisbury. It was a very honorable task for my father. The talks were mainly about the Suez Canal. This had been completed in November 1869. The canal was an important connection, as goods could be transported by sea much faster after its construction. The maritime trading powers of the Mediterranean countries benefited from this, as did Great Britain and Germany, which had economic ties to the Middle and Far East. Austria-Hungary had participated in the construction of the canal and *Österreichische Lloyd*, founded in 1822, quickly expanded to become the largest Austrian maritime trading company and also the largest in the Mediterranean.

Russia was still rather backward in economic matters, which Uncle Nicky tried to change. Nevertheless, Russia was completely excluded from the Suez Canal and trade there. They only had France as an ally and this alliance was opposed by Germany, Italy and Austria-Hungary as a tripartite alliance. Russia and France were allies in order to secure themselves to the left and right of Europe against Germany in the middle, which was becoming the most important economic power in Central Europe.

They were now quite prepared to possibly conclude an alliance with England. These talks between Papa and the Russian Prime Minister were unofficial and my father then traveled on to Windsor to present an initial report to the Queen. After this meeting, he was to have a deep friendship with the Prince for many years and Uncle Nicky also knew that in my father he had an ally at his side who would always mediate between him and England. The Queen was very pleased with Papa, and he also fulfilled her hope that he would be able to speak to Uncle Nicky as confidentially as to his Prime Minister.

Another of Papa's duties, in addition to his command of a ship in the

Mediterranean, was to accompany the Queen on her annual spring voyage to the French Riviera. In 1895 he had not been happy about this task because he was actually happy to be in Malta, also because of the proximity to us. But Aunt Beatrice told him that it was not the Queen who had entrusted him with this task, but that it was an order from the Admiralty. The Queen didn't want to keep him away from us for too long anyway.
In the spring of 1896, my mother and I were allowed to accompany him. We lived in Nice with Aunt Beatrice and her children in the *Villa Liserbe*, near the *Hotel Cimiez*, where the Queen resided. Both the villa and the hotel were situated slightly above Nice and you had a wonderful view. In the afternoon, the Queen went out in a carriage. She soon insisted that I should accompany her. It was of course an honor for me and very impressive. My great-grandmother in the carriage next to me, two liveried servants on horseback in front of us and two behind us. Children came running to us, quickly plucked flowers from the roadside, handed them to the queen and she rewarded each of them with a franc. Some exclaimed "*Madame la Reine!*" with rapture. Every now and then, a new type of automobile whizzed past us, kicking up dust and enveloping us in a cloud that made the Queen and me cough. She was more than indignant about it.

Aunt Alix and Uncle Nicky were going to visit the Queen at Balmoral later in 1896 so that she could get to know Olga. On their journey they also stopped off at Uncle Ernie and Aunt Ducky's in Darmstadt. Mama remarked that it was just like the old days when the Tsar's family came to visit, as half the court arrived with them, including numerous servants and a complete playroom for little Olga, along with her governess and nanny. But contrary to convention, Aunt Alix took great care of the baby and even breastfed Olga herself, in the tradition of her mother, Grandma Alice.

At the beginning of 1897, Mama and I traveled to Nice again with the Queen in the spring. This time we were allowed to stay with her in a newly built hotel, the *Excelsior Hotel Regina*. The building was very imposing and to me it seemed *so* tall that I couldn't really take in all its pomp. Aunt Beatrice accompanied us again with her children and this time also Aunt Lenchen's daughter, Princess Helena Victoria of Schleswig-Holstein, who was twenty-six years old at the time. Helena was called *Thora* or *Snipe* in the family, as she had very sharp and distinctive facial features. She was a cousin of Mama's and very well educated, artistically interested, but very attached to her mother, so that all attempts to marry her off had so far been successfully prevented by her. She always rejected every candidate with good reasons, and this was to remain the case for the rest of her life.

When we arrived at the hotel in Nice, I had to greet the Queen formally as always. She only noted that I had grown very tall in the meantime.
As she didn't think I was old enough to dine with her and the other adults, I was once again allowed to be her constant companion on the afternoon carriage rides. One afternoon, we all drove together to La Turbie, where Uncle Franzjos was staying with the Montenegrin royal family. He had met the daughter of King Nikola I of Montenegro, Princess Anna, during a visit to the Queen in France and immediately fell in love with her.
While we all marveled at *a camera obscura*, a newfangled pinhole camera, at a stand, the uncle and Anna left, and the next morning at breakfast Papa announced to us that they had got engaged. The King of Montenegro came to the Queen and had a great chat with her, as she was also delighted with her uncle's marriage plan.
On the eighteenth of May that year, the couple married in Montenegro. As Anna's sisters, Anastasia and Militza, had already married into Russia and Anastasia in particular had become a close friend of Aunt Alix, Uncle Franzjos now also established good relations with the Russian tsarist family. It was later rumored that Anna had brought a dowry of one million roubles into the marriage.
Of course, we were all happy for the uncle who, after a meeting in London in 1894, hoped to marry the daughter of the American railroad magnate Vanderbilt, named Consuelo. But her mother already had an English duke in mind for her.
In June 1897, the *Diamond Jubilee* celebrations were held in London to mark the Queen's sixtieth anniversary on the throne. At the time, she was Britain's longest reigning monarch, having overtaken King George III, who had reigned for forty-one years, on September twenty-third, 1896. To pay tribute to the other countries of the British Empire, the celebrations became a celebration of the entire empire.
We were billeted with Aunt Louise at Kensington Palace.
On Sunday, the twentieth of June 1897, the Queen had been regent for exactly sixty years and the celebrations began with a thanksgiving service in her honor at Windsor Castle.
Many relatives had traveled from all corners of Europe to take part in the festivities. The Queen then traveled to London and took up residence at Buckingham Palace.
On June twenty-first in the morning, we all gathered in the *Bow Room* in the castle, so called because it had many pillars. The Queen was pushed into the room in her wheelchair and everyone greeted and congratulated her individually. Due to her advanced age, now seventy-eight, and her corpulence, she could barely walk. Nevertheless, she was still an imposing figure who had

presided over England and the family for so many years, and as I was twelve years old at the time, I was better able to join in the celebrations than I had been many years earlier at her *Golden Jubilee*. It was an impressive thing for me and I took it all in with more fascination for my great-grandmother because of my more mature age. She was not only the Queen of Empire, of a world empire, but also the namesake of an age - the Victorian age.
The celebrations in London began with another thanksgiving service at *St. Paul's Cathedral*. On the way there, Papa, as the Queen's son-in-law, was allowed to ride in the guard of honor, the Queen led it in her carriage, Mum sat in one and I shared a carriage with Louise, Georgie and Aunt Beatrice's children. Whenever we visited the Queen, I loved playing with them.
So that we were supervised, the Queen's dressmaker, the old Duchess of Buccleuch, took care of us and also sat with us in the carriage.
Aunt Beatrice's children often behaved very strangely as they grew older, which was also a topic of conversation in our family. As they were half-orphans, the Queen and their mother felt they had to spoil them, and the Queen always called them *poor fatherless ones*. As we drove to the cathedral, Ena kept standing up and bowing left and right, which none of us found particularly funny. The Duchess kindly asked her to stop, but Ena was not to be deterred. Later, it was even mentioned in the press.
Ena was very intelligent, but also precocious, which was often not easy when playing with her.
Nevertheless, the journey through London was very moving, as people had gathered in the streets to cheer the Queen. There were flags with the *Union Jack* on the balconies of houses everywhere, garlands of flowers adorned the streets - it was a sea of color. Children waved little flags and the cheers were all the louder when the Queen passed the crowds in her carriage. We even saw people standing on rooftops waving and raising their arms enthusiastically.
We later learned that thousands of people had already spent the night in the parks the night before, just to get a good spot the next morning so they could catch a glimpse of their queen.
The days of the festivities were officially designated as days off, i.e. public holidays, so that working people could also take part.
We drove past stalls where people could buy flags, special porcelain mugs made just for the day, and a program booklet for the festivities.
It was nine kilometers from the palace to the cathedral and I can only say that I was completely impressed when, before we left, the Queen pressed a button that sent a telegraphic message to every corner of her empire to thank her subjects. And our convoy of seventeen carriages, the thunder of cannons being fired in Hyde Park as it moved to announce that the Queen was leaving

the palace - all these impressions left a lasting impression on each of us. I felt proud, proud of this woman I was allowed to call my great-grandmother, and not even Ena's arrogant behavior could take away that feeling. Even my siblings, especially Louise, sat in amazement in our carriage, turning their heads to the right and left so as not to miss anything.
When we reached the cathedral, people spontaneously sang the English national anthem *God save the Queen*. It must have made the Queen as proud as I was, because she wiped tears from her eyes when we stopped. And perhaps it impressed people all the more that she wasn't wearing a pompous dress, but was dressed in plain black, as she was still mourning her husband and her two deceased children, Grandma Alice and Uncle Leopold. Perhaps this brought her all the closer to her people.
As great-grandma could no longer climb the steps to the cathedral due to her arthritis, but also did not want to be carried up in front of all the people, the ceremony took place in front of the cathedral. She remained in the carriage, as the members of the choir barely had enough room on the steps, because even though the guards, soldiers of the colonial troops in their magnificent uniforms, kept the people back, everyone wanted to be as close to the Queen as possible. The ceremony lasted twenty minutes, after which the Archbishop of Canterbury was moved to proclaim: "Three cheers for the Queen!"
The crowds joined in. Louise said the cheering was deafening and Georgie covered her ears. I couldn't hear it, but I could see the joy on people's faces as the men lifted their hats and the boys their caps.
We finally returned to Buckingham Palace and drove past the people again. A small lunch was served and in the evening there was a large banquet, as many heads of state from the Empire were also present.
When night fell, there was a huge fireworks display and several on the surrounding hills for the people. But the cheering of the people did not die down during the night. On this special day, the pubs were open until two thirty and people naturally took advantage of this to celebrate extensively.
The Queen later said that she had been so moved and touched that she would never forget that special day, and I could understand that, because the people had shown her how much she was revered.
A few days later there was a big garden party at Buckingham Palace and on June twenty-sixth there was a big parade of Royal Navy ships at Spithead off the coast of Hampshire in the south of England. Afterwards, a celebratory lunch was served on the *Majestic*, which Georgie and Louise were allowed to attend with me. The proud ship had only been completed in 1895 and was the largest liner in the world at the time. Papa had taken command of the ship on the seventh of June and therefore knew every detail about it. So he could tell us a lot about it and of course it was a special task for him to be in

command of this particular ship.
Aunt Alix was the only one of the sisters who could not attend the celebrations as she was pregnant again. On the tenth of June 1897, my cousin, Grand Duchess Tatyana, was born. The birth of an heir to the throne had been expected in Russia, but it was only the second child for the Tsar and Tsarina and both were delighted with every new healthy baby.

We met Nona Kerr for the first time that summer and she was soon to become an important member of our family. My mother had never had a lady-in-waiting before. Mark Kerr was a friend of Papa's from the Navy. He had six sisters and Nona was the youngest of them. His father was an admiral, now deceased, but he had also been valet to the Queen. Nona, just twenty-two years old and extremely well-mannered, became friends with Mama shortly before the *Diamond Jubilee* celebrations. They got on so well straight away that my mother hired her as lady-in-waiting for herself and governess for us children. Her first task was to attend a dinner with two hundred and seventy guests in a marquee in the gardens of Buckingham Palace at my mother's side. She was placed between two German officers, and as she spoke no German, the situation was difficult for her to master. She was also a little shy, so the whole thing visibly overwhelmed her. But when she was then introduced to the queen, she was definitely put off. She had never moved in these circles before, but Mama thought she could learn.
Only three weeks later, when we were back in Heiligenberg, poor Nona found herself in a household where German and French were spoken, but very little English. Mama soon left again, leaving us with the task of getting Nona to grow together. She immediately threw her in at the deep end, but Nona tried very hard. For the next nineteen years she was to be associated with us, and when she married in 1915, a lifelong friendship remained with us, but especially with Mama.
Only Papa's enthusiasm for her increased over time, which the rather inconspicuous Nona found difficult to deal with as she couldn't really interpret it. He once wrote to her that he missed her as much as he missed us children and Mama. And after her marriage, he wrote to say how much he regretted her loss. His other lines sounded to her as if he saw her as a daughter that he was losing to his husband. Nona told her mother, but she reassured her each time that it was meant purely in friendship and in gratitude for her work. It was perhaps due to Nona's shyness, her own underestimation of her personality, that she completely misinterpreted praise from my father or simple niceties as if he felt something for her. And of course this shocked her, as he was married. Papa laughed about it, my mother was also just confused and a little amused. Neither my father nor my mother were ever unfaithful to each other,

they trusted each other and had a deep love for each other.
In 1898 and 1899 we lived mainly in Heiligenberg. This was interrupted only by visits to the Queen in January, when we stayed with her at Osborne House on the Isle of Wight. I often went out in the coach with my mother and the Queen and still held a special place in my great-grandmother's eyes.

In the course of 1898, my petite sister Louise was diagnosed with a curvature of the spine, which caused her to walk somewhat crookedly. Mama was very worried about this, but Louise was given massages and had to do movement exercises under the guidance of a doctor, so it soon improved again.
From then on, Louise was to receive lessons together with me, for which Mama hired a Miss Textor. She had a big, broad laugh when she was in a happy mood, but also a very loud voice when she was disgruntled or dissatisfied with what we were learning. I could only tell by looking at her features, seeing her lip movements, but Louise told me that her voice could be really loud for a woman. She also taught a final-year English class at a girls' school and had a huge soft spot for Goethe, so we had to read a lot of him. But her lessons were also very diverse and offered a lot of variety, because she had us put on little plays to which we were allowed to invite friends, mostly from our relatives. Afterwards, she always organized small parties where she served English fruit cake, known as *Simnel* cake, sweet rolls, jam and honey. As a drink, she served much sought-after chocolate with whipped cream. These performances on our part, along with the treats that followed, always became popular afternoon events.
My mother thought I was now old enough to expand my education. She took me to the opera. This was possible after my hearing had improved slightly. I could hear very loud noises from time to time. It wasn't continuous, but when I *couldn't hear anything*, I would lip-read again. Maybe I missed one or two things in the opera, but the music was so loud that I could hear its vibrations, and I was also very happy to be able to accompany Mama. I didn't want to disappoint her by admitting that I hadn't heard much and always said that I had enjoyed it very much.
I was also allowed to have dinner with Mama, Uncle Ernie and Aunt Ducky in the New Palace.
In our free time, we played tennis on the Lawn Tennis court at the New Palace and swam in the Heiligenberg swimming pool until it got too cold for that in the fall. The Queen had brought me a new pony from England. It was called *Cheril* and the two of us were soon inseparable.
Uncle Ernie complimented me on what a quiet, sweet girl I was, never overbearing, conceited or challenging embarrassing situations, which is common to some young girls on the cusp of womanhood. They giggle excessively, are

sometimes teasing and silly, but I am always very self-controlled and polite. Sometimes I think it was because I spent a lot of time at the Queen's side. She was very strict in her traditions and attached great importance to good manners. Being in her company really shaped me as a child and young girl.
When Uncle Nicky and Aunt Alix visited us in Hesse in the summer with their cousins Olga and Tatjana, they stayed with Uncle Ernie and Aunt Ducky at Wolfsgarten Castle.
We always visited them, but I kept my distance from the little ones because I was bored of the children's games. But I understood that Georgie and Louise enjoyed them. I thought most of the things they did or laughed about were just *childish*, but that's not to say I didn't like them all very much. The age difference was still a big hurdle.

Aunt Ducky had games for the adults that were definitely more interesting. Unconventional as she always was, she invented a game called *Find the Treasure*. It was more like looking for Easter eggs. Before she called all the adults to dinner, she would hide some of the food in a part of the neighboring forest, in protected packaging of course. It was a different one each time and she announced in advance which section to look in. So everyone set off on their search, which sometimes took a while, so they had to take torches with them. At some point, someone exclaimed that they had found boiled potatoes in their packet, another found a sandwich and it was amusing, but Mama also found it overly silly. Aunt Ducky had her fun. She didn't embody the stereotype of her strict, resolute mother, the Duchess, but was a rather fun-loving Grand Duchess who literally didn't give a damn about etiquette. She appeared at tea with her favorite horse at her side, which grazed next to her when we sat outside, and she smoked whenever and wherever she liked. At a party in the castle, she was probably bored once and escaped through an open window, had a horse saddled in the stables and then, to the amazement of the guests, simply rode off into the night - in her ball gown. It was often embarrassing the way she behaved, but Uncle Ernie took it with a smile because of her youth. As everyone knew about her more than sad, strict childhood, she was forgiven for escaping the constraints of the court for a Mamaent.
However, it was obvious that Uncle Ernie and Aunt Ducky's marriage was not easy due to their escapades. However, Uncle Ernie also had a secret that no one openly shared, but which was well known to the adults at the time, especially his sisters, and soon also to his wife. Uncle Ernie loved Aunt Ducky, but he loved young men all the more. This homosexual inclination was punishable everywhere. Uncle Ernie therefore often traveled to Capri, where the fishermen's boys often offered themselves to men, young men who were willing to provide amorous services for a fee. Whereas in Germany you

could only live out your urges in secret and always had to be on your guard, this was possible in Capri because the authorities looked the other way.
Uncle Ernie also made advances to male servants at court. Despite everything, they tried to pull themselves together for little Elisabeth, whom the uncle and aunt loved very much, and to be a happy family on the outside.
These inclinations were not unknown in our family. Uncle Sergey was also more attracted to men than Aunt Ella, who accepted this. However, he also appeared in public with his young lovers at the theater, the opera or the ballet and always wore a corset under his clothes. I think Aunt Ella loved her husband very much, so she *overlooked* his escapades.
On June twenty-eighth, Papa was promoted to *Assistant Director of Naval Intelligence.* The *Naval Intelligence Department* was a British secret service of the Royal Navy. It was founded in 1882 under a different name. Captain William Henry Hall was the first director and Papa was now under his command, his right-hand man, so to speak. The aim was to decode secret messages from other naval powers, especially in times of war.
Papa had to move back to London for his job in the fall. He rented a house at *40 Grosvenor Gardens* near his office and Buckingham Palace for us so that we could be close to him. So we all went back to England in October.
At the end of 1898, Mama found out that she was pregnant again. Admittedly, she was a little surprised to give birth to another child after Georgie, who had been born six years earlier, but of course she and Papa were delighted. Louise and Georgie were also thrilled, but I was soon fourteen years old. It's an age when you don't find small children so interesting because you feel more like an adult.

The new year 1899 began with good news from Aunt Alix in Russia, who was also pregnant again. The baby was due to be born in June and of course they were hoping for the birth of another son, an heir to the throne for Uncle Nicky.
Bad news reached us shortly afterwards, for on February sixth, Aunt Ducky's brother *Young Affie* died in Merano, Switzerland, aged only twenty-four. The official story was that he had died of tuberculosis, but the truth was far more shocking.
As hereditary prince of the Duchy of Saxe-Coburg and Gotha, he had to pursue a military career and was a lieutenant in the Prussian 1st Guards Regiment of Foot in Potsdam. However, he was very unhappy there. He soon sought distance from the military drill in numerous love affairs, none of which were in keeping with his rank. In 1897, he secretly married the Irishwoman Mabel Fitzgerald, and when his mother, Duchess Marie, found out, she was furious and urged him to have the marriage annulled immediately. The arguments

with her escalated and his father, who was rarely at home as he no longer had any real relationship with his wife, did not interfere. From his point of view, his wife, who was very resolute, would have sorted it out. When Uncle Affie and Aunt Marie celebrated their silver wedding anniversary in Coburg at the end of January, their son tried to shoot himself with a rifle in his room. Against the advice of the doctors who had been called in, the Duchess left her seriously injured son in his bed in the darkened room while she returned to the celebrations. Fearing a public scandal, she concealed the fact from her daughters and had her son taken to Merano shortly afterwards, where he died a week later. Officially, he was to undergo a cure there.

The Duke, powerless against his domineering wife, was so full of grief over the death of his very sensitive son that he separated from his wife after the funeral in Coburg. To cope with his grief and numb it, he began to drink.

As there was now no heir to the duchy, Uncle Affie wanted to offer the succession to his younger brother Arthur, but he declined the succession for himself and his son. The succession was therefore transferred to Carl Eduard, Uncle Leopold's son. He was only fourteen years old, but at the time it was assumed that Uncle Affie would reign for many years to come.

The Queen had already feared for *Young Affie*'s life in December, because when he visited her, she sensed from his words and stories how much of a mental strain life in Potsdam was putting on him, how little he could cope with the military drill. She had written to Mama about these fears, but had not dared to tell the Duchess. It was difficult to enter into a discussion with her, so Aunt Ducky and her sisters were unable to do anything for her brother. They fell on deaf ears with their mother, and they also knew how callous and cold-hearted the duchess could be - precisely from their own experiences with her.

I also found it all very sad, because Mama wanted to support Aunt Ducky in her grief for her brother. She also didn't understand how a mother could behave like that towards her child.

Then there was the fact that Uncle Affie also got drunk during a visit there in the spring shortly after his son's death and it worried her greatly to see her own son in such a situation. She tried to comfort him, but realized that his marriage was ruined. Uncle Affie had traveled to Alexandria in 1898 and had been bitten on the eye by a mosquito. The resulting infection also caused him health problems, as he could no longer see well in his eye and was often in pain. When he visited us or we met in Malta, he was always a very friendly, funny person, but although he was Duke in Coburg, he didn't speak much German. He never bothered to learn it much either.

Of course, I often met Duchess Marie too, but she always seemed a little conceited and reserved. However, I had noticed that she had never been as

affectionate and warm with her children as Mama was with us.
My father was soon very busy with his work due to the situation in South Africa. The two Boer republics, *Orange Free State* and *Transvaal*, which had merged to form the *South African Republic*, insisted on their independence and the conflict had been simmering for a long time. After the Netherlands ceded its Cape Colony to Great Britain in 1806, the Boers living there quickly became a minority. As the slave trade was banned, they also lost one of their livelihoods and so they retreated into the hinterland from 1836 to 1844. Around six to ten thousand Boers hoped to escape the British laws and preserve their identity. North of the Orange River, they founded the *Orange Free State* with its capital Bloemfontain in 1842 and the Republic of *Transvaal* with its capital Pretoria north of the Vaal River in 1853. When Great Britain annexed the South African Republic in 1881, the First Boer War broke out, after which the Republic regained its independence. Nevertheless, conflicts continued because Great Britain saw its position of power threatened.
A second war was imminent, as the fact that large diamond and gold deposits had been discovered on the territory of the Boer Republics in 1869 and 1886 was particularly significant. Attracted by the possibility of quick riches, many gold miners from the neighboring English colonies, the *Cape Colony* and *Natal*, traveled to Boer territory. Once again, they found themselves under pressure. In addition, citizens of European descent who lived there were denied legal and political equality.
A conference in May 1899 failed, an ultimatum was issued and expired. This led to the *Second Boer War* on October 12th. This was to last until 1902 and end victoriously for Great Britain. The Boer republics had to integrate into the British colonial empire and submit.

We celebrated Christmas with the Queen in Windsor, as she was now so frail that she could only travel with difficulty. It was a special celebration where the whole family got together. At a tea reception in the imposing *St. George's Hall* of the castle, we presented small gifts to the wives and children of soldiers. The Queen was pushed back and forth in her wheelchair by a servant to greet people and speak to them. She then took her tea in her private chambers.
The turn of the century on New Year's Eve was something special. We were at the end of a century and wondered what the new one would bring. We celebrated in a quieter atmosphere and smaller company at *Sandringham House*, the Queen's country estate in the English county of Norfolk. As midnight struck, I felt like I was on the cusp of adulthood. It was a strange feeling, as if with the last seconds of the old century my childhood was coming to an end and with the seconds of the new one I would be more mature, more grown

up. I was soon to undergo changes that only young women could. You grew out of short children's dresses, were allowed to wear floor-length skirts, no longer wore your hair loose, held by a ribbon, but pinned up or tied at the nape of your neck. And ahead of me were court parties, which I was now allowed to attend, and at some point a marriage. It made me very thoughtful, but at the same time I was curious about the next few years, about what lay ahead of me, what life had in store for me. That evening, I said goodbye to the innocent days of my childhood with a small hint of melancholy, as my transformation into a woman would also involve many responsibilities.

The sight of the Queen gave me a tender twinge in my heart, for she was now eighty-one years old, very frail and I wondered inwardly how much longer she would be able to reign. She still had a heavy workload, which Uncle Bertie, as her successor, was not allowed to take part in. She saw it as her sole responsibility to manage the fate of the empire and even said nothing more about the war in Africa than that she would never tolerate defeat. Her ministers accepted this.

However, the recent strokes of fate also took their toll on her. At the end of 1898, Empress Friedrich, her eldest daughter, was diagnosed with breast cancer and was increasingly confined to bed due to the severity of the disease. It was a renewed worry that brought the queen down emotionally.

Uncle Ernie and Aunt Ducky's marriage was increasingly in crisis. It was now an open secret that the marriage was more than unhappy. The arguments between the two usually escalated to such an extent that even crockery was not spared being used as a projectile by Aunt Ducky. Poor Uncle then became an involuntary target. It was said that the staff at the castle were now used to the sound of shattering china. Aunt Ducky's only real passion was riding. The selection of horses she acquired was reminiscent of the stables of a much higher-ranking person, as the stables at Wolfsgarten were soon home to magnificent Lippizaner horses that she bought directly from Vienna, stallions from Russia whose wildness was legendary, and riding ponies from England with the best pedigree. Everyone was impressed when she gave a tour of the stables. For Uncle Ernie, horses were a means to an end, to be harnessed to the carriage, but not intended for sporting use, although he also gave his wife credit for how skillfully she rode. Even at the wildest gallop, she cut a perfect figure on the animal.

I remember a very wild Russian stallion called *Bogdan*. Auntie liked to let him run around the yard and he only listened to *her*, was a tame little lamb in her hands, but a terror to everyone else because he chased anyone who crossed his path across the yard with wild bucking jumps. When Uncle Ernie fled from him once, the stallion even followed him up the steps to the castle, bit him on the backside and tore his trousers, which his aunt found more than amusing. As she doubled over with laughter at the sight of her husband, it was immediately clear to everyone that she was more attached to the horses than to her husband.

Both lived more or less their own lives. For example, her aunt went to horse races in Frankfurt on her own, together with her Lippizaner horses, and dressed in the most sumptuous clothes.

At the coronation of Aunt Alix and Uncle Nicky, she had met Grand Duke Cyril Vladimirovich Romanov and flirted with him in front of everyone. Mama once said that she was doing this as a payback for her uncle's frequent pleasures with men, but she didn't want to talk about it any further because the subject was taboo. It was only Uncle Ernie's business and her aunt's.

But even the Queen in England soon had to realize that her *matchmaking* had gone completely off the rails this time, and when she heard about the marital crisis and was told about the quarrels and escapades, she openly declared that she no longer wanted to pursue her passion in this regard.

In May 1900, Aunt Ducky gave birth to a stillborn child. It was a boy and so Uncle Ernie would have had an heir to the throne, but the aunt had taken no notice of her pregnancy, continued to ride out, which shocked us all, and so it was no surprise to anyone that the child was dead. It was a very hard blow for Uncle Ernie, because he blamed his wife alone for not following the doctors' advice, stubborn as she was, and not stopping riding during the pregnancy.

The marriage was still maintained for their young daughter Elisabeth, but it was foreseeable that the two would no longer get along and would separate.

On the fourteenth of June, Aunt Alix gave birth to little Grand Duchess Maria. Now that the third child was also a girl, the aunt faced increasing hostility from her family. Uncle Nicky was very happy about his little daughter, but the other relatives openly expressed their dismay at the fact that it was not a boy. Uncle Nicky's sister, Grand Duchess Xenia, was particularly hard on my aunt. Since 1895, she had regularly given birth to a son after her first-born daughter, including little Nikita in 1900. And if my aunt never had a son, the succession to the throne would pass to Grand Duke Mikhail, my uncle Nicky's brother. It was very difficult for my aunt Alix to keep her head up when she was constantly being reproached. She couldn't influence the sex of the child because it was out of her hands, even if she prayed about it or put up icons in her bedroom that were said to have an influence on the sex of the unborn child.

In the summer, we kept the Queen company for a few weeks at *Frogmore House*, which is close to Windsor Castle. As the Queen was becoming increasingly frail, Mama had promised to have the baby close to her.

Frogmore House is beautifully situated in the middle of a large garden. There

was a small private zoo with two large ostriches, two kangaroos and a zebra. From time to time, a *brougham*, a small one-horse carriage for two people, drove through the park, its sunshade lowered every time so that you couldn't see inside. It was said that the wife of the queen's *munshi* drove around in it. The *munshi*, called Abdul Karim, was a servant from India who had also become a close confidant and friend to Great-Grandma.
It was a special time because before we settled in *Frogmore*, the Queen had been on a last big official trip to Ireland and now we were with her virtually all the time. She would stop for breakfast with us on her morning carriage ride and then visit the animals in their enclosures. Mostly she stayed in her carriage, as it was getting too difficult for her to get in and out, worked through her papers there too and then went back to Windsor Castle for lunch. She returned to us for tea, and when it got cooler in the evening, she drove through the park again. Sometimes Louise and I accompanied her to church. As Mama was heavily pregnant, she would occasionally go to evening prayers with me supporting her.
Shortly before her confinement, Mama moved to Windsor Castle, where she gave birth to a baby boy on June twenty-fifth. As it was her fourth child, the birth did not cause her too much discomfort, but it was very hot that summer. He was born at six o'clock in the morning and the Queen, of course, visited Mama during the day, as did we. He was given the call name Albert after my great-grandfather as it was the Queen's wish. His middle name was to be Louis. At first we other children didn't want this, because it was Papa's name and then no one would know who was meant, as my mother also called my father Louis in the English form of Ludwig. He should have his own name, but we rejected Mama's suggestion of Nicky, after Uncle Nicky, who was to be his godfather. It would only lead to confusion. In the end, we all agreed that his baptismal name should be Albert Victor Nicholas Louis Francis, also in reference to his godparents, but that everyone would call him *Dick*, which quickly became *Dickie*. My brother was to keep this nickname for the rest of his life. Mama often called my father Dickie when they were alone together, which is how she came up with this nickname for my little brother.
His first name was actually Albert, but after the Queen's death my parents put Louis in this place and Francis in the second.
His birth was a milestone for me, because from that evening on the day of his birth, I was allowed to eat at the Queen's table in the evening.
The next day after dinner at twenty-one, I went with the Queen, Papa, Ena, Arthur of Connaught, Aunt Lenchen and her husband, Uncle Christian, to *the Waterloo Chamber*, a large hall in Windsor Castle, to hear pieces from the opera *Carmen* and from *Cavalleria Rusticana*, sung by the famous French soprano Madame Emma Calvé, who had come specially for the occasion. A

veritable sea of flowers had been set up in front of the stage for the performance and it was a wonderful evening, even if I didn't notice the music as much as everyone else.
On the seventeenth of July, Dickie was baptized in *St. George's Chapel* and kicked so hard that he knocked the glasses off the nose of the Queen, who was allowed to hold him, grabbed a ribbon of her hood with his other hand and tugged at it, which Papa commented on with a mischievous smile and the observation that he was probably blessed with a great fighting spirit. When Dickie was later told this anecdote, he could never stop himself from telling everyone that he was the one who knocked the Queen's glasses off her nose, which he then of course knew how to underline with gestures, although it should be mentioned that the Queen herself did not take offense at Dickie's stomping during and after the christening. From her point of view, the child simply showed a healthy liveliness.
However, the queen was almost blind at the time of his birth and therefore had to wear glasses. She was also shaking a lot due to her rheumatic complaints, which is why my parents were a little worried that she might drop Dickie in the baptism water or on the way to the baptismal font.
The Dean of Windsor, Dr. Elliott, had come especially for Dickie's christening. As it was, as mentioned, a very hot summer, the Queen had buckets of iced water placed under the tables and even had ice placed under the loose covers of chairs. So the dean sat down on one of these chairs until the man, who was already getting on in years, suddenly noticed a terrible pulling pain in his back. His legs became cold and stiff. He still performed the baptism, but afterwards suffered from a very bad inflammation of the sciatica, from which he would never fully recover. For the rest of his life, he could only walk with a cane, which was more like a limp.
With the new little brother, we all traveled as a family to Filey, a small town in the English county of North Yorkshire, which lies directly on the North Sea coast. Mama in particular was supposed to relax in the resort. Then we went back to *Frogmore House*. Shortly afterwards, my father rented a house for us at *4 Hans Crescent* in the *Knightsbridge* district of London. We lived not far from the famous *Harrods department* store, which was destroyed by fire in 1883 and rebuilt in 1894, although it was not completed until 1903. A little to the south of us was *Hyde Park*. Even then, Knightsbridge was a rather exclusive residential area.

Louise and I were still home-schooled together and regularly attended *MacPherson's Grammar School* in Sloane Street, Chelsea, for young girls. There we were taught needlework, good manners, physical training, correspondence, conversation and there was even a fencing class for ladies. In addition

to the lessons, we also visited the poor and needy from the school so that we were trained in charity.
Miss Jackson introduced me to English literature at home and helped me prepare for my upcoming confirmation.
Georgie was educated at the prestigious private boys' school *Mr. Moreton's School* in Eaton Square.

On July thirtieth, 1900, Uncle Affie died of throat cancer at his summer residence Schloss Rosenau near Coburg. It had only recently become known that he was suffering from the disease, and the Queen found it difficult to come to terms with the death of her son at the age of only fifty-five. She had lost many loved ones to death in the course of her life, but now, in her old age and due to her own poor state of health, it hit her all the harder. You could perhaps say that she was simply no longer up to it. She knew that her daughter, Empress Frederick, would not live much longer, and yet she tried to hold herself up, to be the strong queen she had been for so long.
She actually hated wars because she thought it was terrible when men had to fight against men and often lost their lives in battle while still very young. But the *Second Boer War* was unavoidable. Great Britain was not allowed to show any weakness in this conflict and she tried to show the people at home in England, her people, how much she felt for them when the men went to war. She visited the wounded in hospitals, troop farewells and parades, barracks, received widows and their children, the wives of soldiers. Germany, France and Austria openly attacked England for its war policy in South Africa, and this made the Queen all the more upset. During this time, she called on all her reserves, which could not be overlooked.
And when Aunt Lenchen's son died of malaria in Pretoria on October twenty-ninth, the Queen almost despaired at the loss of Christian Victor, who was only twenty-three years old. He had been an officer, had already had military successes to his name and the Queen had only very reluctantly allowed him to go to war. The fact that he had not died in battle but of an insidious illness, like Uncle Liko, was even more terrible for her.
She and the Queen had kept up a lively correspondence since Mama's childhood; her last letter was dated July thirteenth. She saw Mama and us often, but had always kept in touch by letter, even if we only lived around the corner. Now she could no longer write because her hands were shaking so much. She regretted that her rheumatism prevented her from keeping in touch with all her relatives and friends.
On the first of September, the Queen traveled to Balmoral, as she did every year, and returned to Windsor on the first of November. On the eighteenth of December she went to Osborne on the Isle of Wight for Christmas. We all

celebrated the feast together again and everyone noticed how unwell she was. She complained of a lack of appetite and felt tired. Nevertheless, she could hardly get to sleep at night. Although she had already reached a respectable age, we were all very worried about her.
On New Year's Eve, she then asked my father, whom she trusted very much, to become trustee of her private assets. Papa was of course honored to be entrusted with such a task - especially that she preferred him to one of her children. He gladly accepted the task.
She was delighted when Lord Frederick Roberts, the commander-in-chief of the British troops in South Africa, returned victorious on January 3, 1901. Among other things, he had captured Bloemfontain in March of the previous year and Pretoria in June, thus declaring the *Orange Free State* and the *South African Republic* to be British colonies. The Burian commander-in-chief, Piet Cronjé, was forced to surrender. The war was thought to have been won when the Lord returned, but the Boers continued to put up resistance until 1902, when they were defeated. At that time, however, at the beginning of 1901, the Queen was very relieved at the good news. It seemed to lift her spirits for a while, as did the news that Aunt Alix was pregnant again.
But on January eleventh, she was in a very bad way. The doctors told us that she would not recover, and so the family gathered at her side. Kaiser Wilhelm II traveled from Germany when he learned of her condition, although no one had asked him to do so. He always pushed himself to the fore, even at Great-Grandma's deathbed, saying that he had always been her favorite grandson. Mama thought that was outrageous, but people didn't want to argue around the Queen. Many of her children, grandchildren and great-grandchildren gradually arrived in Osborne. My mother and papa did not leave the Queen's side either, but when she died at eighteen thirty on January twenty-second, it was Uncle Willy who had held her in his arms for the last two and a half hours. Mama only remarked that it was the only good thing he had ever done for England.
The Queen's death marked the end of an era. Uncle Bertie would now finally become King, as Edward VII, but as she never entrusted him with duties of state, he faced too great a burden. Sure, the ministers would stand by him, help him settle into his new office, but he was very unhappy about how his mother had kept it from him all these years, only to throw him in at the deep end. Even though he knew, of course, that she would not rule forever.
Empress Friedrich was the only one of her children who was unable to travel, as she was already so seriously ill at the time that she was unable to travel.
We all said goodbye to the Queen at her deathbed before Uncle Willy, Uncle Bertie and Uncle Arthur laid her in the coffin on January twenty-fifth. It had been her wish to be buried in a white dress with her bridal veil, and they

placed some of her favorite items in the coffin, such as an alabaster cast of her late husband's hand, some photographs and a lock of her friend and groom John Brown, who died many years ago.
On the second of February, she was laid to rest for two days in *St. George's Chapel* in Windsor and then buried in the mausoleum at *Frogmore House*, which she had had built for her husband in the Italian style.
The English people mourned the loss of their Queen as much as we did and, due to the upcoming year of mourning, Uncle Bertie would not be crowned until the following year.
Mama, in particular, was very sad because, for one thing, the marriage between her and Papa was the only really good connection that the Queen had ever provided, and for over twenty years she had been like a mother substitute for my mother, a guide, an intimate confidante and a support. As a child, Mum, like everyone else, had seen her as an imposing, almost frightening figure, a patriarch who held not only the destiny of England but also that of her family firmly in her hands. But when Grandma Alice died, grief brought them both closer together.
My mother was to mourn for a long time to come and kept entertaining us with little details she remembered about the Queen. When she could no longer get the Queen's perfume with the scent of oranges anywhere, she wept bitterly over it.
Papa was also very sad, because he and the Queen had become even closer, especially after the death of his brother Liko. She often asked him to come to Balmoral, Windsor or Osborne to sort something out for her. She had even accepted comments and suggestions regarding the *Royal Navy* only from Papa.
Of course, we children also mourned her death, but I don't think Louise did as I did. As the eldest, I was often able to spend time with the Queen when she didn't consider my younger sister mature enough to do so. And Georgie was still too young to really understand her loss.
Uncle Bertie and his wife, Aunt Alexandra, whom we all called Alix, a born Princess of Denmark and the sister of Uncle Nicky's mother, were very welcoming.

We loved spending time with them, but it's fair to say they weren't surrounded by that Queen's flair.
I had always thought of Windsor and Osborne as places where my family and I were always welcome, but now we had to wait for an invitation from Uncle Bertie, as a courtesy, Mama said. You could no longer give advance notice and just turn up. In Buckingham Palace, every room soon smelled very strongly of Uncle Bertie's cigars. He also swept away the strict etiquette and

rules of court life, and with it their aura of power. When we were invited to visit in March, he and his wife were in the process of redecorating furniture, redesigning and refurnishing rooms. My mother found this more than disconcerting, because everything reminded her of her grandmother and had become dear to her. And a makeover was of course perfectly fine, because Uncle Bertie and Aunt Alix wanted to literally sweep out the *old mustiness* and make their home their own. We dined in the large dining room, after which the men were asked to play cards in the next room.
The couple had previously lived in *Sandringham House* in the county of Norfolk. It was known that the marriage was not very happy, as Uncle Bertie often had affairs and took little care of his wife and children.
The aunt loved her children very much, but demanded that her daughter Victoria always stayed with her, so Aunt *Thora* was unmarried. Aunt Alix suffered from severe rheumatism, so she had a stiff leg and was severely hard of hearing due to a disease of the inner ear, *otosclerosis*. She always surrounded herself with many animals such as parrots, dogs and cats to give them all her love.
Unfortunately, she did not get on particularly well with her English relatives. She preferred the company of her Danish relatives. Once a year she traveled to Denmark, where she had bought a villa with her sister, the Dowager Tsar Minnie. In *Hvidore*, she found a refuge from her mother-in-law, as she had never really been able to come to terms with the queen either. Although she was very charitable and was involved in many clubs and associations, her aunt actually lived a very introverted life, which was only interrupted by visits to her sister in Russia, her sister in Denmark and her sister in Germany, Duchess Thyra of Brunswick and Lüneburg, Princess of Hanover.
During the visit in March 1901, I met Aunt Alix's nephew, Prince Andrew of Greece and Denmark, who was called Andrew or Andrea, for the first time. He was three years older than me and the fourth son of King George I of Greece. The king was Aunt Alix's brother. Born a Danish prince, the Greeks had appointed him king after the deposition of King Otto by the National Assembly in 1863. He was married to the Russian Grand Duchess Olga Konstantinovna.
Prince Andreas was very friendly towards me. I was very impressed by the fact that he spoke fluent Greek, German, English, Danish, Russian, French and Italian, but only communicated with his parents in Greek. He mostly spoke English with everyone else.
He also studied Greek and European history at the Ruprecht-Karls University in Heidelberg. As the son of a king, he had aspired to a military career from an early age, was an officer in the Greek army and this was not honorary. Quite willing to defend his country, he showed a great interest in politics, had

a sharp mind and his whole character, our short conversations impressed me very much.
I was only sixteen years old, but there was something about Andreas that I liked straight away. Maybe it was the openness with which he met me despite my disability, his charm, his humor ... I can't say for sure. It didn't seem to bother him in any way that I was deaf, because he only replied that he was short-sighted, which is why he wore a monocle, and that he didn't care about such things. He wanted to pursue a career as a cavalry officer in the Greek army in May of that year, even though he was short-sighted. I was very impressed by his determination and he complimented me because I was so good at lip-reading and speaking. When he called me pretty, I was a little insecure because it was my first compliment from a man who wasn't family. But he made up for my insecurity by saying quite openly that I should be told that I was something special, at least from his point of view. Despite my disability, I had put a lot of energy into learning everything that hearing people found so easy.
At my age, I had of course already thought about love, about marriage, but I was still under the care of my parents, who hadn't even discussed these topics with me yet, because I was still young. But I felt something towards Andreas and suspected that he felt the same way. But after this visit, we unfortunately parted ways again for the time being.

Due to the death of the Queen, Mama now received an annual allowance of 2000 English pounds from the royal court. With Papa's income, we were now quite well off financially. However, my mother had never attached much importance to great wealth and believed that too much money could quickly lead to misfortune and that it also spoiled one's character. There were more important things in life for her, and the increased financial allowance didn't change that.
I had to prepare for my confirmation with the help of Pastor Frisius, the chaplain of the German Royal Chapel in *Marlborough House*. When we traveled to Heiligenberg at the beginning of April, I was very excited because shortly afterwards I was examined by Pastor Matthes from Jugenheim. After passing my examination with flying colors, I was confirmed on the ninth of April in a small ceremony in the town church of Jugenheim.
In April, we were all struck down by the measles and at the same time Uncle Ernie and Aunt Ducky announced that they were now seeking a separation after the Queen's death. Aunt Ducky had already eluded the court several times in recent months by traveling to the south of France, where she lost vast sums of money playing cards at the gambling tables or squandered the money on expensive wardrobes.

Uncle Ernie had founded an artists' colony on the Mathildenhöhe near Darmstadt and was very much looking forward to presenting it to the public along with an art exhibition. He also took advantage of his wife's absence to redesign and renovate everything in Wolfsgarten. After we had all recovered, we visited the castle and I have to admit that I didn't like his leather wallpaper at all. It all seemed too new-fangled and didn't suit the old building at all. But I understood his desire to reorganize his life.
The Queen had known how much of a rift there was between the couple, but she always hoped they would work things out for little Ella. Aunt Ducky loved the little girl very much and began to get Ella used to horses and teach her to ride from the time she was a toddler. Mother and daughter soon shared a passion for riding. But her aunt understood Uncle Ernie's deep affection for the child, as he adored his daughter and even believed they understood each other without words. This was due to the fact that when the little girl was just six months old, they wanted to move her into a new room, in which everything had to be renovated first, of course. Uncle Ernie showed the baby paint samples and she let out little squeals of delight when she saw a purple one. So her room was decorated with this wallpaper. Over the years, he built her a playhouse in the castle grounds, which was not unlike a real little house with a small kitchen and lounge. Adults were not allowed in. And so the tutors and governesses walked up and down in front of the little house until the children had finished playing. Elisabeth longed for a sibling when she saw the rest of us together with ours. She begged her parents to adopt one of Aunt Alix's children so that she would have a playmate. When her little brother was born dead, she was inconsolable. I remember how she could make the Queen laugh. When we were at Windsor and she heard the Queen's carriage coming, she would run to the balcony, wave and exclaim in English: "Granny Gran, I`m here!"
Sometimes there was something in my little cousin's eyes that even Mama, the governess, Miss Eagar, and Uncle Ernie noticed. They were sometimes filled with a deep sadness that was hard to understand, because this little girl was so full of joy and love for everyone. Her parents' quarrels did not pass her by without a trace, or so we all thought at the time. Somehow she suspected that her parents' marriage had broken down.
My mother always said that there was nothing else to do but just love this child and she understood her brother in his idolization of his daughter, who was his little sunshine.

On the fifteenth of May, Uncle Ernie ceremoniously opened his exhibition, entitled *A Documentation of German Art*, which was a great success for our art-loving uncle. I didn't have as great an appreciation of art as he did and found *Art Nouveau* rather uninteresting, but he was so proud of everything he had created that I kept my opinion to myself and simply congratulated him appreciatively.

Aunt Alix gave birth to a fourth daughter, Grand Duchess Anastasia, on June eighteenth. Again it was *only* a girl. As there was no possibility of the laws in Russia being changed to allow a woman to ascend the throne, hostility towards the aunt grew within the family. Tsar Paul I of Russia, the son of Tsarina Catherine the Great, had decreed in 1797 that only male descendants were allowed to occupy the Russian throne. This was probably more out of hatred for his mother, but in traditional Russia there was no question of abolishing this rule. Aunt Alix therefore had to give birth to a son or Uncle Nicky would lose his throne to his brother Mikhail.
In the summer, we children, Papa, Mama and Nona traveled to Russia. We were really looking forward to seeing our aunts, uncles and little cousins again. First we spent some time with Aunt Ella and Uncle Sergey and their foster children Maria and Dmitri in Ilinskoye, where we enjoyed the summer, went swimming and fishing. At that time, Dmitri and Maria spent most of their summers with Aunt Ella, wanting for nothing. My aunt was absorbed in spoiling the children, with Uncle Sergey sometimes putting his foot down, but usually overlooking the children's little foibles with a smile. Both children were taught at home by tutors and house teachers, who had access to the estate's large and very comprehensive library. Like Mama, Aunt Ella also loved to read. They had both inherited this from their mother, Grandma Alice. My mother had made a habit of writing the titles of the books she had read in large, brown leather books so that she could always check what she had already read and also use her notes for reading recommendations. Like Mama, Aunt Ella attached great importance to a good general education. The children were taught mathematics, art, history, geography, dance, music and languages. In addition to Russian, they learned German, English and French. A governess, Mademoiselle Hélène, was hired especially for Maria and was her constant companion and confidante. I was sorry that their biological father hardly looked after them. They didn't say a word about him either.

We then traveled on to Aunt Alix and Uncle Nicky in Peterhof, the summer residence of the Tsar's family. Peterhof is an impressive palace on the Gulf of Finland with a wonderful park, extravagant fountains and water features. It is located right by the sea and we really enjoyed our stay there. Life at the Russian court was quite unusual and overwhelming for us children. One room of the palace was more magnificent than the next, there were a huge number of servants and at times you felt almost overwhelmed by all the splendor and wealth, the precious antiques. The etiquette was strict, but we were given an insight into a world that seemed both unattainable and dreamlike at the time. We traveled in the imperial train, in magnificently furnished carriages with every comfort. While we were allowed to immerse ourselves in this world, which I saw through the eyes of a young woman on this journey, my mother's fears seemed to be completely unfounded. Wherever Uncle Nicky appeared, the people cheered him on, his power seemed consolidated and secure. And the only flaw was the lack of an heir to the throne.

While we were in Russia, we received the news that the Empress Frederick had died on the fifth of August at her widow's residence Schloss Friedrichshof near Kronberg in the Taunus. She was to be buried in Potsdam, but on the thirteenth of August a memorial service was held in her honor in St. Petersburg, to which we traveled on the imperial yacht from Peterhof. From there we traveled on to Narva in Estonia in the Gulf of Finland. Uncle Nicky wanted to make Papa happy and showed him the tsarist fleet during a military maneuver there. For a few days, we lived on the imperial yacht, the *Standart*, which was in no way inferior to the castles and the train in terms of its furnishings. Aunt Alix's children were looked after by a so-called *sailor nanny* - a sailor who looked after the girl on her own and passed the time, and the officers were also very familiar with the aunt and her family. It was not as strict a life as at court. The deck was the little Grand Duchesses' playground. There were even cats on board that had kittens and could be played with, and of course the Tsar's family dogs always traveled with them.

It was a wonderful stay in Russia and we children drew on the impressions of this trip for a long time.

On September tenth of that year, Papa took command again, this time on the *Implacable*. He traveled to Plymouth and prepared to resume service with the fleet in the Mediterranean. We followed him in October and this time he had rented a house, 25 Strada Mezzodi, and had it completely furnished for us. He had also bought a *buggy*, a small two-seater carriage, so that Nona, Louise and I could go for rides. Mama hired a new governess called Miss Grau, who was billeted near us in the capital Valette. She was to help us with our further studies, the home schooling.

Aunt Ducky and Uncle Ernie divorced on December twenty-first, 1901. It was the end of a disastrous marriage that Uncle Ernie tried to save several times.

Aunt Ducky had not really noticed Uncle Ernie's homosexual tendencies in the early days of their marriage. When they were on vacation in Capri, he used to secretly meet the young fishermen who offered themselves for amorous services. Soon, however, the servants in Darmstadt were whispering in the corridors when Ducky walked past them, some even giggling maliciously. Some turned away, avoiding eye contact with her because it embarrassed them. But Aunt Ducky only knew for sure when she entered Uncle Ernie's bedroom one morning without knocking and found him in bed with a teenage kitchen boy. It hit her so hard that she was emotionally devastated for a few days, retreated to her room and didn't want to see anyone else. And when she visited her sister in Romania, Uncle Ernie acted out his inclinations so openly that soon everyone in the palace knew about it. She later said quite freely how uninhibitedly Uncle Ernie slept with everyone. No boy was safe from him, from the stable boys to the kitchen help. This was also the reason for the large turnover of servants at the palace and in Wolfsgarten. The rather sexually inexperienced aunt still believed at the time that only Uncle Ernie practiced such things. She had simply never heard of it before. I had already mentioned Aunt Ducky's very strict upbringing by her mother and governesses. She grew up in Malta at *San Anton Palace*, with every comfort. The white villa was surrounded by a large, stately park. Her father was always at sea. And her mother sent the children outside to play in all weathers; she did not accept illness or lazy lounging on the pillows, i.e. sleeping in late. As a result, Aunt Ducky was blessed with robust health as a child. The Scottish nanny Nana Pitcathly placed a brown and a black leather whip above the beds in Ducky and Marie's nursery, which encouraged discipline. Even if none of the whips were ever used.

I used to stay with them as a child when we were in Malta, and even then I was impressed by the way Aunt Ducky and the others enjoyed their freedom outdoors in all weathers. She even climbed trees. And it was telling that her mother wanted prodigies, but they couldn't meet these high standards. Instead, the pressure was too much. Mama found it strange that when they moved to Rosenau in Germany, the Duchess said that girls should not be older than twenty when they married. Otherwise they would ask too many questions, have too many ideas of their own and think too much. That's why they had to be married off in their teens.

Later, she made another statement that was more indicative of Aunt Ducky's failed marriage. Women should flirt, have fun, but never lose their hearts. Men were not worth it, she said, because if you looked at their lives and then realized the reality, you would turn away in disgust, because all you would see was filth, even in men who appeared good and noble on the outside. But this was surely her own offended heart speaking.

Sexual education was not part of the strict upbringing, which led to Aunt Ducky's plunge into the deep end.

When they married, Aunt Ducky's parents had stipulated that she was to receive an annual allowance of fifty thousand marks from Uncle Ernie, which

he was to pay in monthly installments. If she had outlived Uncle Ernie, she would have been paid eighty thousand marks a year. This also included a comfortable, appropriate apartment and furnishings. In all these agreements, however, no allowance was ever made for divorce.
As Uncle Ernie was living out his inclinations so publicly at court, his aunt soon had no more moral qualms. She met openly with the Grand Duke Cyril and planned a new future with him. At the end of the summer of 1901, she was no longer at court, but lived with Cyril in Nice for a time, came to Wolfsgarten with him only briefly, and appeared with him at parties and family celebrations. On October 16th, she left Darmstadt with little Elisabeth and most of her belongings and moved in with her mother in Rosenau. The Duchess understood when Ducky explained to her why she wanted to separate, and they both wrote to Uncle Ernie asking for a divorce. But he believed that since she now had a lover and he tolerated him, he could live as he wished. In this way, it was possible to make the public believe that the marriage was intact and happy. Nobody needed to be interested in what happened behind the walls. But Aunt Ducky insisted on a divorce through the courts.
On the twentieth of November, Uncle Ernie wrote to his wife asking her to return, but she replied curtly from Nice that she refused.
Mama and all of us, the family, were outraged by what was going on, and especially by the fact that Uncle Ernie had taken a vacation to Capri in October, despite everything.
Aunt Ducky deserves a lot of credit for not mentioning Uncle Ernie's homosexual tendencies in court so as not to damage the reputation of the House of Hesse. She also wanted to protect little Ella and come to an amicable agreement about custody. She even renounced her title so that she could remarry in accordance with her station. As in most cases, she was divorced at fault, but accepted it.
Ella would now live with her mother in Coburg or in her mother's house on the French Riviera for six months and with her father for six months. However, it soon became apparent that the child was so close to Uncle Ernie that when she went to her mother, she would take refuge under a table or sofa, cry bitterly and tell him that only he would show her how much he loved her. And the separations were just as difficult for her uncle, because he and his daughter had a special bond, she was everything to him and seeing her sad was a great burden for him. Of course they wrote letters to each other, but the physical separation soon became a real burden for both sides. Uncle Ernie never said a bad word to Ella about her mother or tried to influence the child. It was my little cousin herself who would not forgive her mother for leaving her father. Aunt Ducky tried to make her stays in Coburg pleasant, but Ella often made her feel how great her longing for Darmstadt and her resentment

about the divorce were.
Mama was very upset about Uncle Ernie's divorce. I don't know if she ever reproached him or just accepted him as he was. But she was sad because Ella suffered so much from not always being able to be with him.
Ella was such a mature child for her age that you sometimes thought you were looking at an adult, not a seven-year-old. I liked her a lot, even though we didn't spend as much time together as my younger siblings because of the age difference. But you can say without a doubt that Ella was simply adorable, and as she was always well-behaved and very well-mannered, her moods were undoubtedly due to the separation, both from her parents and from her father.

After my seventeenth birthday in February 1902, Louise said she was sure I would marry a king one day, because in her view I had the looks and qualities of a queen. I had no such ambitions and did not aspire to such a life, because when I saw how my relatives' lives were burdened with labels and constraints, with constant, exhausting public appearances, it rather put me off. There were many expectations of a queen, because she also represented her country, and for Aunt Alix this even meant being forced to give life to a boy. No, that was definitely not a life for me. I liked to immerse myself in the silence that I was born with and could spend many hours at the beginning of the year watching the storms and raging waves that gripped the island.
After Malta, we stayed in Heiligenberg again from spring to summer.
On June twenty-sixth, the coronation celebrations for Uncle Bertie were to take place in England. Mama and I were invited to attend. On June twenty-second we traveled to England, Nona accompanying us, and in *Flushing, Cornwall*, we were joined by Uncle Henry and Aunt Irene.
They let us stay at Buckingham Palace. But on June twenty-third, Uncle Bertie appeared for lunch looking very miserable. He was pale, had severe stomach pains and no appetite. At first we thought it was the excitement before the ceremony, the stress of the preparations, but in the evening he developed a high fever and suffered terrible pain. The doctors diagnosed acute appendicitis. His life was in danger. They had to operate on him and cancel the celebrations. At that time, such an operation was also dangerous for the patient's life. So we were all very worried about our uncle.
Of course, many distinguished guests and relatives had already arrived for the coronation celebrations. Among them were the Greek relatives of Uncle Bertie's wife, such as Crown Prince Constantine of Greece and his wife, Crown Princess Sophie, a born Princess of Prussia, sister of Uncle Willy. The two were accompanied by Princes Andreas and George, both brothers of the Crown Prince. I already knew Andreas, was pleased to see him again and

called him *Andrea*, like his family. He was now firmly established as an officer in the Greek army.
When we met again, he seemed like a Greek god to me. There was something about him that captivated me, more and more. And he felt the same way and couldn't take his eyes off me. While everyone feared for Uncle Bertie's life and had nothing to do but wait for long hours, Andrea's relatives suddenly seemed to be inspired to bring us together.
Andrea and I got on so well that we both quickly realized that we were falling in love with each other. I realized that my mother didn't like how close we were sitting together, constantly spending time together. She thought I was too young and only saw it as a first fling between a young officer and her pretty daughter. But she expressly did not want anything more.
Uncle Bertie survived the serious operation well, but he first had to recover and so the coronation was postponed. It hurt me a lot to leave Andrea again when we traveled back to Heiligenberg on the fifth of July. At the time, Mama had no idea that Andrea and I had secretly become engaged after Aunt Alix had listened to my woes and thought the union was wonderful. And Uncle Bertie, whom I visited briefly at his bedside, was also delighted with my choice.
In Heiligenberg, no one could fail to notice how happy I was. Perhaps you could say that I was full of the new feelings that were flooding in. I wanted to marry this man, whatever the cost, and it only increased my mother's resentment. She informed Papa, who was in Corfu, how worried she was about my future. He was able to take time off from his commitments at short notice and came to Heiligenberg for five days. The union would make me a Greek princess and Papa was surprised that I was so insistent on getting married. On the other hand, neither he nor Mama wanted to force a marriage candidate on me.
But Mama also wrote to her sisters for advice. I think her biggest fear was that I might make a rash decision out of my youth, but that it would influence the rest of my life and that I wasn't aware of this because of my first love. Even though I kept reassuring her that I was really serious about my heart's desire. And when she found out about the secret engagement, she was disappointed at the high-handedness with which we, Andrea and I, had acted. Aunt Alix then reminded her in a letter how she and Ella had had to fight for their love, their happiness. Mama had also married for love, had followed her heart, despite all the resistance. It gave my mother food for thought. Papa already realized that I couldn't be changed.
We talked a lot about my future during the five days he was with us and he said that my happiness was all that mattered. That was the most important thing.

I was eagerly awaiting a new date for the coronation celebrations so that I could see Andrea again in England.

Andrea, around 1901

I loved my family very much and knew that marriage meant leaving the protective nest and starting my own life. But I longed to stand on my own two feet.

My parents were simply faced with the same problem as all parents. The child grows up and you have to let it go.

The coronation celebrations were scheduled for the ninth of August. I counted the days until we traveled to England. And I felt such relief in my heart when we finally left.

On the way to *Westminister Abbey*, where the solemn ceremony took place, my mother, Andrea, his brother George and I were placed in a carriage. My mother took it with a slight displeasure, I could feel it. As the coronation had been postponed, there were fewer guests from overseas this time as they didn't want to make the long journey a second time, which was quite understandable.

Uncle Bertie chose the reigning name of *Edward VII,* and when we attended the ceremony at the front among the royal guests and relatives, with me as one of the maids of honor, it was very impressive, because with the coronation of the uncle, the *Victorian era* was finally over and the *Edwardian era* began. The Archbishop of Canterbury, Frederick Temple, who performed the ceremony, was eighty years old. He had to kiss the new king on the cheek. As he approached his uncle, he stumbled and almost fell, which deeply shocked many of the guests present.
In the days after the coronation, I tried to spend every minute with Andrea and he with me. You could say we were inseparable. And it almost broke both our hearts when we had to part again. Because on the thirteenth of August, Mama and I traveled back to Heiligenberg.
I suffered terribly, because as Andrea had to serve in the Greek military, we wouldn't see each other for an agonizingly long time, we would only be able to write to each other. And my mother saw how I was suffering. It made her change her mind, because she now also told Nona that she would probably have a Greek son-in-law.
I was actually very happy to have found a man with whom I wanted to share my life. A soul that was my equal. But Andrea loved the military, he wanted to fulfill his duty as an officer, just like everyone else who served there. He had told me that his entire upbringing from a young age was geared towards a military career. In a military academy, he had also been educated by German supervisors and then handed over to the very strict supervisor Panayotis Danglis, who taught him weaponry for large-caliber guns, military history, weapons technology, geography and fortifications. Even when the family was on vacation in Corfu, Andrea had to continue learning while his brothers enjoyed themselves at picnics. But he loved it all and his resulting profession. His only thought was to serve his country.
One of Andrea's sisters was *Aline*, who died in tragic circumstances in 1891 during a visit to Aunt Ella, after giving birth to little Dmitri. Andrea's sister Maria, also known as the Greek Minnie, married the Russian Grand Duke George Mikhailovich, a cousin of Uncle Nicky's father, Tsar Alexander III of Russia, in 1900. His brothers George, Nicholas and Christopher were still unmarried like him.
I was very impressed by how determined Andrea was with regard to his military career and I tried to show the same interest in our conversations that Mama always showed in Papa's profession.
And when we said goodbye, we promised to write to each other.
I wrote to him every day, and when I had been waiting for a letter from him for over a week, my emotions got the better of me. Full of grief, I took refuge in a room at Miss Textor's girls' school, which I was attending at the time,

where another girl found me - my hair disheveled, my face red with tears and my dress wrinkled, I was crouched on the floor, bent over in grief. She tried to comfort me, wanted to know why I was crying so bitterly. I let her in on my grief and confessed that I was afraid for Andrea. If he didn't get in touch, he must be ill, must have had an accident or - and this was my worst fear - he had changed his mind and no longer wanted to marry me. The girl was deeply touched and said it could be because of the post, but I was so devastated that I had to go home.

The next morning, however, I came back to school completely relaxed and at ease. All the bitter tears I had shed were forgotten, because I had received five letters from my lover. It was the post office's fault, the letters reached me slightly late.

Whenever I received a letter from Andrea, I couldn't wait to read it. I would run into my room, lock the door, lie down on my bed and read his lines over and over again until I could almost memorize them. My mother found this behavior very strange, but she tolerated it, even though she still thought it was all a crush that could quickly fade away. She often said things like how easy it was to win and influence the hearts of young girls. But I kept reassuring her how serious I was. And she had to realize it slowly, just as I awaited each of his letters, almost pining for his written words.

In September 1902 Papa became *Commodore*, i.e. commander of a group of ships and their captains during the Tenth Fleet Maneuvers off Argostoli, the capital of the island of Kefalonia in Greece, and in November he became Director of the *Naval Intelligence Department*. It was another milestone in his career and it filled us all with pride.

That year we celebrated Christmas in Kiel with Uncle Heinrich and Aunt Irene. We drove around with Uncle Heinrich in his steam car, a new type of automobile that was powered by a steam engine using steam. Coke, brown coal, wood or oil could be used as fuel for the boiler. There were only fifty of them in the world at the time. Every now and then we had to stop to fill up with water at farmhouses, but it was very interesting to get around in this vehicle. My mother was also always open to technical innovations, as was Papa.

We also sailed on Uncle Henry's yacht. Relatives were also present at Christmas, such as Empress Auguste Victoria, Uncle Willy's wife, who went to church with us and drank tea with us in the officers' mess on the yacht. Afterwards the presents were distributed. She gave me a very beautiful and elegant fur coat and muff. I was delighted, but I was even more pleased with the gifts that arrived from Greece. The King sent me a beautiful bracelet, the Queen sent me real fine silk for a dress and a fine letter opener and from Andrea I received a wood-carved duck's head as a handle for an umbrella and a beautiful brooch. It was exactly to my taste. I was amazed that he knew or suspected exactly what I might like. I hadn't sent him a present yet because I simply didn't know what I could give him. I was a bit ashamed, but I would have to think of something and talk to my Mama. She was surprised that I hadn't come to her with it before Christmas. After all, I was expecting presents from Greece because of the circumstances and Andrea's relationship with me.

As Papa now held a high position, we moved into a house at *70 Cadogan Square* in *Knightsbridge* in London in January 1903. This rather upmarket residential area was close to the posh *Belgravia* district. I was to complete my studies by taking piano lessons from various tutors and being taught music history, art and English literature. I also had lessons in French and Greek. Andrea wanted to visit us soon, but it was unclear whether he would be able to come at the beginning or middle of March.

Uncle Bertie was very pleased to have us always in England, as he thought highly of my father and considered him to be one of the best officers in the *Royal Navy* and invaluable in the positions he held.

On the tenth of March, Uncle and Aunt Alix invited us to celebrate their fortieth wedding anniversary. There was a small family dinner and then a ball with four hundred guests. The ball season hadn't actually started yet, but I enjoyed waltzes, polkas and quadrilles, even though I wasn't a very good dancer due to my disability. There weren't many other opportunities for distraction, as Andrea had postponed his visit until May, although he couldn't give an exact date. He explained it was due to his service in the Greek army, as there was slight political unrest in Greece.

The months became long, the waiting time almost unbearable. It depressed me so much at times that I couldn't really get myself to do anything, nothing brought me joy.

In April, we moved to *Sopwell* in *Hertfordshire. Sopwell House* was a very special building, as it was a so-called widower's house for the Earl and Countess of Verulam, and Papa rented it for three months. The grounds belonging to the house, the park, were very large. My father bought us one of the first automobiles with an engine, a so-called *four-seater Wolseley Wagonette.* It was a very exclusive vehicle and Louise and I usually went for short drives with our father.

And finally Andrea announced that he would be visiting us on the eighth of May. He arrived without an aide and when he finally stood in front of me again, I could hardly believe my luck. We were finally reunited. And my parents, who also knew how much Aunt Alix and Uncle Bertie approved of our relationship, finally agreed - on the tenth of May they officially announced

our engagement. I was now eighteen years old, Andrea twenty-one. Uncle Bertie, who was in Scotland at the time, was delighted and was of course happy to give his blessing.
Uncle George and Aunt May, the Prince and Princess of Wales, hosted a small dinner party for us at *Marlborough House* and it was there that Uncle Bertie officially announced our engagement.
On the fifteenth of May, Mama took Andrea and me to a *Te Deum*, a thanksgiving service in honor of our engagement. This service took place in the Greek church on Moscow Road in *Bayswater*, a district of London. Two *archimandrites*, heads of the Greek Orthodox Church and comparable to abbots, welcomed us. The ceremony was quite short. But the delegations of high-ranking personalities from the Church and from London, such as the Honorable Secretary of the *Byron Society* at a reception in the Greek Embassy, were long. Everyone made a speech, including the Secretary, who told Andrea that it was a great honor that his choice had fallen on me, Princess Alice, daughter of Prince Ludwig von Battenberg, a special officer of the Royal Navy and granddaughter of Princess Alice, Grand Duchess of Hesse, whom they greatly admired, and whose memory would always be in the hearts of the British. This choice was therefore a great honor for Andrea. My fiancé was visibly uncomfortable and very intimidated, but he thanked the secretary in a firm voice, trying not to show his uncertainty.
A few days later, Uncle Bertie and Aunt Alix invited us to Buckingham Palace for a dinner followed by a visit to the theater. The uncle was sometimes a bit strange in his humor. That evening he turned up for dinner in a freshly ironed white shirt and jacket. As he began to eat, some spinach fell onto his shirt. A small stain formed, but he carried on eating, not noticing it at first. Then he saw the stain, dipped his napkin in his glass of water and deliberately rubbed it so that it was now much bigger. After the meal, he said he had to change his clothes. Aunt Alix didn't say a word about the stain, but Andrea and I were literally dismayed. Uncle Bertie returned in a fresh, clean shirt for the theater and just said that at least it was worth changing his shirt. He was also the only person I knew who could pour vast quantities of Worcester sauce over his meat at dinner.
Papa chose Darmstadt as the location for the wedding celebrations. It was quite central for our relatives, if you want to put it that way. They could reach it easily from all directions. The date was set for the seventh of October. Uncle Nicky was able to go hunting with the Austrian Emperor in Styria in September beforehand and would already be *nearby*.
Andrea didn't have much herself, but I was a worthwhile match for him, even if that didn't count for him. All the relatives wanted to give us a carefree start to our future together as a couple and so the wedding presents would be

correspondingly generous.

Of course, we received many congratulations on our engagement and Mama only heard how the old Grand Duchess of Mecklenburg-Strelitz, Auguste Caroline, a former Princess of Cambridge, very much regretted that I wouldn't wait for her grandson Adolf Friedrich, who was the same age as Andrea at the time, but wasn't thinking of getting married. She also called me pretty, but also deaf. Which could certainly be difficult for *her Fred*, but if other princes didn't mind, the Greek one should be happy with me.

Her Fred would become Grand Duke of Mecklenburg-Strelitz in 1914, but had to abdicate in 1918, and as he was severely depressed afterwards, he shot himself in the same year due to his melancholy and a failed affair. He would not have been a good match for me. And as his brother was also to die in the same way, the problem of severe melancholy and depression seemed to run in the family. Mama, however, dismissed the Grand Duchess's tip with a smile.

Andrea left for Darmstadt on the nineteenth of June, because with the permission of the Greek king, his father, he was allowed to serve with the Hessian *Red Dragoons*. I would have loved to travel to Darmstadt with him, but my mother joked that I would be spending my whole life with Andrea, so I could probably wait a few more months. Nevertheless, I was eagerly awaiting the big day.

On the seventh of July, French President Emile Loubet came to England on a state visit. Mama and Papa took me to the ball, which was held in his honor with around a thousand guests at Buckingham Palace. The famous Australian soprano Nellie Melba also sang at this ball. I danced a lot with my father and we stayed there until three in the morning. It was a welcome change.

At the end of July, we finally traveled to Darmstadt. Nona accompanied us to help plan the wedding and Andrea visited us in Heiligenberg when his military commitments allowed him to take time off. In August, he was able to do this for seven short visits with us, as he also wanted to help with the planning. And in September, he was granted a few more days off in view of our upcoming wedding.

I couldn't wait for the wedding. In England, I had been so homesick for Heiligenberg and longing for Andrea. I also had many friends in Darmstadt, all of whom I was now seeing again.

Me in 1903 before my wedding

I was a bit afraid of becoming lonely if Andrea was involved in the military after the wedding, because I was still young. I had to get used to it, Mama explained, because she herself had also gotten used to Papa often not being at home. Maybe it would put a strain on me, but it would make being together again all the nicer and separations were good for a marriage. I understood what she was trying to tell me and realized that. But I was entering a completely new phase of my life. It was exciting and scary at the same time.

Love's happiness, love's sorrow and the end of the old world, 1903- 1922

Our wedding ceremony was to take place in the Russian church in Darmstadt. This was a special honor, because this church had been built on the Mathildenhöhe at the request of Aunt Alix and Uncle Nicky. Uncle Nicky had donated money from his private fortune so that he and his family always had a suitable place to pray when visiting Darmstadt. They did not want to do without the Russian Orthodox services when visiting relatives. As the church was financed by the Russian tsarist family, it also belonged to them. The church has the style of the Yaroslav churches, it is not massive, has gilded onion domes and richly decorated, gilded roof ridges. The earth on which it stands was brought to Darmstadt from various governorates in Russia. The marble in the plinth area comes from the Caucasus. Inside and on the roof ridges, everything is decorated with small tsarist eagles. The icons were specially painted by the famous Russian church painter Karl Timoleon Neff. The foundation stone was laid on October sixteenth, 1897 in the presence of Uncle Nicky and Aunt Alix, and the consecration took place on September twenty-sixth, 1899, also in the presence of uncle and aunt.
Duchess Marie of Saxe-Coburg and Gotha donated an altar cloth, the iconostasis and the church flags from her private church in London. She also donated a wood-carved sarcophagus with the tomb of Christ to the church. The interior decoration of the church was only completed in 1903, shortly before our wedding, and I was delighted to say "I do" to Andrea in this very place.
It was a huge effort for Uncle Ernie to accommodate all the guests. Aunt Alix and Uncle Nicky arrived with their daughters, Grand Duke Paul, Uncle Sergey, Aunt Ella and their foster children Marie and Dmitri on the fifteenth of September, with Uncle Nicky leaving again on the twenty-fourth to continue hunting with the Austrian Emperor and to discuss political problems. However, he returned for the wedding and the Russian relatives stayed with us until the end of October. They also brought the imperial Russian choir with them to perform national folk songs and Gregorian chants for us. Aunt Alix and Uncle Nicky gave Andrea and me the most beautiful and precious wedding presents. One was a million roubles, about 2,530,000 marks at the time. A qualified teacher earned about two thousand marks a year back then. So it was a very generous gift. I also received jewelry worth 250,000 marks. It was a tiara, necklace, brooch and bracelet made of diamonds of the purest water and alternately set with light green aquamarines.
Mama gave me her diamond stars as a wedding present, which could also be

worn individually, for example pinned in the hair. They were also available as a necklace, tiara and bracelet. I also wore the necklace as a bandeau in my hair.

Our best men were King George of Greece and Papa.
Uncle Bertie was unable to attend in person due to state business, so Aunt Alix and her daughter Toria and Aunt Beatrice and Ena came on his behalf.
Uncle Ernie accommodated Aunt Alix and Toria in the *New Palace*, as well as the Russian relatives.
The entire Greek family, including Queen Olga's sister, Duchess Vera of Württemberg, lived in the *Old Palace*. The rather large palace directly in Darmstadt also became the home of Aunt Irene, Uncle Heinrich, their children, Duke Aldophus of Teck, who stood in for Uncle Bertie, and Prince Albert of Schleswig-Holstein. They were joined by Aunt Beatrice and her daughter Ena.
Of course, a few friends from smaller houses arrived for the wedding itself, such as guests from Austria, Danish and French princes. Of course, all the guests brought their servants with them so that, as Uncle Ernie said, it soon became quite *crowded* in old Darmstadt.

With the bandeau made of my mother's diamond stars in my hair, 1903

For little Ella, who was of course also in Darmstadt for my wedding, the presence of her cousins from Russia and the Prussian cousins was a welcome change. My two brothers also enjoyed having so many children for company. They were able to have fun together all day long under the supervision of the nannies and governesses.
Louise, who was now fourteen years old, preferred to join the adults or have fun with Grand Duchess Marie and Dmitri. But in general, meetings of all relatives were always held in high esteem in my family. Due to the distances to the other places where we lived, we always kept in good contact by letter and family celebrations were always a big reunion.

There had already been a few festivities before our wedding. One advantage of Darmstadt was that the strict etiquette at court did not apply here, as it did in Russia, for example. The distinguished guests were able to move around freely and didn't have to stick to a strictly pre-planned time slot. This meant that everyone could spend the days leading up to the wedding in relative peace.
Only for Uncle Nicky, three hundred and fifty Russian detectives and minders had to patrol the city to ensure his safety. We thought that was a bit excessive, but he was the Tsar, one of the most powerful men on earth, and his safety always came first.
Uncle Ernie organized a large gala dinner for all the relatives, guests and their servants in the castle and on the evening before the wedding, Papa and Mama invited everyone to a wedding ball and buffet, which was attended by two hundred and sixty people in the ballroom of the *Old Palace*. The only blemish was the fish that was served, as Mama immediately noticed on first tasting that it was anything but fresh and had it cleared away immediately. Papa wore his uniform of the *Grand Ducal Hessian Field Artillery Regiment No. 25* and looked very proud in it.
The Duke of Teck seemed somewhat unsettled by the distinguished guests surrounding him. He constantly wrote to his wife and asked my parents behind closed doors whether there would be enough to eat before the upcoming visit to the opera in the next few days or whether the food would only be served afterwards. He was reluctant to make an unpleasant impression in society with a growling stomach. And he wasn't used to always showing up in uniform. So he asked whether he always had to appear like this in the company of Aunt Alexandra, because she was a queen after all, or in front of Aunt Alix, because she was a tsarina. And whether he always had to greet her exactly when the King and Queen of Greece were standing in front of him. He was only thirty-two years old, but soon confused like an old man and

probably not the best choice to stand in for Uncle Bertie. He was called *Dolly* in the family. I don't know the reason for this, but in the company of kings, tsars and their wives, he was visibly uncomfortable being called that. His sister was Crown Princess May of England.
There were three ceremonies for our wedding. One was a civil ceremony under German law, one in the old Protestant-Lutheran chapel in the castle and one in the Russian church on Mathildenhöhe.
The civil wedding ceremony took place on October 6th at twelve o'clock in the *Altes Palais* in Darmstadt. The alderman of the city council, Dr. Glässing, performed the ceremony on behalf of the Lord Mayor. There weren't many guests present, just the two witnesses, as mentioned, Papa and the King of Greece, my father-in-law, Mama, Aunt Alexandra, the Queen of Greece, my mother-in-law and the Greek Minister Namgabe.
The other two ceremonies followed on the seventh of October. Uncle Bertie had wanted a fourth one at the British Embassy in Darmstadt, but Andrea and I objected that this would be too much of a celebration for us. It was all very exhausting for us. Even though he said that, as someone with British roots, he would have liked to throw me a small party there too.
A wedding is something very beautiful, but when the seemingly endless preparations are over and the big day has finally arrived, you want to enjoy it a little and not rush from party to party.
On the seventh of October, the sun was shining and the weather was generally very nice. First we got married according to the Protestant-Lutheran rite in the chapel in the *Old Castle*.

Andrea wore his red dragoon uniform for the ceremonies and the *Grand Cross of the Royal Victorian* Order, which Uncle Bertie awarded him for the wedding. My wedding dress was made of white lace decorated with bouquets of myrtle and orange blossom.

Thirty guests attended the wedding ceremony in the castle chapel, who always entered in pairs. Those of lower rank led the way, those of higher rank followed at a suitable distance. As Uncle Ernie no longer had a wife at his side, Aunt Alix took on this role as his sister. Uncle Nicky escorted Aunt Alexandra into the church, as Uncle Bertie was unable to attend. They were followed by Andrea and his parents, then my parents and I, with Papa leading me.
At our entrance, a wedding song was sung, which the composer William de Haan, the director of the music society in Darmstadt, had composed especially for us from words from the Book of Ruth and rehearsed with the choir of the court theater. For the ceremony, the guests formed a semi-circle around

Andrea and I left the church in the carriage, which stopped every now and then so that we could thank the people from Darmstadt who had gathered cheering on the Mathildenhöhe and wave to them. Uncle Nicky called out in front of the church that everyone should follow him to catch us in the carriage outside. Everyone ran after him, especially Uncle Ernie. And of course the cousins were only too happy to race the two adults. Uncle Nicky's guards were obviously unfamiliar with the custom of bags of rice and, when they saw one, suspected that something bad might be hidden inside. They overlooked the fact that all the guests were holding bags in their hands. And the satin slippers looked to some like flashing knives from a distance. So they hurried towards the crowd, but while Uncle Ernie ran out of breath anyway and stopped, Uncle Nicky ran head first through the cheering crowd. Some of the children following him slipped and tumbled onto the grass, laughing. When Uncle Nicky reached our carriage, he threw his bag of rice and a pair of slippers. I was just about to stand up again to thank the people with a nod of my head when the bag hit me right in the face, but I caught a pair of slippers unerringly. When my uncle appeared next to me, laughing, I hit him over the head with the slipper several times and told him loud and clear what I thought of him. He was so amazed at how I, an otherwise quiet and controlled person, could get so loud despite my disability. So he stopped, then burst out laughing and calmed the guards, who had reached him in the meantime. I sat back down in the carriage, smiled at the people, waved and Andrea gave me a respectful smile. He realized at that Mamaent that his little mistress could go out of her way when she had to. Of course, I resented Uncle Nicky a little, but it was soon forgotten.

In the evening there was a big family dinner, without the servants. It was very relaxed and laid-back, with Uncle Heinrich being the first to grab his glass and *raise his glass* to us.

Andrea and I then embarked on our honeymoon, which we started with another gift from Uncle Nicky. He gave us a *Wolseley*, just like the one my father had bought for our family. It also had satin slippers attached to the back, so Andrea and I drove it to Heiligenberg at night, where we wanted to stay for the time being.

Uncle Ernie invited the guests to stay with him in Wolfsgarten from the fourteenth of October. They all paid us a short visit in Heiligenberg for one day, then we were there for eight days on our own. Uncle Ernie organized a big evening party at the castle in Darmstadt to mark the departure of our guests. Andrea then had to return to his military duties with the Hessian army and my parents let us use their apartment in the *Altes Palais* for the first time. We were to stay in Germany for a few more weeks until Andrea's service was over.

Some of our guests in the garden of the New Palace, October 1903: front right is Aunt Alix with her daughters and little Ella, next to her on the left is Georgie and Duchess Vera von Württemberg, Uncle Ernie stands on the left with cane, next to him on the right is Andrea's brother Nicholas and his wife Elena, Uncle Nicky stands on the steps above Aunt Alix, Aunt Ella stands on the right next to Andrea's father, fifth from the top left is Uncle Sergey, next to him on the right is Toria, Aunt Alexandra and Marie, Aunt Ella's foster daughter, next to Aunt Alix on the left is Aunt Irene and slightly above her Dmitri, Aunt Ella's foster son, my mother-in-law, Queen Olga is on the left next to Uncle Sergey and the other Greek relatives, like Andrea's siblings, are at the far back left

A souvenir card, published for our wedding, 1903
Of course, we received lots of congratulations on our wedding in the days and weeks that followed and my Mama helped me to answer them.

On November fourth, Uncle Nicky met Uncle Willy in Wiesbaden and on November seventh at four-sixteen in the morning, the train with Uncle Nicky and his family left the station in Egelsbach. Uncle Ernie and little Ella were traveling with them. They wanted to spend some time together in Uncle Nicky's hunting grounds in Skierniewice. The Tsar's family owned a very comfortable estate there, like a hunting lodge. The children played together in the forest and went on many excursions with their governesses. The adults went hunting, organized picnics or went to the theater and opera. Uncle Ernie, who had organized the whole wedding so perfectly for us in Darmstadt, had earned some peace and quiet, although he also appreciated and enjoyed family gatherings.

One evening, the adults had a little get-together by torchlight in front of the estate and Ella's governess and governess, the lady-in-waiting Baroness Georgeina von Rotsmann, who had taken on this task with great dedication since February 5th, 1902, wanted to make her protégé happy. So she let Ella sit by the window in her nightgown and take a look at the adults in the park. The night was cool, but it wasn't for long, so no one thought Ella might catch a cold. She was in perfect health.

On November fifteenth, the little girl woke up with a severe cough, a sore throat and chest pains. Her governess thought she had a cold and blamed herself. The baroness loved Ella very much and affectionately called her *my*

baby. They sent for the tsar's personal physician, Dr. Botkin, but he said it was just a harmless cold. The child had tired herself out playing and running around in the forest with her cousins and simply needed some rest.
For this day, a Sunday, a visit to church was planned at ten o'clock, then Uncle Ernie was introduced to the members of the *Klastitsky* Cossack Regiment and they had breakfast together. Then they went hunting in Remitsa. Pheasants, partridges and hares were shot, which, like all game, were prepared in the estate's kitchen. Uncle Ernie worried about his little daughter and often looked after her, but under the care of her governess, the Russian nanny Mrs. Eagar, and the visits of her little cousins, she seemed to be doing better.
We had lunch. In the evening there was a small concert and ballet in the theater. They did not think she was seriously ill, but as a precautionary measure they removed the cousins from Ella's room as sleeping companions because of the risk of infection if she caught a cold. When the adults returned at twenty-four o'clock, she already had a high fever, which rose to over forty degrees.
In her delirium, Ella demanded to see her mother and fantasized about playing with her cousins. Uncle Ernie immediately sent a telegram to Aunt Ducky in Rosenau, Coburg, to inform her that Ella was ill.
Her condition deteriorated rapidly in the hours that followed. She cried out that she must die. Uncle Ernie never left her side, holding his little girl's hand, calling her *Babysweet*, as he did in his letters to her when they were apart.
Soon she could hardly breathe, was writhing in the sheets and a doctor called in from Warsaw found that her heart was getting weaker and weaker. She was given injections of camphor and caffeine to strengthen her heart. Aunt Alix stayed with Uncle Ernie and Ella, as did Uncle Nicky, because sleep was out of the question that night. Another telegram was sent to Aunt Ducky saying that Ella's condition was now life-threatening.
When the sun rose, there was no more hope. Ella kept her eyes fixed on her father until the very end, who encouraged her and was shaken by such violent crying fits that Aunt Alix thought it would be better if he left the room briefly so as not to frighten the child so much, as she knew that the end was approaching. Leaving her beloved Papa alone was certainly all the more difficult for her. But my uncle stayed with her until she died at nine thirty after a short, serious illness. It was without doubt the worst day of his life, as the *sunshine of his life*, as he always called her, had died.
An autopsy was ordered and it was determined that Ella had died of *typhoid fever* or a rapidly progressing form of *childhood cholera*.
Aunt Alix got a terrible headache and was heartbroken that her brother had just lost his child while visiting them. She had to lie down.
Uncle Ernie collapsed and was prescribed bed rest to cope with the shock.

Nevertheless, he sent a telegram to Aunt Ducky informing her of Ella's death. What was planned as a happy family vacation now had to be cut short. Uncle Nicky sent his daughters back to St. Petersburg accompanied by their nanny. Aunt Ducky only received the last telegram on November seventeenth; the other two had arrived shortly before. She had been sitting at breakfast in Rosenau and wanted to pack something quickly and travel to Poland to see Ella. She had actually been waiting for a telegram to tell her Uncle Ernie when they would be back in Darmstadt. Now she was in a panic, worried about her child. Her mother brought her the last telegram while she was packing her suitcase and Aunt Ducky could see from her teary eyes that it contained something terrible - it was the news of Ella's death.
In the meantime, Aunt Alix had been diagnosed with a middle ear infection, which meant she couldn't leave and had to stay in bed. Uncle Ernie informed us all by telegram and prepared for his departure.
Uncle Nicky gave him a silver coffin for Ella with a glass lid, in which she was laid so that she looked like a sleeping little Snow White with her dark eyes. The coffin lid was closed and then a prayer was said in the presence of a pastor. Uncle Sergey had also made a special trip. He stood guard as the coffin was carried to the station by Cossacks and Uhlans, who were also there to honor Ella. Uhlans fired salutes at a pond. The coffin was placed in the same compartment as Ernie, who brought the coffin home with Baroness Rotsmann. At two forty in the afternoon, the train departed for Darmstadt.
When we received the news of Ella's death by telegram from Uncle Ernie in Darmstadt, the news came as a shock. Mama immediately agreed to help organize the funeral, and of course Andrea and I were there to support her straight away. I remember how we were all overcome with grief, bursting into tears and hugging each other. My siblings couldn't believe that their cousin was dead either. We also had to comfort them in their grief.
Papa was in London and Mama of course informed him immediately.
It had been such a beautiful wedding, a wonderful time with all the guests and relatives, and now the grief lay like a thick, black, impenetrable veil over Darmstadt. On November eighteenth, the Darmstadt newspaper reported on Ella's death in a special afternoon edition.
After the autopsy, it was clear what had killed my cousin, but there were still rumors as to whether a poisoned meal for the Tsar could be to blame for her death, because Uncle Nicky had a habit of always giving priority to the girls with *Ladies First* when children were at the table. But it was more likely that Ella could have eaten berries in the forest while playing that contained the bacteria that caused the disease. Baroness Rotsmann had always kept a close eye on her protégé, as had Mrs. Eagar on the Grand Duchesses, but perhaps it had happened in an unobserved Mamaent. No one could say for sure. And

speculation was pointless now, it didn't help anyone.
So Mama, Andrea and I waited for Uncle Ernie, the baroness, Aunt Ducky, who was boarding the train in Frankfurt am Main, and Ella's coffin at the station in Darmstadt. They arrived on November nineteenth.
Ella's funeral took place immediately. It was half past three in the afternoon when six horses, draped in white cloths, brought the coffin to Mathildenhöhe. It was a rainy day, the sky was gray and cloudy, as if it too was weeping. From Rhein-Neckarbahnhof through Rheinstraße, Alexanderstraße, Mühlstraße and Erbacher Straße, we and many relatives who had traveled there accompanied Ella on her last journey to the mausoleum on Rosenhöhe. The streets were lined with crowds of people who all wanted to pay their last respects to their little princess. Many were crying and Uncle Ernie thought he could hear it. Some Darmstadt residents had always seen Ella skipping and laughing through the streets on her way to school. What's more, her early death at the age of just eight really touched everyone's heart.

Aunt Ducky paid her last respects to Ella by placing her Order of the House of Hesse, which she had received at her wedding, with her daughter in the mausoleum.
Shortly afterwards, Ella was laid to rest in a grave on Rosenhöhe in the immediate family circle. Uncle Ernie had a large stone angel placed at her head to guard her eternal sleep, and a picture of the sleeping Snow White and the seven dwarfs was carved on the gravestone.
Something in my uncle also died with Ella, so that many, many years later he would mourn her again and again in quiet Mamaents. Then he would mention anecdotes about her and say that he still missed her.
The baroness also found Ella's death difficult to deal with. When we were in Ella's room, she looked thoughtfully at the books she read to her in the evenings, like *Heidi*. She wanted to process her grief and remember the girl. So she wrote a fairy tale in which a little princess who lives in a playhouse climbs the ladder to heaven. As Ella also loved the fairy tales by the Brothers Grimm, she gave the book the title *Once upon a time ...*
Mama kept emphasizing how glad she was that she had gotten us all through the childhood illnesses without having to lose one, because losing a child was the worst thing in the world. But we all understood her uncle. Aunt Ducky was grieving too, but in her own way, and she had never been as close to Ella as he was.

A phtotograph that expressed the loving bond between Ella and her father

Mama was a support to her brother, but I often had the feeling that although she suffered with him, she was hit harder when Queen Victoria died. She once said that she wasn't afraid that Uncle Ernie would let himself be overwhelmed by his grief for Ella or even despair or break down. I thought that was a bit

hard-hearted of her.
Aunt Ella and Uncle Sergey arrived over the next few days to be with Uncle Ernie, who was very quiet and introverted. We only celebrated his birthday on November twenty-fifth in a very quiet way with a small meal, which he took little pleasure in. The first Christmas without Ella was also very hard for him to bear. Mama left for London with my siblings to visit Papa, while Aunt Ella and Uncle Sergey traveled back to Russia. So Andrea and I were the only ones to celebrate with my uncle.
At the beginning of 1904, we packed up our things to set off on the long journey to Greece. We would travel most of the way in the *Wolseley* that Uncle Nicky had given us as a wedding present. We were about to start our journey when we were informed that the Royal Greek yacht *Amphitrite* had to pick up Queen Olga from Odessa first, as she was visiting her Russian relatives.
So we had to leave Darmstadt later. We said goodbye to Uncle Ernie, drove off and on the long drive I thought a lot about my new home, a country I had never visited before. It would all be new to me. We boarded the yacht and were warmly welcomed by my mother-in-law. On the sixth of January, we reached Piraeus, the country's third largest Mediterranean port. We were surprised by a heavy storm and rain in the Corinth Canal, so we were briefly delayed off the Peloponnese peninsula. Grand Duke George Mikhailovich of Russia and his wife, Grand Duchess Marie, the *Greek Minnie*, as she was known, a sister of Andrea's, accompanied their mother-in-law and spent time with me and Andrea on board the yacht. They had two children, but they had stayed in Greece because they were still too small to travel to Russia. Little Nina had been born in 1901 and Xenia in August 1903. I found it remarkable that Minnie had no problem leaving the baby alone for a long time.
Andrea let me know that Minnie and George weren't really happy together. She had always emphasized before the wedding that she didn't love him, but George adored her and hoped that love could grow from her side over time. Unfortunately, you could sense that this would never be the case, even after only four years of marriage, because she was rather cold towards her husband and more distant than affectionate towards me.
We disembarked in Piraeus. My father-in-law King George I of Greece was also waiting for us there. We were taken to Athens. Together with my mother-in-law, after an official reception at the port in Athens, the king escorted us to a cathedral where we were greeted by a *metropolitan*, a senior bishop who presided over an association of dioceses, and other high-ranking members of the *Holy Synod*. We took part in a *Te Deum* to which Greek ministers, diplomats and court officials had also been invited.
The Athenians had already cheered us on the way to the cathedral and when

we left the cathedral, the cheers erupted again. On the way to the palace, too, the streets were lined with people waving and welcoming us. I learned that our arrival was a day off for the people. The schools were therefore closed, as were the stores, so that the Athenians could give us a warm welcome.
The royal family lived in a palace *on Syntagma Square* in Athens, which was also known as the *Old Royal Palace*. In 1871, the king also bought a plot of land twenty kilometers north of Athens near *Dekeleia* and had a summer residence built for his Russian wife in the style of Peterhof. *Tatoi*, as the country estate was called, was more like a summer house than a palace. Andrea was the only one of his siblings to have been born there.
There was still a *crown prince's palace* in Athens, where Andrea's brother Konstantin or *Tino* lived with his wife Sophie and their children George, Alexander, Elena and Paul. George was thirteen years old, Alexander ten, Elena seven and Paul three. Sophie was heavily pregnant and was due to give birth to little Irene on the thirteenth of February.
The palace in Athens, where we were first taken, was quite beautiful. Andrea pointed out to me that he had contracted typhoid here through unclean water pipes when he was just eight years old. So of course my husband was deeply saddened by the fact that little Ella should have died from it. They shared the same age of contracting the disease, but he had survived. It showed me once again how sensitive my husband was, as he had already been very caring to Uncle Ernie in his grief in Darmstadt.
The mayor made a speech for us in the palace and called it a great joy that a princess of noble blood would now become an ornament to the Greek nation, which honored me greatly.
In the evening, a large fireworks display took place, which lit up the entire city.
The king informed me that he had already sent a telegram to London to tell my parents that we had arrived safely in Greece. I thanked him for this as, like Andrea, I was overwhelmed by our welcome but also very tired from the journey.
I also found out that evening that I was allowed to call Christopher by his nickname *Christo*, George, the *big George*, because he was really very tall and to distinguish him from his father. He lived in Crete and Minnie still had a house in Athens so that she could get away from court life. I only got to know many of the family members, especially the children, that evening.
Andreas' brother Nikolaus and his wife Elena, Ellen or Helena, as they were known in Greece, had a seven-month-old daughter, Olga, and Helena was also pregnant. She was expecting the birth of her second child in May.
My father-in-law attached great importance to a close-knit family life and so everyone met regularly for Sunday lunch. The family stuck together. My

father-in-law was also very friendly towards me, showed me around, introduced me to everyone, including the distinguished guests, and was very sensitive to my deafness. He also said that everything must be confusing for me, because I had to get to know a new country and new faces. I didn't know anyone here and had to find time to settle in.
The king was not actually held in high esteem by the Greeks, as he had been installed in this country, was not a king by birth and often did not behave in a manner befitting his status. He kept official occasions to a minimum and loved to stroll through the streets of Athens without a guard. He had survived an assassination attempt in 1898, but did not see the point of being shielded like Uncle Nicky. He was a democratic monarch, progressive in this respect, thought highly of the constitution and for the rather quiet man, politics was important, but not everything.
His wife Olga was very popular with the people, as she was involved in charitable work and had founded a Christian hospital in Athens, two military hospitals and a Russian Orthodox hospital in Piraeus. She was sixteen years old when she came to Athens to marry the king, and her trousseau consisted largely of valuable dolls. Her rooms were filled with magnificent icons and she was very Christian, but her kindness always came from the heart.
My parents-in-law's marriage was extremely happy and you could see that in their family life. Once a year, my father-in-law went on vacation in France to *Aix-les-Bains*, a well-known thermal spa in the *Auvergne-Rhone-Alpes* region. The municipality boasted the largest freshwater marina in France and was a popular vacation destination for many aristocratic spa guests from Europe.

My parents-in-law, King George I of Greece and Queen Olga, around 1904

However, the king went there alone while his wife visited her Russian relatives. Tino also often accompanied his father there and his wife Sophie was probably unsure at first whether she should go with him, as she told me. But the king just told her not to be unsure because it was a men-only vacation and to just ask the queen what she thought about traveling with the gentlemen. Of course it was all right.
Sophie, as Uncle Willy's sister, had married Protestant and Orthodox like Andrea and me. But her brother, as Emperor of Prussia, forbade her to visit him in Berlin. She was simply denied entry to Germany because of her change to the Orthodox faith. She took it in her stride, as she did not hold her brother in high esteem and did not want to be intimidated by him. Berlin was a cosmopolitan city at the time and Sophie found Athens rather provincial, the Athenians often very slow to organize, she noted, which is why her charitable commitments often came to a standstill.
Andrea's brothers were all soldiers in the Greek army.
Shortly afterwards, Christo told me how interested he was in the occult. He was fascinated by spirits and tried to make contact with them at séances. When I arrived in Athens, he was just sixteen years old. Due to the small age difference between us, we got on very well straight away, as he was a very calm and level-headed young man.
Ellen, who was a Russian grand duchess by birth, was very distant towards

me because she saw herself as being above me. I came from a line that had been founded through a morganatic marriage and this was a thorn in her side. From her point of view, my marriage to Andrea had only elevated me to a royal highness, but not one by birth. My mother's lineage, who was the daughter of an English princess, didn't count for her. You could perhaps say that she saw me as an *upstart*, nothing more.

But Ellen also often behaved coolly towards her sister-in-law Sophie, as she had to show her respect as the daughter of Emperor Frederick III of Prussia, but still considered herself to be above everyone else. Ellen perfected that which was alien to my mother-in-law because of her birth, to elevate herself above others or even to hold them in low esteem. We were only to find each other later in philosophy. Now, in 1904, shortly after my arrival in Athens, I did not feel respected or esteemed by her.

The palace was centrally located in Athens. It was quite an imposing building, mostly made of marble, but offered hardly any comfort. The rooms were large and draughty.

There were few fixed rules. One was that if there was an official ball, guests were invited for eight thirty in the evening and entered the ballroom as a family at nine o'clock on the dot, half an hour late.

We settled in with the parents-in-law in the palace. Christo, the youngest, still lived with his parents and Andrea and I were allocated a small apartment. Nicholas, Andrea's brother, and Ellen still had the so-called *Nicholas Palace* in Athens, where he retired to.

In the future, we would also spend time at the Tatoi country estate with its game enclosures where deer grazed, the pine forests that surrounded it and the vineyards.

On February twenty-fifth, my nineteenth birthday, Andrea woke me up early in the morning. It was still dark outside. He congratulated me, kissed and hugged me, confessed that my present was in the bedroom. And so I turned on the light and my eyes fell on a motorcycle that he, in his often exaggerated sense of humor, had brought into the room at night while I was asleep. My husband was always good for a surprise and I was delighted with his gift.

Uncle Ernie came to visit us in Greece in March and stayed until April. He was present when we celebrated the baptism of little Irene in April, who had been born in February.

Uncle Ernie seemed to blossom somewhat in Greece, but one sensed that it would take him a long time to get over Ella's death. He also had to think about the succession, because without a wife and child, a son, the grand ducal house in Hesse could not continue to exist. But the divorce and the loss of his daughter were still too recent. He did not immediately feel the urge to go looking

for a bride again.
I was in contact with my mother and the other relatives by letter and so I received the news that Aunt Alix was pregnant again. The baby was due to be born at the end of July and, of course, it was hoped that this time it would be a son. My aunt was definitely receptive to the supernatural. She, Uncle Nicky and Aunt Ella had travelled to the Diveyevo Abbey in Sarov in 1903, where the monk and mystic Serafim was canonized during a ceremony. The Mother of God is said to have appeared to this monk, who is also one of the most famous monks in Russia for his good deeds. During the ceremony, Uncle Nicky was given a seventy-year-old letter written by Seraphim before his death in 1833 *to the Tsar, who was coming to Sarov*. In this letter, the monk described the end of the tsar's life and prophesied that Russia would be free again at the end of the same century. I never found out more, but Seraphim can probably be compared to Nostradamus in this respect. His prophecy could be interpreted in many ways. But Aunt Alix was so moved that she went to the holy spring in the nearby forest, bathed in the water and prayed for the birth of a son. There were many people at the time who were convinced that the water from this spring could free them from all imaginable ailments. Aunt Alix also draped many consecrated icons around her bed, as I mentioned earlier, because her deep spirituality meant that she grasped at every straw. It was not just about an heir to the throne per se, but also about her popularity among the Russian people. She often didn't show her grief, as she was a rather introverted woman, but you could see her acting cheerful, although she probably often shed tears over the burden she was given.
Prince Franz von Teck, the younger brother of Crown Princess May of England, visited us in May. His baptismal name was actually *Francis* in English, but as he was also related to the House of Württemberg, he was called *Frank* in the family. He was a *black sheep* in his family, as he did not really value good behavior and had already had to leave schools as a child. His money problems were legendary, as he gambled, bet on horse races and had proven himself militarily as a major in the *Second Boer War*, among other things, which earned him a certain reputation and livelihood. Like his parents, he loved traveling and indulged in a certain amount of luxury, so it made sense for him to pay us a visit in Greece. In the meantime, he had become chairman of the *Middlesex Hospital* in London, where they specialized in caring for cholera patients. As the patients were mostly from the working or lower classes, they had no money to pay for treatment, so the prince collected donations. He was also quite successful at this. The well-known English nurse *Florence Nightingale* also volunteered at the hospital. Her name meant quite a good reputation for the hospital.
I found Frank's commitment very interesting and appreciated it. We got on

well and it was a pleasant visit where we spent most of the time in Tatoi. Frank thought that Andrea and I were a very beautiful couple, you could see our happiness. He also constantly complimented me on my good and radiant looks, to which Andrea simply said that he was a charmer and knew what a woman wanted to hear. My husband was undoubtedly right, because Frank was known in English society as a womanizer and his affairs were numerous.

On the twenty-fourth of May, Ellen gave birth to little Princess Elisabeth. I took part in Ellen's Greek lessons and I was amazed at how quickly she returned to her studies after the birth, with great concentration and ambition. Russian nobles were not used to looking after their children themselves. They loved their children, but were not afraid to hand over even the youngest ones to governesses or nannies. It was simply a tradition. My Aunt Alix was the exception, as she always took a lot of time for her girls, even breastfeeding them herself as babies, which was unthinkable for Ellen. She had time for other things when the children were being looked after, so we both learned Greek quite quickly and soon became fluent. It was also necessary, because it was the language of the country we lived in, and it was the only way to get involved in something. It was assumed that a princess from the royal house would take on a charitable task or even several.
The Royal Greek School of Needlework and Lace in Athens was founded in 1897 by Lady Olga Egerton. Mrs. Egerton was a Russian princess by birth and the wife of Sir Edwin Henry Egerton, British Ambassador and Minister to Greece from 1892 to 1903. His wife, a very good embroiderer, had studied ancient Greek embroidery and lace-making techniques, for which she had also traveled to the Greek islands to learn the Byzantine style for both. The aim was to provide girls and young women from poor families with work that would enable them to earn a living and support their families. A committee was formed and Mrs. Egerton was soon appointed chairman.
Traditional handicrafts were made in this school and later sold.
At first the school had been housed in a private building, but as the number of students grew, a new house was built specifically for the classrooms on a private property on *Michail Vada Street* in Athens. Wealthy Athenian women supported the school with donations through the committee, and when I enrolled there were around two hundred students attending the school. The main rules were to work neatly, efficiently and mannerly and to use commercially acceptable designs that would sell well. The English embroiderer Louise Pesel had risen from a designer to become principal of the school, a post she held from 1903 to 1907.
Ellen and my mother-in-law were already patrons of the school and I now followed them. I was able to withdraw into my own world and concentrate

fully on my work and I enjoyed it very much. I learned how to decorate batiste with embroidery, but also wool, linen and silk. The patterns came from Greek and Byzantine antiquity. The teachers traveled through the centers of Europe to find out which patterns and designs were in demand and would also be in demand in the near future. The products were not only sold in Athens, but were soon exported to London, Paris and even New York.

The training of the schoolgirls was expensive, as they were offered the materials and lessons free of charge. They only received a wage once they had mastered their craft. In order to keep these costs down, i.e. to recruit, train and later employ more young women and girls, who could then sell the finished handicrafts for a profit, new schools were soon established, such as in Volo, Affya and other towns and communities. Hundreds of people were quickly employed in Greece. New subjects were added, such as the use of lace and embroidery on clothing and so-called openwork, which took a long time to complete by hand because the patterns were so intricate. It took a lot of skill and experience to create such pieces.

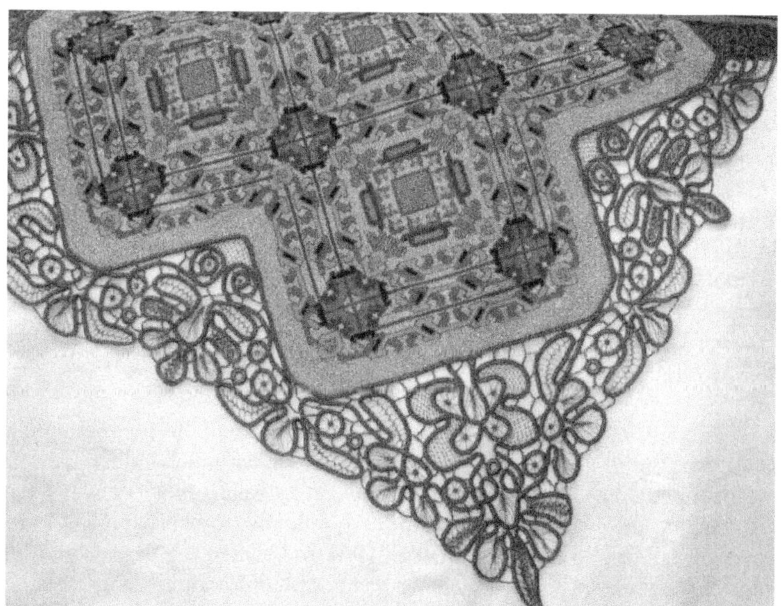

A traditional cutwork embroidery, based on an antique model from Cyprus, around 1903

It wasn't just about making tablecloths, but also many other things, such as decorations for parasols, clothes, books, blankets, runners, cushions, bags, among other things. The work was very varied and it was a good way for me to pass the time, as Andrea was very conscientious about his service in the Greek military. This kept him very busy, but I also needed something to do. Soon I was spending hours there, immersing myself in learning how to embroider, how to mix colors and learning all about the different ways of working.

On July 1st, 1904, Papa was appointed Rear Admiral. He steadily climbed the career ladder in the *Royal Navy*. Georgie, who was now twelve years old, was keen to follow in Papa's footsteps and my father was visibly touched by this. Mama was also very positive about my brother's wishes. However, he had to wait a little longer before he could attend the *Royal Naval College* in Dartmouth to start training in the *Royal Navy*.

The early days of our marriage were relatively carefree. Andrea loved riding. He had a wing adjutant, Captain Menelaos Metaxas, who was also a good friend and his right-hand man. I often traveled with him and Andrea to the *Actaeon Palace Hotel*, about six kilometers outside of Athens. There you could go for rides in the surrounding countryside, but Andrea and his aide were better riders than me. They rode fast and I tried to follow them at the same pace with my horse. At one point, Andrea stopped the horses and asked Metaxas to help me off my horse because he was afraid I might break my neck. I didn't fully understand him straight away as he spoke too quickly in Greek. So Metaxas asked my husband to repeat it in English, and instead of telling me exactly word for word, Andrea just told his aide to tell me the truth. In other words, that I simply wasn't suited to her wild rides, that I didn't have my horse under control like she did. It wasn't a statement I took offense to, because it was a fact. I could ride, because I had been taught from an early age, but I preferred slower rides and so I always stayed a little behind them with my horse.

It was a tradition in the Greek royal family not to spend the summer months in Athens, but to go traveling. These could often last much longer and drag on for months until you returned. Since visiting relatives was always very important to me and I also longed to see my family, my husband and I took up this tradition. So in the summer of 1904, we visited my parents and siblings in *Hertfordshire*, a county in England north of London, where Papa had rented a house. We then traveled with Mum and my siblings to Wolfsgarten to visit Uncle Ernie. In the meantime, Uncle had gone on a *gentle kind* of bride hunt, if you want to call it that. He had inquired about unmarried princesses and met Princess Eleonore zu Solms-Hohensolms-Lich from Lich near Giessen. *Onor*, as she was called, was already thirty-two years old and a

daughter of Prince Hermann zu Solms-Hohensolms-Lich. My uncle found her very warm and was quite taken with her. Even though the two of them had only formed a tenuous bond, it seemed to make him happy again. That made us all very happy, because Onor seemed to distract him from his grief and give him courage for a new future with a wife and possible children.
Unfortunately, our vacation was marred by the fact that I contracted a bad fever and had to stay in bed for many days. Andrea was very worried about me, but I was actually blessed with quite robust health. So although I recovered quickly, I still needed some time to rest and recuperate afterwards.
When Mama told me that Aunt Alix had finally given birth to a son on the thirtieth of July, I wasn't as happy as I would have liked to be. It wasn't until a little later that I congratulated Aunt Alix on her son by letter. It seemed that a burden had been lifted from my aunt in Russia. The baby was christened *Alexei* on the third of September. Just a few days after his birth, however, it was discovered that the little boy's navel would not stop bleeding. The bleeding was eventually stopped, but for my aunt it was an ominous black cloud gathering in the sky. She was gripped by the fear that her little son, whom she had waited so many years to give birth to, might be suffering from hemophilia. Now it is not unusual for a baby to bleed a little longer at the navel and for the wound not to heal quickly, but haemophilia hovered over our family like a sword of Damocles and so Uncle Nicky and Aunt Alix prayed that Alexei would be healthy. Otherwise, he was a strapping boy, a well-behaved baby.
Mama was deeply saddened, because on February twenty-sixth of that year, Aunt Irene and Uncle Heinrich had lost their youngest son Heinrich to the same disease in a tragic accident. Their son Waldemar also suffered from it and only Sigismund was not affected by hemophilia.
My mother had not passed the disease on to us children and so I could actually be sure that my children couldn't get it either. Because my mother was not a carrier.
In our family, Aunt Beatrice had passed the disease on to her son Leopold. Her other two sons were healthy. And her daughter Ena could also be a carrier. But it was such an insidious disease that you never knew who of the male offspring it could affect. And Queen Victoria, my great-grandmother, had been the first to bring it into the family.
At that time, haemophilia was still so unexplored that it was difficult to help with bleeding. Painkillers were given priority, but there was no real hope of a cure or at least relief or even a therapy.
On top of all this came the joyful fact that I was sure I was pregnant in September, and after an examination by a gynecologist, he confirmed my suspicions. The baby was due to be born in April next year. My parents were very

happy, as were my siblings and Uncle Ernie. Andrea was of course the proudest man in the world. He was looking forward to the baby and was happy that my fever had not harmed him.
We stayed in Wolfsgarten and Heiligenberg for a long time and only arrived back in Athens in mid-October, where we told the family the good news straight away. Everyone rejoiced with us.
I immersed myself in school work again, devoted myself to needlework and Andrea resumed his military service. In anticipation of my first child, I also made some clothes for him.
Many visitors from abroad often came to Athens, as Greece itself is a country steeped in history and, of course, its capital. The country literally courted travelers and wanted to present itself as cosmopolitan. Many archaeological sites were opened to visitors to get them excited about the country and its history.
Unfortunately, as I was pregnant, I was soon unable to travel much or get to know the country. I also missed some official appointments, but I wanted to concentrate fully on motherhood.

On the second of February 1905, Uncle Ernie married Princess Eleonore in Darmstadt. Unfortunately, I was unable to attend this wedding due to my pregnancy, but I wrote to wish them both all the best. I had been able to meet Onor briefly in Wolfsgarten and she seemed to me to be a really loving woman who would make my uncle happy again. She was in the middle of life due to her age and was, as they say, down to earth. There was nothing negative to say about her. I didn't begrudge my uncle the fact that he could now settle down after his more than turbulent marriage to Aunt Ducky.
This February, however, we also received terrible news from Russia.
Uncle Sergey had made a brilliant career in the Russian military. He had been with the *Preobrazhensky Life Guards Regiment* since 1882. In this very prestigious regiment he rose to the rank of major general in the town of Preobrazhenskoy. He quickly became the commanding officer there. He was adjutant general of the Imperial Guard, also known as *Svita*. His brother, Tsar Alexander III, certainly helped his career to date, but Sergey was also a determined man who lived for the military.
In the spring of 1891, his brother appointed him Governor General of Moscow, which was a great honor for his uncle, but he was reluctant to accept the position. Firstly because he had been very popular in his regiment, and secondly because he and Aunt Ella loved the tranquil life in St. Petersburg more than that in the big city of Moscow. Sergey acted on behalf of the Tsar and was a political hardliner, as they say. He was at one with his brother's desire for a firm hand on the people. In one of his first official acts, twenty thousand

Jews were expelled from Moscow, mainly craftsmen and merchants. This was done in three stages and took a year. First the unmarried Jews, those without children and those who had lived in Moscow for less than three years were affected. Then families with up to four children who had lived in the city for less than six years. In the final stage, all families with many children were affected, especially white-collar workers, but mainly people who had called the city their home for over forty years in some cases. Young Jewish women were allowed to stay in the city if they registered and hired themselves out as prostitutes. Soldiers usually came at night, surrounded the houses and drove people out of their homes and apartments in a very aggressive manner. In January 1892, hundreds of them of all ages and genders stood at the train station in Brest at minus 30 degrees Celsius, with the few possessions they could take with them, and were transported away. Many fled to the west or south of the country, but most emigrated from Russia.

The Jewish factory owners, who mainly produced and processed silk in their factories, were forced to leave. In turn, hundreds of Russian workers lost their jobs, and at the same time it ruined this branch of production for which Moscow was known.

The uncle also did good things for the city, was committed to creating comfortable dormitories for students, supported charitable schools for blind children in his high position and much more. However, his political actions often had a very negative connotation when professors at universities were spied on to determine whether they were loyal to the tsar and also politically compliant with the regime, the tsar's autocracy.

My mother and other relatives were also very skeptical about the treatment of Moscow's Jewish population. If I had known back then what we would be facing many, many years later in terms of anti-Semitism, I probably wouldn't have been able to stop shuddering.

I would give my uncle credit for roaming the city incognito to see for himself the living conditions of the poor and for moving Aunt Ella when he told her about it.

However, he soon became a target for revolutionaries, which is why he, his wife and their two children lived in *St. Nicholas Palace* in the *Kremlin*, where it was safer for them all.

On the fifteenth of February, the family came out of the *Bolshoi Theater,* revolutionaries wanted to carry out an assassination, but saw the children in the carriage and Aunt Ella. So they gave up their plan that day. They only wanted to kill the uncle, not the children or his wife.

On February seventeenth, Uncle Sergey drove to his office in the governor's house at around two forty-five in the afternoon. He had asked his adjutant not to accompany him because he was married and had children. His uncle was

claim to this territory and the war was to be very costly for Russia. Uncle Nicky was to lose the war in the summer of 1905 and *Port Arthur* fell to Japan.
Aunt Ella was looking for distraction and a task after the death of her husband and soon became involved in the hospitals, where she cared for wounded Russian soldiers.
My mother wrote to me that my aunt was a very strong woman and that she would emerge stronger from this trauma, build a new future for herself and overcome her grief. Because she saw a meaning in everything, even in the death of her husband, as I mentioned earlier. I only knew my aunt like that and was now all the more impressed by her character. I would often take my cue from her strength later in life. She was an impressive role model for a woman who loved her foster children, supported them, of course, because they were also mourning the loss of their uncle, and yet in her own grief still found joy in family gatherings and didn't let fate weigh her down.

On April eighteenth at one o'clock in the morning, I gave birth to little Princess Margarita in the royal palace in Athens. Mama had arrived in Athens the night before so that she could attend the birth and see her first grandchild straight away. Her mother-in-law was also present at the birth. It was good for me because I was in labor for a very long time. Queen Olga told Andrea that he should support me quietly, because men should also see the suffering they put their wives through, and from her point of view it was not right to stay away from it all the time. So Andrea was by my side, but then couldn't bear it any longer, left and then came back. But he wasn't nervously able to endure all the long contractions, even if only as an observer. It is the fate of men that they just sit by and can't share or empathize with the pain. For most of them, a child was simply born. It was very positive that my husband was able to experience for a while how painful and exhausting such a birth can be.
The baby was healthy and Andrea and I were very happy about our little girl. My father had been in command of a cruiser squadron on the *Drake* as a rear admiral since the first of February. She was the flagship of the squadron and so he came to Athens on the ship to see his grandchild and attend his christening on the eleventh of May.

Despite the exhausting birth, I recovered quite quickly and so Mama left for Darmstadt again on the sixteenth of May. When Papa had to leave again, he was very sad because he regretted how often and for how long the family had been separated. His work had kept him so busy that he had also missed Louise's confirmation in Jugenheim. From his point of view, Mum still had a

female confidante in Louise, because I had left the family far too early. Nevertheless, he was happy to see me happy.
Due to my pregnancy, childbirth and postpartum period, I was unable to attend the opening of the *International Archaeological Conference* in April. I was only able to attend one day of the inauguration of the new library at the *British School of Archaeology*. I also missed Uncle Willy's visit, which was more spontaneous and not welcomed by his sister Sophie in particular. When Aunt Alexandra from England visited us, I would have liked to spend more time with her, but that wasn't possible for me either. And finally, I also missed the *Panhellenic Games* in May. Everything seemed to be concentrated around the time of my pregnancy and the birth of Margarita. I didn't regret that I didn't see everything, I was too happy with my baby and devoted myself entirely to caring for her.
In all the joy of the new life, I soon realized that there was also political trouble in Greece. On the thirteenth of June, Greek Prime Minister Theodore Delyannis was just getting out of his carriage to enter parliament when a man rushed out of the crowd of people in the street, as if to greet him, and plunged a knife into his chest. Delyannis died an hour after the attack. His murderer was the owner of a house where people could gamble. He had murdered Delyannis because he wanted to crack down on such establishments with tough rules, which meant a lot of money for the owners - revenue that they would lose if these houses were closed down by law.
Delyannis was buried just four days after the assassination. My father-in-law, Nicholas and Andrea followed the coffin to the cathedral, while many mourners lined the streets, who appreciated Delyannis during his lifetime and condemned the assassination.
It was a great shock to have to experience such a cowardly murder in my own country after Uncle Sergey's violent death.
I was glad that we traveled to Heiligenberg in August to introduce little Margarita to my siblings, Aunt Onor and Uncle Ernie. However, only a few days after our arrival, Dickie noticed that life in Heiligenberg was much more pleasant and quieter without a constantly crying baby. You had to forgive the then five-year-old boy.
Dickie was preparing for his entrance examination for the *Royal Navy* Cadet School, he loved his little niece straight away, and Louise was equally fascinated by the little girl. She thought Margarita was very cheerful, laughed a lot and cried very little.

Aunt Onor and Uncle Ernie also loved looking after Margarita. They were also keen to have children together and Onor cuddled the little one so warmly, playing with her, that Mama thought it could almost be her own. The Erbachs

were of course also very taken with the little one when they visited us.
My husband loved animals very much, especially dogs. But he also had a cockatoo that could talk and traveled with us. It was naturally very popular with my brothers because you could talk to the animal and it listened very docilely when you taught it new words. Andrea and I left the animal with the relatives and handed Margarita over to my mother, which was very difficult for me. But Andrea wanted to visit his grandfather King Christian IX in Denmark, who was already eighty-seven years old. He was suffering from lumbago and very bad back pain. So we went to Copenhagen for two weeks in mid-August. Andrea's grandmother, Queen Louise, had already died in 1898. We also met my husband's Danish relatives there. However, my grandfather was in a very bad way. He died in January 1906. So in retrospect, it was good that we had visited him again that August.

We returned to Greece in September. At that time, I suspected that I might be pregnant again. But since you generally wait for the first three months, as complications can still occur and you might lose the baby again, I kept my hunch to myself for the time being.
Andrea had to resume his military service and was transferred from the second to the

First Cavalry Regiment. He was appointed commander of an *escadron*, the smallest tactical unit of the cavalry. Such a *squadron* comprised around one hundred and fifty horses and five officers. Andrea's job was to train recruits. He had to take up his post in the capital *Larissa* in the Greek region of *Thessaly*. The town is beautifully situated in a valley basin, shielded by Mount *Ossa* and the River *Pinios* runs through the valley. The famous *Mount Olympus* is also nearby. We would live there from the fall of 1905 to the spring of 1906, because of course I went with my husband.
Andrea was soon to discover that the people there were, as they say, *simple folk*. Most of them were farmers from the mountains, rough-hewn, who had never left their herds of goats and had never met a horse in their lives. They knew donkeys, which they used as beasts of burden. It was only the children who rode them. In other words, Andrea had to turn a bunch of farmers into soldiers and teach them how to ride a horse. He was in charge, but I found it strange to recruit and train these farmers, who lived so remotely, for the military.
I had my little Margarita to look after. She was a very attentive child, loved to romp around with Billy, the biggest of Andrea's dogs, and was soon able to walk a few steps by the hand. My husband sometimes treated his dogs like children, spoiling them very much and talking to them like a child. I liked animals, but I was never as fond of them as he was. Margarita seemed to have

inherited her passion for dogs from her father, as she was not afraid to choose the biggest of them as a friend.
Our cook had a tame little monkey that my daughter and I sometimes played with. But our life in Larissa was more tranquil than in Athens.
Andrea and I often went on little trips around the area in a car he had bought, taking Margarita with us, who loved these trips, whooping and squealing with delight.
It wasn't easy for me to bring up a baby or toddler because I didn't hear my child crying or calling for me. Maybe that's why I was a bit of a mother hen, constantly checking on her, even when she was sleeping, because I was afraid she might wake up and ask for her Mamamy. When she was playing, I always kept an eye on her. I could speak, but it was never like the voice of a healthy person. As I was well aware of this, I made an effort to teach Margarita to speak, perhaps over-enunciating the words. Andrea loved how much I cared for our child and he also told me how proud he was of me that I didn't always leave her in the hands of nannies and wanted to teach her to speak myself. Margarita had to learn early on that her mother couldn't hear her, but in some quiet Mamaents when I was thinking, when I was for myself, I wished I could hear her voice, just like her father's voice. The first word is something special from the mouth of a child and I would have loved to hear it. There were Mamaents when my disability did weigh on me a little and I felt a little sad. But I think it's the same for everyone with a disability. If you can't walk, you learn to live with it, but in some situations you certainly wish you could walk.
In the fall, I learned that Aunt Ducky had married Grand Duke Cyril on October 8th according to the Russian Orthodox rite at Lake Tegernsee. Our former aunt could now call herself Grand Duchess, but Uncle Nicky's *wedding gift* to them was the revocation of all royal privileges for Cyril and his title within the Navy. Aunt Ducky and Cyril were first cousins. Marriage under these conditions was forbidden under Russian domestic law. The couple were not allowed to enter Russia, so they stayed in Coburg at Rosenau Castle and had three children together.
After the disastrous marriage with Uncle Ernie, I didn't begrudge Aunt Ducky her happiness again, but she had started an affair with Cyril when she was still married to my uncle.

In April 1906, we celebrated Margarita's first birthday and I was heavily pregnant at the time. The baby was due to be born at the end of May.
Andrea and I first traveled back to Athens, where he stayed, while I retreated to Tatoi to prepare for the birth, for which my mother-in-law was at my side, as she had been for Margarita's birth. We were actually invited to the wedding of my cousin Ena von Battenberg in Madrid, Spain, on the seventeenth of

May, as she was marrying King Alfonso XIII, but I was unable to travel due to my pregnancy, so Andrea had to go alone.
The wedding was not under a good star, as there was a national crisis in Spain at the time. The Basque country and Catalonia were demanding their independence, anarchists were turning against the king and threatening violence. Riots broke out and Catalan nationalists demonstrated in Barcelona the day before the wedding. On the day of the wedding, the situation escalated and an anarchist named Matteo Morral carried out an assassination attempt on the wedding couple. It happened in the main square, the Calle Mayor in Madrid, where many cheering people had gathered; twenty-three people were killed in the bomb attack. When I heard about it, we were all very worried about Andrea and, of course, Ena and her husband. Fortunately, nothing happened to them, but people who had been cheering the couple died, which must have been very stressful for Ena. The best day of her life ended in disaster.
Poor Ena was also to pass on haemophilia to two of her sons, including the crown prince, her first-born son Alfonso Pius. This was another reason why the marriage was very unhappy, as her husband did not forgive her for passing on the disease, even though it was not her fault. He took refuge in affairs and had five children out of wedlock. In view of what was to come in their marriage, the assassination attempt on their wedding day of all days was a bad omen.
I was just relieved that Andrea was healthy. But he stayed in Madrid to support Ena and her husband. I fully understood that.
On the thirtieth of May 1906, at eleven forty-five, I gave birth to little Princess Theodora. Andrea only saw his little daughter a day later, when he had returned from Spain. We showed her to Margarita, who immediately took her little sister to her heart. But as she understood *dear Dolla* when we told her what the baby should be called, Theodora got her nickname and from then on we called *her Dolla*. The birth wasn't as stressful as the first, but I still had to rest afterwards and tend to the puerperium.
During the last few weeks of my pregnancy, I had missed the opening of the Olympic Games in Athens in early April. The Prince of Wales, George and his wife May had dropped in briefly on a visit to the Royal Family in April as they were passing through from India to England and I had seen them briefly, introduced them to Margarita, but had not been able to attend the banquet at which Uncle Bertie, who was accompanying them, spoke. I regretted this somewhat, but it was in the nature of things that you didn't show yourself in public with a big belly, heavily pregnant, back then. And it would have been too much trouble for me.
I was now looking after my two children, but I soon wanted to devote myself to charitable work again. A society was training young girls to become nurses

and this organization urgently needed donations, which I wanted to collect for them.

Mama was unable to attend the birth of her second grandchild. She was visiting Aunt Ella in Moscow at the time. They traveled to Ilinskoye together with the foster children, but my aunt was now living under the constant protection of armed soldiers. Mama found a completely changed person, who stood in stark contrast to the energetic woman she had known before Sergey's death. Aunt Ella didn't like being under protection day and night, even if Uncle Nicky had only ordered it for her safety. She was also still in mourning. Nevertheless, she got involved, seeking diversion by setting up one of the guest houses in the estate park as an infirmary for soldiers who were physically restricted by their wounds in the Russo-Japanese War. Many of these soldiers were now in wheelchairs and Aunt Ella looked after them very touchingly. My mother told me this in her letters from Russia.

Some members of the Tsar's family were not impressed by her commitment because they thought Aunt Ella mothered these men far too much and demanded too many carriages from the family estate to take her charges out. She wanted to give these desperate people hope, to distract them from the physical limitations they had had to endure while fighting for the Tsar and Russia. That's why she didn't care about negative criticism. Nona, who accompanied Mama, also felt that a form of carelessness had gone out of Aunt Ella, as she did not laugh and could no longer be cheerful from the heart. My aunt had a very big heart, so the fate of her protégés weighed on her immensely.

But there was also a heaviness in the country. When Mama and Nona traveled on to St. Petersburg, they heard about the assassinations of army officers and high-ranking officials. These had become a daily occurrence since the war began. When Mama and Nona arrived at the train station, they were told that a general had been shot just before their arrival - on the train, with his wife and mother sitting next to him.

Aunt Alix and Uncle Nicky were also in a bad mood and desperate. Firstly, of course, because Uncle Nicky had to realize that the war was lost for Russia. And then it was now clear that my little cousin Alexei was suffering from hemophilia. It had become an open secret in the family, the family doctor and two nannies were in on it. His sisters now had to be very careful when playing with him. Aunt Alix saw her eldest daughter Olga, who was almost eleven years old, as someone who had to look after her little brother. Mama thought she was putting too much of a burden on the girl, as Olga was still a child herself. But when Alexei fell, dark bruises immediately appeared on his skin, the area swelled up and the pain became so unbearable for the now two-year-old that he just cried.

Nevertheless, her nieces seemed cheerful to her mother because they were always trying to cheer up her mother and father and distract them from their worries.
Mama and Nona stayed until August, visiting a parade of warships with Uncle Nicky and Aunt Alix in Kronstadt, a military seaport, only a few of which had returned from the war.
All in all, Mama found her trip very stressful and depressing. She was looking forward to finally seeing her second grandchild.
At least there was good news from Darmstadt, because Aunt Onor was pregnant. Uncle Ernie and she had been looking after Dickie while Mum was away. My little brother enjoyed this attention, spent his days at Wolfsgarten riding, playing in Ella's cottage and had quickly become the favorite of all the servants as he was very polite for his six years, never begging for anything.
Georgie was now a cadet at *the Naval College* in Dartmouth. My father had accompanied him there, seeing in him the way he had started his career in the Navy many years before. He was allowed to travel to Heiligenberg in the summer, with my sister Louise accompanying him.
Andrea and I visited my family in Heiligenberg in October. Everyone was very happy to meet little Dolla too. And Margarita had already been so excited during the trip that she could hardly shake it off in Heiligenberg. Papa was also able to take a few days off from his commitments. Family reunions like this were always something special. We reminisced and learned new things about each other's lives, but after Mama's report from Russia, I was also depressed. My children were both healthy, but I had an inkling of how unwell Aunt Alix was, worried about her young son, as was Uncle Nicky. My aunt was also prone to migraine attacks, suffered from facial pain and back pain. The emotional burden intensified her mental suffering all the more. My mother once described her personality traits as highly neurotic, but I don't think she meant it in a derogatory or spiteful way. She just didn't understand her sister that well in these matters. Mama was a stranger to any kind of mental stress.

I was proud of Georgie, who presented himself to us in his uniform, and I saw the sparkle in Papa's eyes. For my father, it was certainly one of the most beautiful experiences to see his son like this, with the same energy and ambition that he had once had in him.
Louise, now seventeen years old, had no thoughts left for a possible marriage. There was no man in her life to whom she felt attracted, and my mother seemed relieved about that. She should take her time, Mama said, because she still needed her by her side. My sister was a welcome companion to her and also enjoyed looking after Dickie. When Papa was too busy at work,

Mum could fall back on Nona or Louise, who always organized everything, was always ready to help and never refused to do anything.

On November 8th, Aunt Onor gave birth to the heir apparent, George Donatus, who was quickly nicknamed *Don*. Uncle Ernie and his wife were overjoyed at the birth of a son and heir. They chose the middle name Donatus because it means *the one given by God.*
We all celebrated Christmas together and enjoyed this time. We went sledging, ice skating and had snowball fights. Everyone was able to switch off a bit and just enjoy seeing the whole family together.
My mother was happy about her two healthy grandchildren, her little nephew, and yet at Christmas she remembered how her grandmother, the Queen, didn't want to let her two sisters go to Russia. Mama now feared that she hadn't been so wrong.
We received the news from Greece that Ellen had given birth to a baby girl, Princess Marina, on December thirteenth.

My father received a promotion to an active Vice-Admiral on the twenty-fourth of February 1907 on *HMS Venerable*, a battleship and now under Papa's command flagship of the British fleet in the Mediterranean. Papa was well on the way to becoming an admiral, but was still subordinate to him in his function. But he also proved himself in this position, so that on the twelfth of August that year he was given the same command on the prestigious *HMS Prince of Wales*.
Ever since I was a child, I have always been impressed by the way my mother managed her life alongside a man who was hardly ever at home. It was her job to have his back. She organized every move, planning ahead for the next few months every time my father took up a new command or a new post. Every new home in England was lovingly furnished by her so that my father always returned to a comfortable home, she planned family reunions well in advance and also wrote countless letters to relatives and friends to keep in touch. Only the constant uncertainty sometimes got on her nerves. It concerned the simple fact that, as the wife of a member of the navy, you usually didn't know where he was being transferred to or to what post. She commented that it sometimes made her very tired when she had to organize too much, but she didn't want to burden my father with it, because he should be able to concentrate fully on his career.
My brother Dickie was counterproductive when it came to moving house, as he had become an animal lover who owned a dog called *Scamp*, a little lamb called *Milly* who followed him around like a puppy, and lots of white mice. Their prolific breeding drove my mother to the brink of despair, but also

ensured that there was always a replacement on hand if one of the animals escaped or died. Dickie insisted that his animal friends had to travel with him. They couldn't stay in Heiligenberg on their own. So Mum had to organize this too, but she took it in good humour because she also saw that my brother took very good care of his animals. He never forgot to feed them or look after them. He was also the youngest, which made me feel a bit sorry for him. When Georgie left for the English navy, he was left with just Mama, Louise and Nona. Aunt Marie Karoline's children were all grown up too, and it would be some time before he could play with little Don.
At least he got on very well with Margarita, who shared his love of animals.
Another thing I always admired about my mother was her constant literary appetite. Wherever she went, she always had one or more books with her. I have already mentioned her leather books, in which she wrote down the books she had read. These leather volumes were titled *Books I've Read,* and within three months she usually managed to read twenty-one books, including historical books as well as novels or dramas. The remarkable thing was her ability to remember each of the books she read and their contents in detail.
When we returned to Greece in the spring, we noticed for the first time that the press was also turning against the royal family based on rumors. It was said that the royal princes were all receiving financial benefits from the state that they were not entitled to. Andrea and his brothers were accused of doing nothing for the country, which meant that they did not deserve such funding. One newspaper argued that they were not interested in Greece's problems. And financial subsidies for doing nothing were a privilege of Russian grand dukes. Another paper even said that one would never hear from the royal princes, especially not in times of crisis. When Thessaloniki, or Salonika for short, was the target of terrorist attacks in 1902, carried out by a Bulgarian revolutionary committee, the princes had not intervened, although they were all militarily engaged, according to the newspaper, instead strolling around the boulevards of Paris and enjoying their lives. The town of Anhialo had been burned down, but allegedly no prince had visited the refugees, and the Greek population gave the shirt off their backs for these people. Moreover, Andrea and his brothers were supposedly richer than any other European prince.
This was a direct attack on the royal family and of course also affected my father-in-law, as these rumors and accusations were unbelievable. The British ambassador, Sir Francis Elliott, who was in Greece from 1903 to 1917, had the task of putting Greek affairs in the right light for the office in London. He was loyal to the royal family and stood behind my father-in-law. He said publicly that the princes always did everything they could, but that their room for maneuver was limited. In his view, the attacks were symptomatic of a country

in which disrespect was seen as a form of independence and freedom was confused with the freedom to publish lies in order to do harm.

It was quite an uncomfortable situation and, of course, hard to bear for my father-in-law and the family in general. From the trips Andrea and I made, you could say that we preferred everywhere else to Greece at that time.

In the summer of 1907, we were invited to England. The annual horse racing season was always opened by the King on the eighteenth of June at Ascot. The spectacle was also known as *Royal Ascot* and many members of the aristocracy frolicked around the racecourse alongside the royal family. Ladies presented their most beautiful hats and dresses. It was actually too much showing off for me, too much pomp, but Andrea and I were invited to Windsor by George, Prince of Wales. Uncle Ernie and Aunt Onor were also there. This invitation was something special for me, because although I was born in England and was part of the family, I was treated like any of the other royal guests at Andrea's side. It was a bit strange for me, but I always looked forward to family reunions. We were driven to Ascot on June nineteenth in a Landau bearing the emblem of Windsor Castle, which we shared with May, Princess of Wales. After the races there was a party at the castle, which May noted was attended by all manner of nobility. Aunt Onor and Uncle Ernie also felt a little lost among the gathering of high chiefs, as even the King of Siam had been invited.

In the following days, we moved to Buckingham Palace. We were invited to a ball at the Russian Embassy. The King's birthday parade took place in the summer, as Uncle Bertie's birthday was in early November and the weather was usually no longer suitable for such an outdoor celebration. Andrea was allowed to ride directly behind her uncle in the parade, which was a great honor for him. I rode in the carriage of Aunt Alexandra, the queen, as did Aunt Onor and Toria, the queen's unmarried daughter. We followed the King and his entourage on horseback in carriages *along the Mall*, the grand avenue in London from Buckingham Palace to the *Horse Guards* parade ground near Whitehall.

In the evening, Aunt Alexandra invited Onor and me to Covent Garden to the Royal Opera House, with Toria accompanying us again. They were performing the opera *Un Ballo in Maschera*. Of course, this was a really special invitation, as we were sitting in the Queen's box, but I wasn't that keen on the opera, which is and was due to my disability.

On the first of July, a ball with five hundred guests was held at *Grosvenor House*. The house is located in *Park Lane* in London and is one of the most magnificent town houses in which the *Dukes of Westminster* have always resided. The Duchess of Westminster had invited guests to this ball.

Hugh Grosvenor, the second Duke of Westminster, had been married to

Constance Edwina Cornwallis-West since 1901. Her father was a British colonel and she came from a very distinguished family. Her sister Mary Theresa, known as *Daisy*, had married the German Prince Hans Heinrich XV von Pless in 1891. The aforementioned Daisy had opened the door to high society for her sister, as she organized very exclusive hunts on her estates in Silesia and her balls and parties were so highly regarded that anyone who was invited could count themselves lucky. The list of her friends ranged from the German Emperor, Uncle Willy to Uncle Bertie, Ducky, her sister Marie, the Queen of Romania and all sorts of other names of distinction. Like Constance, she had also married rich, but Daisy outdid everything as *the fixed star of* society.
However, the high chiefs, or rather their descendants, were to regret their friendship with Daisy in the 1930s when Daisy published her memoirs, in which she revealed many a tidbit from the world of the aristocracy.
Constance also presented herself as urbane and the perfect hostess.
The days in London were very exhausting and I was somewhat relieved when we traveled to Germany on the third of July. We had taken our two daughters with us, but they had been in the hands of nannies most of the time, so when we went to Heiligenberg, Margarita was particularly pleased to see Louise and Dickie again. Dolla was still too small, although she was always happy to receive attention. My two little girls were very close. When outsiders saw them, they were often mistaken for twins because of their very light blonde hair.
In Heiligenberg, Mama was very pleased to have her two grandchildren around her again and she said she had to write to Georgie at college straight away to say that I had grown, but was also a bit wider, which made Louise look even thinner. I replied that it was because of the birth of the children and she laughed about it, saying that any woman would be happy to come up with that excuse.
Dickie, now seven years old, was a very headstrong child. He was the only one who could stand up to Mama when she reprimanded him or told him off, which he didn't like at all. Whenever they got into a fight and Mama started arguing, giving him a lecture, he would hang a cardboard board around his neck on which he had written the letters *IAO*. Everyone asked him what it meant and he explained that it meant *I am offended*. This was his way of letting my mother know that he didn't think her rebuke was okay, because he marched around the house for hours with the board around his neck. He was also very annoyed when my mother always spoke so loudly, which I couldn't hear. From an early age, my mother had told me not to let on if I didn't understand something in a conversation, not to ask people to repeat it, but simply to try to follow the conversation again. Dickie was the only one who didn't think this was okay, because he said you could see from my face that I

hadn't understood something and then people could repeat it. But sometimes I was also glad not to hear Mama, because she also liked to interrupt conversations when she felt she had to say something.
Dickie was once asked what he wanted to be when he grew up. Aunt Alix suggested a sailor, like Papa and Georgie, a soldier or a train driver, because little boys often had the latter wish. My brother immediately replied glibly that none of that interested him, because a sailor could drown, a soldier could be shot and a train could derail. So everything was too dangerous for him, because he wasn't very brave.
Mama brought up Dickie, he had a nanny who was actually more of a companion. She once confessed to us that she had always wanted to be a teacher as a child. That's why she took great pleasure in teaching Dickie, because she had actually wanted to teach us all, but that was never possible due to her limited time. So my brother now had a little school desk, to which she had attached a sheet with a timetable. Mama was an excellent teacher because she was very well educated in history, although she didn't focus on kings or queens, but rather on social developments and circumstances. In geography, she could tell us a lot about countries and people. Languages were never a problem for us, as we all grew up bilingual. German and English were the basis, French had to be taught.
Mama encouraged Dickie's talent for pantomime, theater and amateur performances, because he loved to dress up and often performed little plays he had rehearsed himself.
But maybe Mama took so much time for him because he was the youngest and often alone.
Only occasionally did their arguments escalate to such an extent that she banished him to a closet, where he was only allowed to come out when he was good again. She thought it was her last resort to tame him, but she was usually afraid that he might be scared in the wardrobe. She would then check on him, but he would always say that he was not yet well-behaved again and had to stay in the cupboard, which made her even angrier. At some point, he called for her and said that she could let him out now because he was good again. Half an hour or a whole hour could have passed.
My mother wanted to send him to a school when he was a little older, but because of his sometimes erratic behavior, she was afraid he wouldn't behave there.

Mama loved to have portraits of her loved ones. As she had already had several pictures painted of all the family members, she now asked me to sit for one too. She had hired the Hungarian painter Philip de Lázló especially for this. He had recently moved to London and had also painted Uncle Bertie's

portrait there.
So I had to sit as a model from the fifteenth of July until the twentieth. While drawing, the painter sang Hungarian songs and was accompanied by Conny Pauer. She was a singer and sister of the famous musician Max Pauer. Her father was the Viennese pianist Ernst Pauer. The singer lived with her family and her brother in Jugenheim near us.
I didn't really feel like sitting in a chair for hours for a portrait, always in the same position. I also didn't like de Lázló's work because he didn't capture the person's whole expression for me. He would make a sketch, then fill it in and, from my point of view, his lines looked quite stiff. But I wanted to do Mama a favor.
Every now and then the time got too long and I asked Louise to sit for me.

The finished portrait of me, 1907

We traveled back to Greece in August. Andrea had a house built for us in Tatoi so that we could be on our own.
My father had been in command of the *Prince of Wales* since the twelfth of August and was in the Mediterranean. In the fall, Papa was able to take a few days off on his way to Malta and visit us in Tatoi.

Andrea, his brothers Konstantin and Christo had to go on maneuvers after Papa's departure and I stayed in Tatoi with the children.
In December, we went to Athens because Andrea's brother George was getting married. His bride was Princess Marie Bonaparte, a great-grandniece of the former Emperor Napoleon I of France, who was called *Mimi*. She was twenty-five years old and very rich. George was thirteen years older than her and the wedding had been arranged.
The bride's father, Prince Roland Bonaparte, had mentioned his only daughter as a marriage candidate at a lunch with my father-in-law in September 1906. They wondered whether George and Marie wouldn't be a good match, as the princess wanted to marry, but her father was very picky. He had rejected a prince from the noble Parisian Murat family, as well as Prince Hermann of Saxe-Weimar-Eisenach and Louis II, Prince of Monaco. Princess Marie's mother was a Blanc by birth, who had died at the birth of the child, but left her husband a proud 8.4 million francs. The Blancs had become rich with casinos in Monte Carlo. Marie's father was *president of the Society of Geography* and Botanists in Paris, and as he only had his daughter left, he only wanted the best for her - a royal son. It was said that the princess had suffered from phobias and hypochondria in her youth because he was so overprotective.
George met Marie for the first time on July nineteenth, 1907, at the Bonapartes' house in Paris. The couple were given twenty-eight days to get to know each other better, and then they became engaged.
Prince Bonaparte was more than astonished when George waived a *bridal clause* in a marriage contract that guaranteed him financial support from his bride in the event of a divorce. After all, Marie received eight hundred thousand francs a year from a fund and would inherit sixty million francs on her father's death. But George had fallen in love with her at first sight and the money meant nothing to him. He thought it was worse that Marie hoped they would live as a married couple in Paris. George had to dash this hope, as he had royal duties to fulfill in Greece, but he promised her vacations in her home town so that she could visit her father.
When the couple arrived in Athens in December, there was a scandal because Andrea's brother Konstantin felt disturbed by the press at the train station. He loudly told them to go to hell. His statement meant that the newspapers did

not report on Mimi's arrival. Instead, his words were interpreted to mean that he had said them to the couple, which was of course an infamous lie, but found its way into the newspapers in similar wording.
George and Mimi were first married in a civil ceremony on November twenty-first in Paris and on December twelfth in a Greek Orthodox ceremony in Athens.
I found my sister-in-law very nice, but also a bit special, because she was very interested in psychoanalysis, was a friend of Sigmund Freud and was also concerned with sexual problems that people were trying to find out about in a person's psyche. She also planned to write books on the subject and was completely open and free in her approach. So she immediately offered to analyze anyone's psyche in conversation, which I found a bit intrusive. And I also didn't think that sexual matters should be discussed so freely.
From the first Mamaent we met, however, Mimi noticed that Ellen seemed very proud and conceited to her, which I didn't comment on. I didn't like that kind of blasphemy. Nevertheless, the two women were very similar because they both seemed proud to me. Mimi was to receive a reprimand shortly afterwards when the family was resting in the afternoon and Ellen wanted to go through a door when Mimi approached her and simply pushed her way in. She lifted her skirt to one side as if she didn't even want it to touch Ellen. The English ambassador reported the incident to Uncle Bertie in a letter and the uncle dismissed it with the remark that Marie was very rich and had already secured her position among the king's daughters-in-law. He was proved right, because Mimi behaved as she wished, knowing her status. She was above reproaches, but didn't take them to heart because they simply didn't interest her.
I was a stranger to arrogance, so I stayed out of any arguments between my sisters-in-law.
Mama was in Russia in the summer of 1907 to visit Aunt Ella in Ilinskoye. My aunt had decided to help needy people out of her deeply religious convictions. She planned to open her own monastery, with her as headmistress, but her plan was not yet fully developed. In the meantime, however, she had become a vegetarian, which Mama found strange. From her point of view, her sister was mortifying herself by deciding to give up fish and meat from then on.

I was to spend more of 1908 outside Greece again. In March, I traveled to Malta with Margarita and Dolla to visit my parents. Papa carried out his duties conscientiously, but he had recently started suffering from gout attacks, which became so bad that he was partially confined to a wheelchair.

My private trip degenerated into a minor diplomatic conflict. My father-in-law had given me a Greek medal to present to the British officer and captain Robert Hornby. Actually, such awards were of an official nature and had to be made by the King himself. Of course I did my duty, but when they found out about it in England, Uncle Bertie was not very happy. I hadn't given any thought to why the captain was receiving this award, nor to the fact that I wasn't actually authorized to present it. It also put the poor man in a tight spot, because he didn't know whether he should wear the medal when he met my father-in-law or not.
I traveled back to Greece at the end of March.
On the third of May, Aunt Ella's foster daughter Marie married the Swedish Prince Wilhelm, Duke of Södermanland, in Tsarskoye Selo. Marie was Andrea's niece, as her late mother Aline had been his sister. So the Greek royal family was invited to the wedding, as were my parents and siblings.
I had already met Maria and it was a little depressing that Aunt Ella was pushing her into this marriage. The prince and Marie didn't get on particularly well, and they hadn't spent enough time together before the wedding, but my aunt probably thought he was a good match because his father was King Gustav V of Sweden. Marie no longer had the same high expectations of Ella as a special person. In fact, she was never to forgive her for the misfortune she had forced her into by marrying her.
The wedding was celebrated in the palace of Tsarskoye Selo, but under her jewels, wrapped in a magnificent dress of the Russian Grand Duchesses, which was so heavy with the embroidered fabric that she could hardly lift her feet, Marie looked very unhappy. I couldn't be angry with Aunt Ella for her decision, because in my eyes she was still an impressive woman. But unfortunately the marriage was not to be a happy one. Marie's son, Prince Lennart Bernadotte, was born just a year after the marriage, but as Prince William was an officer in the navy, Marie often had to stay alone in Sweden and in 1913 she left her husband. The divorce followed in 1914, her son stayed with his father and she rarely saw him.
Even at the wedding, it was an affront to Marie when her father, Grand Duke Paul, turned up with his second wife Olga, who was not befitting his rank, and their children Vladimir, Irina and Natalia.
During our visit, I quickly realized one thing. It was not easy for my two aunts there to combine their traditional roles as Tsarina and Grand Duchess with their efforts to help the people. Aunt Ella had a certain amount of freedom, but Aunt Alix was always struggling with the demands placed on her, which she found difficult to live up to. First she had to withstand the pressure when she only gave birth to girls. Then God finally gave her a son, but he was ill and the public was not allowed to know. If people had found out that the heir

to the throne suffered from haemophilia, my aunt would have been treated with hostility again, because she had brought the disease into the family. Aunt Alix was also a very shy, reserved woman, rather introverted. However, a tsarina had to represent herself and appear in public at appointments, which put a lot of pressure on her, as she quickly blushed when she was approached. Her relationship with her mother-in-law was not easy, and she only got on with a few people at court. Only Uncle Nicky's sister Olga was a good friend to her, as well as a few ladies-in-waiting and the personal physician Dr. Botkin also got on very well with her aunt.

At the automobile races St. Petersburg - Moscow, at the finish line in Moscow,
Andreas standing on the right, a lady-in-waiting sitting on the right, me sitting on the left,
1908

Uncle Nicky and Aunt Alix had been acquainted with a monk called Grigori Yefimovich Rasputin since the first of November 1905. He had been introduced to them in Peterhof and Militza and Anastasia, two friends of Aunt Alix and former princesses of Montenegro, had recommended him because he was said to have healing powers. Uncle and aunt let this monk into their lives, because when Alexei suffered from a hemorrhage in the spring of 1907, Rasputin prayed for him and the very next morning Alexei had recovered and the bleeding had stopped. They called him *Father Grigori* and he called them

Mama and *Papa*. My aunt raved about him and believed that God worked miracles through this man. As the doctors were often powerless against the bleeding and their methods, such as mud baths, did not help, Aunt Alix clutched at any straw she could find. And the monk's prayers also managed to alleviate her migraines and relieve the emotional strain. In her strict religiousness, she saw him as a savior.
Aunt Ella was rather skeptical about this, especially since her sister and brother-in-law let this man into their lives so completely, as he also became a good friend and confidant of the girls. Rumor had it that he even visited them in their bedchambers, with them sitting on his lap in their nightgowns. These were lies, but the rumors grew, because by letting Rasputin into the palace, envious people arose who looked askance at his relationship with the tsar's family. With his position at court, he could afford a good life in St. Petersburg, but he also attracted attention through his drunkenness, polygamy and faux pas in society, which prompted his uncle and aunt to admonish him to keep his temper. For my poor aunt, this man was like a Messiah who led her out of the darkness and into the light.
It was not until many years later that it was discovered that it was not his prayers that stopped Alexei's bleeding. Whenever the monk was summoned, he forbade the administration of any medication and so the painkiller aspirin, which was commonly used at the time and whose blood-thinning effect was not yet known, was discontinued. Nevertheless, the monk was perhaps able to exert a kind of autosuggestion and thus cure the aunt's migraines when she had an attack, among other things.
At the beginning of July, Andrea, our children, Mum, Louise and Dickie were accommodated in *St. Nicholas Palace* in Moscow. The servants were quartered in the nearby Tsar's Palace in the city. The conditions there were not nice. Everything was a bit run-down and Mama's maid, Edith Pye, whom we all called *Pye-Crust*, which translates as *pie crust*, had to sleep in a bathroom on a cot, which she found very uncomfortable. Along with Nona, she was a close friend of Mama's and was to remain in our family for a long time.
While Andrea was playing bridge with Nona and other ladies one evening, which was very humorous, I had a very lively conversation with Aunt Ella. She revealed to me that she had undergone an operation at the beginning of the year because she was suffering from *endometriosis*. Because too much tissue had formed in her uterus, which was benign, the uterus had to be removed. Such an operation was very risky at the time, as blood transfusions were not yet known. Like Aunt Alix, she also suffered from nerve pain in her face and migraine attacks, which she hoped would now improve. She hadn't told anyone about the exact reason for the operation so that none of the family would worry about her. Even her mother hadn't told her anything specific.

My aunt Ella had become very thin, looked tired, but finally wanted to put her plan for her own convent into action. She was in the process of selling all her jewelry and luxurious things, along with many of her private possessions, and had already sold her wedding ring to fulfill her dream. She had used the proceeds to buy property in the city, on which two houses stood. One was to be used as a hospital and she wanted to live in the other building with the nuns. She also planned to build a church.

Her aim was to found a convent where women from all walks of life could come together to pray and help the poor in the spirit of *St. Mary* and *St. Martha*. She would create her own nun's habit for this purpose, which was to be white.

Sisters were to be trained in the hospital to care for the poor and sick in the city's slums. At the same time, community facilities such as kindergartens and an orphanage were to be supported. People were to be able to obtain medicines free of charge from their own pharmacy.

Aunt Ella took up something that her mother had already created in Darmstadt. Grandmother Alice had recruited women who were known as *Alice Sisters*. These women trained as nurses and worked in districts and communities. They could take a vow and work for two or five years, after five years they could renew their vow.

My aunt had the foundation stone for her church laid in a solemn ceremony on the tenth of June. We took part in the ceremony and the long blessing that followed.

Mama thought her sister's idea was a very good one, and that Aunt Ella wanted to fill her life with an important task of the heart, but she still doubted whether her sister would really become a nun herself and thus abbess of her convent. The other family members feared that Aunt Ella might overburden herself with her task and exclude herself from the family. But my aunt proved them all wrong, determinedly carried out her wish and two years later she was a nun.

In 1908, she gave away many of her private possessions within the family, finally renouncing all worldly possessions.

The conversation with her and what she was up to impressed me so much that I wanted to follow her example, but only in a charitable sense. When she said that she was on her way to leave the world of splendor that had been placed in her lap to enter a much larger one by dedicating her life to the poor and the sick, we all knew that she would reach her goal with a strong will.

On one of the last days we spent in Moscow, our aunt took us to visit the fortress-like *Abbey of St. Sergius*, which was a few kilometers outside the city. To get there, we had to take a rather long train ride, then we drove on in small carriages on uneven roads with lots of potholes, crossed a forest where

traders were selling wool to pilgrims at stalls and at some point we finally reached the abbey.
When we arrived, we were welcomed by the archimandrite and the priests. They led us into the church, which was already filled with people, and began the liturgy. It was only a short service after the archimandrite took Andrea with him and showed him the sarcophagus with the bones of *St. Sergius*. The rest of us followed them after a while and everyone who belongs to the Orthodox faith knelt down in front of the coffin, prayed and touched the ground in front of the sarcophagus with their foreheads. Then we kissed the relic of the saint. It was very moving and a nice idea of Aunt Ella to invite us there.
St. Sergius of Radonezh is the most famous saint of the Orthodox Church. He lived from 1314 to 1392 and was a hermit who founded a chapel of the Holy Trinity and had many followers who lived with him in a community of hermits who rejected everything worldly.
After Moscow, we traveled on to St. Petersburg, where we left Margarita and Dolla in the care of Mama, Louise and Aunt Alix in the Winter Palace, because Andrea and I traveled on to Sweden and Denmark to visit relatives.
We returned to Russia at the end of July and met up with our daughters and the rest of the family, as well as Aunt Ella, in *Haapsalu* in Estonia. The city is also known as the *Venice of the North* because of its many waterways. Nomme is a village near the town where Tsar Alexander III often spent his vacations with his family. There is beautiful nature around the town of Haapsalu, as well as many holy springs. Aunt Ella had traveled with her to take the water from the springs as part of a drinking cure to strengthen her body for the tasks ahead.
After a longer stay there, we traveled back to St. Petersburg to spend some more time with Aunt Alix, Uncle Nicky and their children.

It was a wonderful stay. The children in particular had a lot of fun together and it was after this stay in Russia that Dickie remarked that he wanted to marry Marie one day. We smiled at his crush, but my brother would have feelings for her for the rest of his life and a picture of her was always on his bedside table. Perhaps he would have married her if the story had turned out differently.
Marie was very pretty, a little chubby, but unlike her sisters she was rather quiet and introverted, something in which she was very similar to her mother. Olga, the eldest, could sometimes be a bit stubborn, Tatyana was the one who was always worried about everyone, which is why the sisters often called her *the governess*. Anastasia was a pixie from whose jokes no one was safe. Aunt Alix thought that the girls were enough company for themselves, so there wasn't much variety in their lives. The two younger cousins were called *little*

pair, the two older ones *big pair*.

I think my cousins and my little cousin led a life of luxury, where they didn't miss out on toys or other things, but it was a *gilded cage* in the true sense of the word. My aunt taught them to be frugal, but they still had everything they could dream of. But this only applied to things you could buy.
My aunt was often ill, so the girls rarely saw her and her few friends were limited to ladies-in-waiting, the officers on the imperial yacht or other servants. Uncle Nicky's sister Olga often picked up the girls to spend time with them. But other children were rarely invited to the palace and the world around them, the real Russia, remained foreign to them. They never walked the streets
St. Petersburg, except for parades or other public occasions. Mama remarked that they had not been able to experience *real life* outside the palace walls.

At the end of August, Andrea and I traveled back to Greece with our daughters, making a brief stopover in Constantinople, where local Greeks greeted us warmly, but the Sultan had no time to welcome us. The Greek press reported this affront just one day later.
We then stayed in Tatoi for the rest of the year. There I learned that Aunt Onor had given birth to a second son on the twentieth of November, the little Prince Ludwig, who was to be called *Lu* by everyone.
Mimi, the wife of Andreas' brother Nikolaus, was also pregnant. The baby was due to be born in December.

Rhallys was deposed, Venizelos was secretly brought into the city and assigned the role of advisor for the time being. In the meantime, there was also a crisis in the Greek part of Macedonia, where people were also rebelling against the Ottoman authorities.
The country was shaken by unrest and my husband had to painfully realize that he and his brothers were being stripped of all their high titles in the Greek military, as he put it, and that they were not wanted as supporters in any way for the political situation. It was all the more difficult for the king. He had to come to terms with the insurgents and accept Venizelos' presence and function. He was effectively condemned to act like a puppet. Andrea wanted to stand by his father, but after long discussions with his father and brothers, he came to the conclusion that they all had to retire from the military.
On September 1, 1909, Andrea, Nicholas and Christo signed their letters of resignation for the Greek military and George his for the Navy. The press wrote that they had had to bow to the will of the people, but the British ambassador corrected this by publicly stating that they could no longer serve side by side with the other officers in the old tradition.
Constantine, as crown prince, followed his brothers' example a few days later and resigned as commander-in-chief of the Greek military. He was criticized for his aggressive attitude towards other subordinates and for neglecting his military duties, which he should have performed during the autumn manoeuvres. Given the situation for the royal princes in Greece, it had not been possible for the annual maneuvers to take place normally. The criticism only served to discredit him as well.
Konstantin and his family left for Paris shortly afterwards. On their departure, people stood at the harbor and shouted that they didn't want to let him go. Rumor had it that the family were on their way to Uncle Willy in Germany, but the latter had strictly refused Konstantin's wife Sophie, his sister, entry for all time. Of course, the public knew nothing about these internal family affairs.
Nevertheless, Constantine's friends were outraged that he fled to Paris of all places, which in their eyes stood for pure pleasure-seeking instead of looking after the interests of the country. They did not think it was appropriate for his status and age. In other words, the family enjoyed themselves in the cosmopolitan city while the riots raged in Athens. In the eyes of most, this was behavior that did not befit a crown prince. The British ambassador Elliot agreed and condemned the trip in the strongest terms. Kosta and his family were not due to return to Athens until April 1910.
Nikolaus had been a colonel and inspector of artillery. He now joined the Russian army, which was made possible by his wife's Russian origins.
Christo went to Germany to study there for three years. George had been a

rear admiral in the Navy and was now able to devote more time to his travels to visit relatives in Denmark and spend time in France on his country estate with his wife Mimi.
Konstantin's son George began a career with the 1st Regiment of Guards on Foot in Berlin. Unlike his mother, Uncle Willy had nothing against his sister's children.

My father-in-law seemed like a broken man during this time. He looked back on forty-six years of regency and would have liked to have reached a round jubilee of fifty years on the throne. But he now felt so humiliated that it pained him to have to receive even one soul in the palace. He spoke openly to the British ambassador about how the thought of abdicating bothered him.
Andrea and I had actually wanted to travel to Berlin in mid-September, but now he thought it would be better if we stayed in the country. He was afraid that otherwise we might all be refused entry and refused to return. But this also applied to his brothers and their families who had left the country.
On September twenty-seventh, a rally of the guilds of Athens and Piraeus took place *at Champ de Mars-Parc* in Athens. About fifty thousand people gathered there to listen to the reading of a resolution welcoming the activities of the military league. This resolution was solemnly presented to the king and the crowd cheered him when he accepted it. The people demanded changes in the government. Rumor had it that they were planning to replace the king, which turned out to be just that. The British ambassador commented that people were indulging in fantasies every day.
But it wasn't until Christmas that my father-in-law's position as King of Greece was consolidated again.
My parents, to whom I wrote about the events in Athens, were very worried about us, but they also understood Andrea's concern that we could leave the country in this precarious situation but not be allowed to re-enter. I missed them all very much and would have loved to go to Uncle Willy's in Berlin for Christmas, but I had to turn down this invitation too.
Even my father, now in his position as Vice-Admiral of the Royal Navy, could not visit us. It was hard to have him around, in the Mediterranean, and yet we were not allowed to see each other.
My brother Dickie was now attending *Locker's Park School* in Hertfordshire. It was a prestigious boarding school for boys from the age of ten and Mum had prepared him well for it, as the other pupils all came from prestigious families, but Dickie had a different status as a prince. He was used to Sunday lunches with the King at Windsor Castle, as my mother put it, rather than dinners in the fine restaurant at the *King's Arms Hotel* in Berkhamsted. You had to be careful how you behaved towards the other boys, what you said and

how you said it. He would attend the school for three years and my mother missed him the first few days he went. She was proud of how well he fitted in there, studied hard and was on his best behavior, but she had taught him the first few years, admittedly very well, otherwise he wouldn't have been accepted at the school, but she missed that closeness to her little boy. In her letters to him, she often couldn't hide her loneliness and longing, which was a great burden for my brother. Because he missed her too.
When she wrote to him that diligence and zeal would distract him from his grief at being separated from her, she tried to reassure herself.
The school was run by a principal called Percy Christopherson and his wife, who were both very understanding but also strict. My brother often wrote to my mother about how unfairly he felt he had been treated and she replied that he should see the principal as a person who also made mistakes and would surely see them.
My mother wanted to strengthen Dickie's character, but there were some things he couldn't learn at school on his way to adulthood. If he remembered birthdays in the family on his own and wrote a card to the person concerned, she praised him. If he forgot a birthday because he was still a child, she reprimanded him too harshly. She instructed him in letters about what he had to write, to which address, how the letter had to be structured and often overwhelmed my little brother with her high demands.
Of course, there were also arguments between the boys at the boarding school, little scuffles, but Dickie was kept out of them because of his status. Nobody dared to involve him in anything like that and my brother didn't know anything like that either. As he grew up, however, he would encounter situations in which he had to stand up to others, which he then found very difficult.
As Christo was in Germany for his studies, Louise and he were able to get to know each other. He visited her in Heiligenberg and they simply got engaged. My parents were more than horrified by this. They understood that they had feelings for each other, but Christo was actually penniless, living off his father's support, and my parents didn't want to bear any financial responsibility for the couple. Without further ado, they had to break off their engagement, which plunged my sister into deep grief.

Louise, 1909

Even though she understood our parents' decision, she had already dreamed of a future at Christo's side and had hopes that were now literally shattered. And poor Louise feared that she would end up as an old maid.

In winter, we traveled to Tatoi. We spent the holidays there with my parents-in-law and the dejected Christo, who was mourning my sister Louise. Nikolaus, Ellen, Andrea and I were invited to evening parties at the British and Belgian embassies in November, which we gratefully accepted. It was the first time since the coup that we dared to go to such events again.

On the night of January 6, 1910, the telephone rang and startled us all out of our sleep. We were told that the entire central section of the royal palace in Athens was on fire. The fire had first spread to the orthodox chapel of the palace, then to the upper corridors and finally to the central section. Everything was completely destroyed.
The two British battleships in the Bay of Phaleron were fortunately still there and the crews were called to help, so that eventually four hundred crewmen assisted the fire department by bringing in earth and sand in buckets to smother the fire.
We immediately went to Athens to help extinguish the fire and possibly save some of our belongings. Twenty armed sailors soon arrived, as it was feared that the fire might be the work of insurgents, in which case the king would also have to be protected. But my husband thought this was commendable in

the tense situation Athens was still in, but nevertheless inappropriate. He feared that it could have a negative effect if such a military presence was combined with the protection of the king. So he sent the men away. And he was proved right, because just one day later it was written in the press that these men were undermining the interests of the people in their aggressive stance.

We were able to save the archive, important documents and papers, some pictures and furniture. My father-in-law's rooms were almost completely cleared out without any damage. But most of the personal belongings in my mother-in-law's rooms were destroyed or fell into the hands of thieves. At midnight, the roof of the castle collapsed, which meant that nothing could be saved as it was no longer possible to enter the building. At three thirty in the morning we traveled back to Tatoi.

The British ambassador Elliot then had to inform Uncle Bertie that, after he had been at the scene of the disaster for half an hour, the first rumors circulated that the king had set fire to the palace himself in order to gain sympathy from the people. Allegedly, he wanted to let everything go up in flames on Christmas Eve so that the people would feel even more sympathy for him. Of course, this was another terrible rumor, because the castle had been the home of the king and his family, so they now had to take up residence entirely in Tatoi. It was absurd to think such a thing of my father-in-law, and I found it more than absurd that someone would deliberately set fire to his home in order to regain popularity with the people.

It hurt us all and Andrea objected that it was insulting enough that he and his brothers all had to wear civilian clothes for public appearances instead of their uniforms. Since Andrea no longer had any military obligations, he was able to spend a lot of time with me and the children, which our two girls enjoyed as much as I did. Nevertheless, I knew how much my husband was suffering from the situation. His heart belonged to the military and he saw himself deprived of a task that he considered very important in his life.

On the tenth of February, George's wife Marie gave birth to little Princess Eugénie in Paris, as the couple were mostly abroad and Marie preferred her hometown of Athens.

In April 1910, we traveled to Corfu, where we lived in *Mon Repos* Castle. Here my father-in-law received constant encouragement from the population that they wanted to keep him as king. He was delighted, but we were all exhausted by the recent events and I wrote to my parents saying how much we longed to be able to leave the country again.

Margarita, left, and Dolla, right, April 1910, Corfu

Andrea was very skeptical about Venizelos and was curious to see what else this man literally had up his sleeve. He was right in his assumption that Venizelos was striving for more power. After all, he founded the *Liberal Party* in 1910, which was progress-oriented.

The *military league* had already been disbanded in March, as its officers were exhausted and wanted to devote more time to politics instead of fulfilling their military obligations. Many of them became members of Venizelo's party. Some calm returned to Athens and my father-in-law bowed to the demands for reform at the end of March by convening a new National Assembly in Parliament to work out reforms in a revised constitution that would have a positive impact on Greece itself in terms of the population and foreign affairs. This new National Assembly was based on an agreement between Venizelos, the *Military League* and the King. At the first session, my father-in-law had to appoint Venizelos as Prime Minister, as he won the majority in the elections.

Venizelos had thus consolidated his position of power and was sure of his influence over the king.

Andrea commented on the development by saying that all this unrest had cost him his job. And I could only reply that it had happened just as he was about to make a career in the military.

Aunt Alexandra, who had been on vacation in Venice, came to visit us on

Corfu on the twentieth of April. We received news from England that Uncle Bertie was in a very bad way.
He had been on vacation in Biarritz, France, in March and collapsed there with chest pains. Having always been a bon vivant who loved to eat and smoked twenty cigarettes and twelve cigars a day, he had long suffered from his obesity and chronic bronchitis. Now, at the age of sixty-nine, this lifestyle had left its mark.
His condition did not allow him to return to England quickly and so he was only brought back to London on April twenty-seventh.
Aunt Alexandra had to travel to England immediately to be by her husband's side, Andrea and I accompanied her with Margarita and Dolla.
In the late afternoon of the fifth of March, we all arrived in London, Andrea, the children and I drove to *Chesham* in *Chiltern*, a district of *Buckinghamshire*, where my parents had rented a house. It was about forty kilometers from London.
Uncle Bertie suffered several heart attacks in the days following his return to England and died at Buckingham Palace on the sixth of May.
Even though my uncle's death hurt me a lot, I was somehow relieved to be able to escape Greece for a while.
Uncle Bertie's son George, the Prince of Wales, inherited the royal dignity on his death and was formally proclaimed King George V of England at *St. James's Palace* on the seventh of May and took the oath of monarchical allegiance. Aunt May thus became Queen Mary of England at his side. The official coronation celebrations were postponed to 1911 due to the year of mourning.
The couple had six children, one girl and five boys. Their youngest son Prince John was almost five years old and had been diagnosed with epilepsy a year earlier. He also showed signs of autism, which was very distressing for his mother. She was so ashamed of this child that she largely shielded him from the outside world, as she feared that his unruly behavior, which was due to his disability, could damage her reputation. I felt very sorry for the boy, because his siblings also saw him as a burden. In 1917, his mother had to banish him to a farm under the care of his nanny, where he hardly received any visitors and died in his sleep from an attack of epilepsy in 1919.
Papa, in his capacity as the uncle's personal aide-de-camp, walked in the procession on the way to the laying out in the chapel at Westminster directly in front of the coffin, which was pulled by horses, with the uncle's favorite dog, Caesar the terrier, beside him. Andrea walked behind the coffin with others, while I rode in a carriage.
The official state funeral for Uncle Bertie took place on the twentieth of May. Many heads of the European aristocracy, relatives and friends traveled to

England and my father-in-law, Konstantin and Christo also came. Mama, Nona, Dickie, Papa, Andrea and the children, like many others, attended the funeral service at St. George's Chapel. Georgie had been given time off from college for the funeral and had traveled from Portsmouth. Nine kings from Europe alone paid their last respects to Uncle Bertie.
Papa remarked after the funeral that things would now change at court. Uncle Bertie had had countless affairs and so the most elegant women had always come and gone at the English court, albeit often with dubious reputations. His son, on the other hand, was absolutely faithful to his wife, held marital values very highly and placed more value on collecting stamps or hunting than seeking his pleasure in traveling like his father. He lacked verve, according to his father, and did not seem as impressive as his uncle.
For me, Uncle Bertie's death meant that from then on I was just one of many cousins of the king at court. It alienated me somewhat from this world, even though I felt so estranged from my new home in Greece.
We stayed in England after the funeral. Mama found our daughters very entertaining, as Dolla had a great imagination, told her about fairies who lived in the trees and whose stories she told in full, having made them up herself. Dolla was able to dream herself into worlds of her own invention from an early age, completely excluding herself from everything that surrounded her, while Margarita was rather lively and always approached everyone, never showing fear of anything. Unfortunately, Margarita also tended to mock and tease her little sister when she went back to her dreams. I often reprimanded her for this, but Mama thought I shouldn't interfere. Dolla would eventually stand up to her big sister who set the tone.

On June twenty-fourth, Mama, Andrea, Nona and Louise were invited to Prince Edward's confirmation in Windsor. He was the eldest son of Uncle George and now Prince of Wales. It must have seemed strange to outsiders how we women all sat there in black mourning clothes, Andrea in evening dress with a black tailcoat and the Knight's Cross on her ribbon, which had been awarded to him honorarily by Uncle Bertie at our wedding. My husband couldn't help joking that we must look to others like a collection of widows accompanied by a magician.

Andrea and I felt that we didn't really need to return to Greece, because the way things were going, they didn't need us there and at least we didn't have to deal with the situation there when we were traveling, but could gain some distance. The next few weeks were therefore a mixture of amusement for us, followed by indecision and a certain increasing listlessness, which affected Andrea more than me.

So we traveled from London to Paris. We were able to live there at ease, as the city was not in mourning like London and we were also far away from the Greek press. The wife of Prince Karl Joseph zu Isenburg und Büdingen, Princess Bertha, was spending her summer vacation in Paris and she took us under her wing, so that we went from one invitation to the next. Princess Bertha, née Lewis, came from New Orleans and had married the Prince morganatically in 1895. I was familiar with the noble family of von Isenburg-Büdingen from Birstein in Hesse.
We had a great time until I got the flu and had to stay in bed. This also delayed our departure from Paris, so we didn't get back to Heiligenberg until the fourteenth of July and missed Louise's twenty-first birthday by a day. It wasn't too bad, because I still felt weak. On top of that, Andrea now also had a cold. Papa was able to take a few days off, and Georgie and Dickie also traveled from England.
When Andrea and I were feeling better, we were finally able to enjoy our days with my family. We visited Uncle Ernie, Aunt Onor and their two sons in Wolfsgarten and I rode out with Louise every morning before breakfast.

Andrea and I were a little worried about our future. My husband felt committed to his home country and couldn't really enjoy the days in Hesse, as the uncertainty weighed heavily on him. His brothers Christo and Nikolaus, who were also in Germany, were also unsure whether it wouldn't be better to return to Greece.
At the beginning of August, Andrea decided to travel back, even if it was only for a while, to show some *goodwill* with his presence on site. His brothers followed his example, which Louise acknowledged by saying that Christo in particular, whom she was still very fond of, was always under his brother's proverbial slipper and always emulated him. But I didn't see anything wrong with that, because Andrea was the older of the two brothers and such behavior was normal. Neither of us knew which was better. I didn't have much desire to go back to Athens, but I didn't want to let my husband down either. However, he also knew how much I loved spending time with my family and so he decided to come back to Darmstadt in September to pick me and our daughters up so that we could travel to Athens together.
But shortly after his arrival in Athens, I received a telegram in which he threw his plan overboard and wrote to me that I would have to travel back to Athens alone with the children. Without further ado, I had to look for a nanny who could accompany me and the girls on the journey. I telegraphed this to Andrea, but he did not receive the telegram. Instead, I received another one from him in which he made it clear how torn he felt and asked if I had received his

telegram. I didn't understand what he was getting at with his last words and I was overcome with fear that he might want a separation because the situation in Greece was bothering him so much. For a while, I felt like I had been shunted off, abandoned in Darmstadt, to suggest to myself that we were no longer a couple. I complained to Louise and my mother. But both of them reassured me that they must have meant that I had to meet him on the way back, but that he had never spoken of separation.
My mother also objected that I belonged by my husband's side despite the tensions in Greece, or precisely because of them, although she also liked having me around with her two grandchildren. But she had always followed her husband, no matter how hard times were. Of course I knew that and I loved Andrea, but at the same time I didn't really feel at home in Athens. The ongoing problems in the country didn't exactly help to change my feelings in that regard.
I knew about Andrea's inner turmoil and yet I couldn't share it because I didn't feel as committed to Greece as he did. I didn't feel very homesick for this country, which was characterized by the same inner turmoil as my husband.
I didn't mean it selfishly, but I was afraid of new tensions in Athens, because they were hanging in the balance. I was also very outraged that my husband and his brothers had lost their military posts. None of them were interested in any privileges, because they only wanted to serve their country.
So I tried to enjoy the time with my family to take my mind off my worries.

Aunt Alix and her family traveled to Cowes in England in July for the annual regatta, accompanied by Aunt Ella. They also met the royal family in Osborne and then came to Darmstadt, where Uncle Ernie made Friedberg Castle near Bad Nauheim available to them. My aunt suffered from heart problems and severe neuralgia in her face. Her sciatica and migraines had also worsened. Aunt Alix was to undergo a bathing and drinking cure in Bad Nauheim to improve her ailments. They arrived on the thirtieth of August and were to stay until the twenty-fourth of October, with a trip to Hemmelmark to visit Aunt Irene and Uncle Heinrich in between. Uncle Nicky wanted to meet Uncle Willy in Potsdam for a few days.
It was a big family reunion and we were all very happy about it. It was especially wonderful for the children. There were plenty of playmates, the adults chatted, played tennis with the children or we went on excursions in the surrounding area.
My aunt's ailments were certainly largely mental, but this did not include her back problems, which were so painful that she was usually unable to walk long distances and had to be pushed in a wheelchair.

Alexei was a happy little boy and enjoyed the company of my daughters and the sons of Uncle Ernie and Aunt Onor. However, due to the attacks of hemophilia, he was also a very fragile boy who could not walk long distances. In the meantime, two so-called *Sailor Nannies* had been hired to look after him. Uncle Nicky thought it made more sense for a man to look after Alexei so that he didn't injure himself while playing and running around, to carry him, push him in a wheelchair or ride him around on a specially made bicycle with a seat in the front. One of these male nannies was called Nagorny, he had stayed in Russia. The other was slightly stocky and his surname was Derevenko. He had come to Darmstadt with them. Because Aunt Alix pampered her *baby* and let him get away with a lot, Alexei often behaved out of character or took advantage of his status as heir to the throne. He tended to order others around and patronize them, pulling pranks that were very unpleasant. He threw things into wells, asked servants to fish them out and had even pushed one or two people into the water. Sometimes he called Derevenko *the fat man* and even called after him. Alexei was still a child who had already been punished enough by his suffering and so many things were held against him.

Mama often thought Aunt Alix was a bit careless, but like all of us, his illness came first and this was so bad for my aunt that she didn't want to suppress his zest for life even more by constantly reprimanding him. He had to live with restrictions that he didn't accept with other children, like his sisters. Riding a horse, riding a bike, running around wildly, climbing trees, playing soccer and much more was denied him, as every little injury could inevitably lead to a bad seizure.

And when he had one, called for his mother, told her he wanted to die so that the pain would finally stop ..., who could blame my aunt for her negligence in his upbringing, for her lack of strictness?

The girls were used to taking care of either their mother, if she was ill, or their brother. So Olga and Tatyana in particular, aged fifteen and fourteen, were very sensible. Marie was a dreamer, very much like my Dolla, and Dickie was still in love with his Russian cousin, so he wanted to be by her side all the time.

Anastasia was a whirlwind who had to be pulled out of a tree more than once. She thought up jokes all day long, but she could also cheer people up, which was certainly good for her mother, and she felt very close to Alexei.

Alexei, on the right, with Uncle Ernie's sons, Lu in the baby carriage and Don on the left, 1910

On the occasion of the Tsar's family's visit, Aunt Onor and Aunt Alix took many photos of the children, which could then be bought as postcards for a good cause by the people of Hesse. A large part of the proceeds went to charitable institutions under the direction of the *Red Cross*, among others, but a lot was also donated to children's homes under the patronage of Aunt Onor.

them a chance to show how well they could behave and they never disappointed me. Sometimes I longed to hear their voices just once. They had had to learn to live with a mother who had to show strictness in her own way instead of using a loud voice or verbal requests not to do something. I usually just lifted a finger. That was enough, because my two treasures were very considerate, rather low-maintenance little girls.

Louise took Margarita and Dolla to the carnival celebrations and followed the procession, throwing confetti, colorful paper balls and ribbons into the crowd, as they told me later with joyful gestures.

Once they took my sister to the beach at Phaleron, where they climbed around on the small rocks to catch crabs.

The first lessons had begun for both girls and so they received their first lessons in Greek and English from their nanny, although both of them already spoke it very well alongside German. For their physical training, they received gymnastics lessons from a Swedish teacher.

I would have liked to plot for my sister to get her together with Andrea's brother Christo, because they both still had feelings for each other and yet his unsettled financial situation was too important for me to achieve anything. Aunt Alix had called Christo a tall, chubby boy and other voices in the family criticized his short-sightedness, the plumpness of his stature. I didn't share these opinions, and Louise had to love him and accept him as he was. What mattered to her was his character, how they got on. But the family was against marriage, there was nothing to be done about that and so I felt very sorry for my sister. Perhaps she had come to Greece with the hope in her heart that I could help her. My parents-in-law had no objections to them getting married, but they also understood my parents. But poor Louise wasn't getting any younger, as she herself pointed out, and she certainly didn't want to end up as an old maid who spent her life at her mother's side, even though she naturally appreciated their company.

While Louise was in Athens, I went back to the needlework school in the mornings because I wanted to improve my technique. And my presence there was very welcome, which also had a positive effect on my husband. In any case, I thought it was important to go there for this reason too.

In March, elections were due to be held in Athens again. My father-in-law didn't want to be in Greece during this time. So he urged Andrea, Louise, Christo, Minnie and me to accompany him on a four-day cruise in the Mediterranean on the royal yacht until the votes were counted. We were more than relieved to receive the news that Venizelos had been re-elected.

Some calm returned to Greece. The press fell silent and there were no more negative headlines about the royal family. The hostilities towards the king and the crown prince were simply treated as if they had never existed.

The only criticism levelled at my sister-in-law, Crown Princess Sophie, was that she was not concerned enough with the Greek population, that she was not involved enough in the people's problems, although she had long been committed to reforesting forests that were destroyed every year in the hot summers, and she was one of the co-founders of the Greek *Organization for the Protection of Animals*. Like my mother-in-law Olga, she also ran soup kitchens for the poor and patronized hospitals and orphanages.
So the hostility in the press was probably more for the purpose of writing something at all and a pure defamation of a more than committed member of the royal family.
My sister left on the sixth of May and was glad that the tensions in Greece had calmed down, as she, like the rest of my family, was always worried about us.
This summer we were first in Tatoi and then traveled on to Corfu, where we enjoyed a quiet, tranquil life with our three children.
Uncle Ernie had traveled to Russia with his family to visit Aunt Alix in April. Mama took this trip in July 1912, with Nona accompanying her.
My family loved meeting each other and Aunt Irene was more accessible to my mother than Aunt Ella and Aunt Alix in Russia, because Hemmelmark was easier to reach than making the very long and arduous journey to Russia. Of course, my mother wrote to me about everything she experienced on the trip. She first visited Aunt Ella in Moscow, who now ran the first convent for women, led by an abbess, in Russia. She was very proud of what she had created. Aunt Ella had changed her life from the ground up, lived directly with the sisters and wore her gray uniform with the white veil of her order like a royal robe, Mama thought. She had arrived in life in her own way and loved her *Martha and Mary garb*, as she called it herself.
The small house near the convent, which corresponded to the environment surrounding them, was not exactly inviting because it was full of bugs. And after a sleepless night, Mama and Nona moved into Ella's little house with her. There was only one large lounge there, furnished with simple wicker furniture. They ate in the room and received guests, most of whom were old friends of Aunt Ella's or members of other convents. My mother had learned some Russian, but it was nowhere near enough to understand the people, and as soon as her sister left the room, she could no longer converse. Understandably, this was a great tragedy for my mother as she loved to speak. And so she noted in her letter that she had never known the feeling of being *speechless* before.
The summer was very hot and my mother was slowly getting to an age where traveling was a little more difficult for her. She heard about the conflicts in the Balkans, was worried about Andrea, me and the children, but also

immediately had to worry about Aunt Alix, whom she met after visiting Aunt Ella in Peterhof.

She found her sister had changed, as she was becoming increasingly neurotic and difficult to deal with, as she did not allow any criticism of her trust in the monk Rasputin. Mama had to accept that her sister described herself as a careworn woman who only found support in the monk's prayers. Her life revolved mainly around her own fragile health and that of her son. When asked how she was feeling, she replied that the doctors were satisfied with the condition of her heart, but that she had pain in her back and legs and that the massages, although very gentle, did not bring any relief. They even suspected that she was suffering from a vein problem. However, her heart pain was so bad that she had hardly been able to walk herself for three years and was always pushed in a wheelchair. She only walked herself on official occasions. She said she got shortness of breath and palpitations if she had to walk for long periods by herself, and for my mother this was more a form of psychosomatic illness than a real ailment. Her sister had undoubtedly become a real hypochondriac, which horrified my mother. There was always something new, like the nerve pain in her face, which became unbearable for Aunt Alix when she was mentally stressed and ended in migraine attacks.

So during Mama's visit, her sister spent most of her time lying on a chaise longue or a bed in her room. Once someone had dared to tell her that she could face real sorrows, that the Lord could give her severe trials and then she would have nothing to oppose them. It hurt my aunt very much, but even from my mother's point of view she was a *Queen of Sorrows*. And she already found it strange in her sister's letters that she was only ever told how Alexei was doing, and it was the same now during her stay in Peterhof. Everything revolved around the boy. He had injured himself and could hardly walk after an attack of hemophilia. It was understandable for Mama to be worried about her sister, but when she left in August, he was a little better.

My mother was never insensitive to the suffering of others, but she also believed that you shouldn't worry yourself to death every time, but always believe in a cure or recovery. In other words, *burying your head in the sand* didn't help at all.

A few years later, when fate really hit Aunt Alix and her family hard, she revised her opinion of her sister, but at that time, in the summer of 1912, her sister just seemed very strange in her behavior and had become something of a stranger to her.

As Aunt Alix could not tolerate criticism, she did not accept any interference or suggestions when she coddled her son, but the girls always had to take a back seat. Olga and Tatyana had been at the opera with their father when the Russian Prime Minister Stolypin was shot there. They had both witnessed his

death not far from them.
For Mama, she said, the only thing that made the visit bearable was the presence of the always cheerful girls and Alexei when he was well. Uncle Nicky was friendly, but usually too busy to spend time with her. They often only saw each other at meals. Mama didn't want to burden her brother-in-law with her thoughts about her sister and kept her opinions to herself.
Both Mama and Uncle Ernie had tried to persuade Aunt Alix not to let Rasputin into her life any longer, as they thought he was a danger, but it was no use. His presence also divided Ella and Aunt Alix, as the older sister was not at all happy about the monk's influence on the younger one.
When Mama was back in Germany and traveled to Aunt Irene's in Hemmelmark, where Louise and Dickie were staying, she felt a bit like her grandmother Victoria, who had warned her granddaughters not to marry in Russia. She wrote to me that she finally understood her grandmother's fears.

In October of that year, my husband, his brothers and I were given the opportunity to become more involved in the country again, albeit in connection with the two *Balkan wars*.
There had already been a crisis in the run-up to the *First Balkan War*.
In 1908, Russia suffered a diplomatic defeat when Austria-Hungary annexed Bosnia and Herzegovina. Some of these territories had previously belonged to the Ottoman Empire under international law. Austria-Hungary had already occupied these territories and some towns in July 1878. In October 1903, Austria and Russia then decided *to* get a grip on the unrest in the Balkans by means of the so-called *Mürzsteg Protocols*.
Subsequently, in September 1908, the Austrian and Russian foreign ministers agreed that Austria would gladly hand over Bosnia and Herzegovina, but in return the Russian warships would be given the right to free passage through the Bosporus and the Dardanelles. This sounded promising for Austria-Hungary, as it had been administering the provinces for thirty years and the administrative treaty with the Ottoman Empire expired in 1908. The Ottoman Empire had been weakened by revolutions in its own country and internal reforms for Bosnia and Herzegovina seemed tempting, as this would allow Austria to put its own stamp on the provinces. There were also several trouble spots nearby. Crete demanded annexation to Greece, Bulgaria, which was under Turkish sovereignty, declared itself fully sovereign and Prince Ferdinand I of Bulgaria was proclaimed tsar.
In July 1908, officers, so-called *Young Turks*, forced the reintroduction of the 1876 constitution in the Ottoman Empire, which was a clear affront to Austria, as parliamentary elections were to be held that also affected Bosnia and Herzegovina. Formally, the two provinces still belonged to the Ottoman

numerous defeats and so a second war meant an even greater weakening for the empire.

Like many Greeks, Prime Minister Venizelos was inspired by the desire to expand the Greek empire and possibly reach as far as Constantinople. The Turks also occupied territories in Thrace, Macedonia and the Aegean. Furthermore, the question of Crete, which they wanted to annex to Greece, was still unresolved.

Andrea left Corfu for Athens on the second of October because he wanted to do his bit and perhaps finally take up a military commitment again. So he approached the Ministry of Defense and offered himself as a volunteer if he was needed. Venizelos needed capable men and arranged for all royal princes to resume their duties in the Greek military. Constantine was appointed commander-in-chief. It was moving for my husband and his brothers to finally be allowed to fight for their country again, which I understood, as it was their homeland that they had to defend.

Andrea and his other brothers were officially reinstated in the Greek military on October twenty-first. My husband was appointed lieutenant colonel of the third cavalry regiment. Even before the whole thing was made official, they had already all traveled to Larissa in the Thessaly region, where there was a field army that Constantine now commanded. Around one hundred thousand men had been recruited there, including infantry and cavalry. This force also consisted of reservists and auxiliary troops, but around eighty thousand men were militaristically trained, i.e. soldiers who belonged to the army.

It was natural for the female members of the royal family to become involved in charitable work and so I was expected to get involved in the needlework school in Athens and its outposts. There were now a lot of busy women there and so I instructed them to make clothes for the soldiers and refugees that the war would bring with it. Just one month after the outbreak of war, eighty thousand items of clothing had already been produced. So-called bashliks, traditional caps made of wool, leather or fur, were also made, which are pointed at the top but have two long pieces of fabric on the sides that can be tied around the neck to ensure a good fit. When I later traveled around the country during the war, I saw many soldiers wearing these caps that we had made at school.

I accompanied my husband and his brothers when they traveled to Larissa, but I was soon needed nearby in Elassona, where reservists needed warm clothing, which I wanted to collect for them with donations, and I wanted to set up a hospital there where first aid could be provided for injured soldiers. So I wrote to Mum and she organized the sending of two trained nurses from the *Alice Hospital*, which her mother had once set up, from Darmstadt. I soon wrote to Mum about my impressions, which were hard to bear.

In Larissa, on October twenty-second, I heard about twenty soldiers who had reached Elassona, some of them seriously wounded. After a fourteen-hour journey over some very bad roads, they finally reached the town. They had to cross the mountain pass near Melouna on the border, which was notorious because there were stones there that blocked the road when they fell from the slope; at any time the slightest tremor could send large boulders crashing down onto the pass, burying everything beneath them. Several of them were so badly wounded that they could not be taken to the military hospital in Larissa, which encouraged me to set up a small hospital in Elassona.

I organized a car and drove to Elassona, where I immediately looked around for a suitable house. I was told that there would be no heavy fighting in the area for the next two days, so I hurriedly had some supplies brought in from the hospital in Larissa, also to set up an operating theater for emergencies. I was accompanied by Madame Agyropoulo, the wife of the prefect of Larissa, in whose house I was living there, a surgeon, his assistant and Sister Margarethe from Darmstadt, who had been trained in first aid surgery and had just arrived but wanted to help immediately. We set off for Elassona at eleven o'clock and arrived there at half past four in the afternoon. The road conditions were wretched, so we were literally shaken to the core as we drove close to precipices, over stones and then got stuck twice in sandy riverbeds, so that we could only continue after an hour.

When we drove through villages, people greeted us in a friendly manner, came up to us to kiss us on the cheeks, some cried with joy that help had come. The people here had suffered under the Turks for a long time, some had sustained injuries and showed us scars that bore witness to the military severity of their rule. They cried out that they would now be freed from the oppressors or that God would no longer allow it, because five hundred years were enough.

When we arrived in Elassona, settled in and I finally saw the Greek flag flying on the roof of my hospital, it filled me with immense pride. It was one of the most impressive Mamaents of my life.

But we were not yet fully equipped to really help all the wounded.

On October twenty-first, the Ottoman troops were defeated at the Sarandaporos River, which flows through the Greek regions of Epirus and Western Macedonia.

We were told in Elassona about the heavy fighting and that many wounded could arrive in the next few days. As my hospital was not yet fully equipped and could not cope with a very large number of wounded soldiers, I organized the provision of a school. So we had to plunder abandoned houses of former Turks to get mattresses, comforters and long pillows so that two men could lie in one bed. We were soon well enough equipped to take in at least one hundred and twenty wounded. Overnight I called for more nurses from Larissa.

I sent my surgeon and his assistant to the battlefield to provide first aid to the wounded. I had to requisition a car from the general staff for this and signed the order myself, although it was actually beyond my authority.

The army actually had good surgeons and male nurses who could apply the first bandages on the battlefield, but they were simply unable to organize the transport of wounded to the nearest town in the chaos of war and had no idea how to quickly set up a hospital at the front. They were not in a position to improvise, produce and provide food and even more bandages. You could say that they lacked organizational skills. The Athens Red Cross was slow and so were the associations from other countries. There was no really well-equipped hospital closer to the battlefield than the one in Athens.

So I had to go to the military authorities to get everything they needed to provide a well-equipped operating theater in twenty-four hours. It wasn't difficult for me because I had to stand up for my cause. I found the poor conditions unacceptable when men risked their lives to defend their country. Then you also had to offer them the best possible care if they were injured in the fighting.

Officially, however, nobody in Larissa and Elassona felt responsible for organizing the transport of wounded from the front to a hospital, for feeding and caring for the seriously or slightly injured. There was no milk, soup, coffee or tea, chocolate or cognac for the wounded to give them at least a little pleasure.

I put the blame on the French General Eydoux and the Chief Physician Arnaud, who had been instructed to organize everything quickly before the outbreak of war, when it would come to that, and everyone knew that the French did not want to deal with the affairs of the Red Cross. The Queen and we other female members of the royal family argued, pointed out the conditions, begged for help, but even when they were accused of just putting you off, they both argued that they would take care of it if necessary.

Until dawn at six thirty we heard shots in the distance, the fighting had been going on for a very long time. The first wounded arrived about two hours later through my surgeon Meerminga, who had brought them to Elassona in the car. When they arrived, only Sister Margarethe was standing by, the other nurses had not yet arrived, and as there were many wounded, Madame Agyropoulo and I took the initiative and we tied aprons around our necks, put on nursing caps and began to help the doctors. We took the first wounded to the school, where mattresses were ready and we had already prepared bandages. So we changed the first bandages, and after the doctors had treated the wounds, we applied new ones. The wounds were often terrible. Some were

very deep, gruesome injuries caused by grenades, broken bones and bullet wounds. We also had to assist the doctors during operations, some of which were hard to watch, then we ran down the corridor in a hurry to comfort the dying and bring other wounded to the operating theater. It was terrible to hear the wounded screaming in agony, writhing on the mattresses, tormented by pain, but we had no room left to take these hopeless souls to so that the others would not witness their death throes.
There was no real light, just one or two bad lamps. Everyone was calling for something to eat and drink. It had also been raining terribly for many hours, so they were all wet and freezing.
More and more wounded were brought to us, so that soon there were two hundred and fifty men. From eight thirty until three thirty at night, we received the wounded and the dying and tried to accommodate them all.
After a long search, I found an oil lamp in the corner of a room and took some oil from another and a small pot so that I could provide something to drink with some water and a can of condensed milk from my private property. It was only slightly warm and certainly not very drinkable, but at least some of the men got some warm liquid. I went from man to man, handing out small sips until everything was used up. Then I made some more, but I couldn't give everyone anything.
I had to assist during an operation while a dying man lay next to me on a stretcher. On the side, I tried to make and heat something to drink again, stirred the pot and the man begged me to hold his hand, which I tried to do as well as I could, while the blood from the wounded man on the operating table dripped onto my apron and shoes. I didn't have time to think, otherwise I might have wanted to cry in the face of all the horror that surrounded me and the others. This went on for three days and three nights, with only short breaks where I sat down on a chair, leaned my head against the wall and dozed off for a while. From time to time we could go to a nearby farmer's house to sleep there, but it was draughty, cold and there was nothing to eat. I stayed in the same clothes all day and never got to change.
During the whole time, I only ate a crust of bread every day and drank a cup of Turkish coffee.
And new wounded soldiers kept arriving. Soldiers often died on the way, then we pulled their bodies out of the wagon, some of their comrades not even noticing their death and not pointing it out to us. The cold and wet weather also meant that many did not make it to us. Weakened as they were by their serious injuries, they had nothing more to offer against the cold and wet.
I had to have another four houses equipped to accommodate some of the less seriously wounded, whom we covered with blankets and used their jackets as pillows. We could barely provide them with food, but I offered all the

pass and the streets were littered with the corpses of the Turks, piled ten feet high, like a wall. Even if he was perhaps exaggerating a little, I understood his joy at the victory, but could only describe it as terrible.

On the twenty-sixth of October, the king came to Servia to inspect the troops and thank them for their bravery. He was received with great honor in the city and had already been to Elassona and Kozani, the three cities that were now back in Greek hands.

The king was followed by his sons and in Kozani, schoolchildren lining the streets had probably already cheered them on and given them a warm welcome. It was similar in Servia. The people greeted their king and celebrated my husband and his brothers exuberantly.

There was a thanksgiving service in a beautiful little church and the bishop wore his finest vestments. I was now able to rest for a few days and finally sleep in a real bedroom again under blankets made of lace and embroidery.

During this brief period of rest, I received the news from my mother that Alexei had been very unwell and had been struggling with death for a while. On the fifth of September, Aunt Alix was with her family in the Bialowieza hunting ground in the Grodno and Brest region when Alexei tried to jump into a rowing boat and fell on one of the oarlocks. A hemorrhage developed within a few minutes, but Alexei was immediately taken to his room and after a week the hemorrhage disappeared. In mid-September, they traveled on to Spala, their other hunting ground. There they took a ride in carriages, Alexei sitting in one with Aunt Alix. The hemorrhage reappeared on the uneven paths of the forest and rapidly increased when my cousin's hip was knocked against the inside of the carriage. They stopped the ride and immediately returned to the hunting lodge, but by then the bleeding had worsened to such an extent that Alexei lost consciousness from the pain. His groin was very swollen, he quickly developed a very high fever and in a very short time he was in a very bad way. He was delirious, writhing in pain, his heartbeat weakened. Aunt Alix sat at his bedside day and night until the doctors had little hope left. On October tenth, with a heavy heart, it was decided to issue a bulletin officially announcing the Tsarevich's condition. Although they spoke of an accident, they could not keep the fact that he was dying a secret. Uncle Nicky sent for a priest and my little cousin received the last rites.

In her distress, Aunt Alix turned to Rasputin and sent him a telegram via her lady-in-waiting Anna Vyrubova, telling him how bad things were for her son. Rasputin received it on October 12th in his home town of Pokrovskoye in Siberia. He replied to her immediately in a telegram, assuring Aunt Alix that her boy would not die. The doctors should not torture him too much because he was praying for him.

Alexei felt better just one day after receiving these lines from the monk. On October nineteenth, the bleeding had disappeared, as had the swelling in his groin, but he was still unable to move his left leg properly or walk again. Orthopaedic massages should help him to be able to stretch his leg again soon.

Mama was just as skeptical as I was about this supposed miracle cure, but we all knew that Uncle Nicky could not banish Rasputin from his wife's life, because if he did and Alexei really died of a hemorrhage, in her eyes it would surely be her husband's fault, because he had sent away the only person who helped her son. My mother expressed this thought cautiously, but I'm sure everyone in the family saw it the same way we did. Aunt Alix had fallen for this monk in her constant concern for Alexei. Of course I was glad to hear that he had recovered, but I found it worrying how anyone could cling to a person and his supposed healing powers like that.

Christo and I had done seances from time to time, laid cards, but I saw it more as a pastime with something that was fashionable at the time, but didn't really believe in the power of spirits on the living. Andrea didn't like it when people got involved in such occult things. It worried him too much to play with something that could turn a person's head in such a way that they would never get rid of it. You often couldn't get rid of the famous spirits you called up so quickly.

I was a down-to-earth person and didn't let that confuse me. Which is not to deny that prayers can help and support a person, but they are certainly not able to heal someone. But Aunt Alix seemed to be becoming increasingly entangled in such mysteries.

The war progressed and our troops achieved their next success when they captured Giannitsa in central Macedonia on October thirty-first. Now the army marched towards the city of Monastir.

I wrote to my mother again on the second of November and at that time I was in Verria, west of Salonika. In Kozani, French engineers had made my work easier and had already built a new military hospital before we arrived, as well as some additional accommodation. We were given all the necessary materials such as bandages, beds, blankets, nightgowns, lamps, cups, wash bowls and much more. Everything was neatly packed and we were able to store it in a large storage room. Before we arrived in Kozani, there had already been some things left in the room, but the Turks took it upon themselves to rummage through everything and make a mess before they withdrew.

Four buildings that stood close together, forming a square, had also been vandalized and the floors were dirty. Madame Agyropoulo and I organized a cleaning crew of women who lived in the city. They wiped the floors clean and swept everything out. Some Greek soldiers who were present spontaneously agreed to set up two hundred beds, which we then equipped with mattresses, blankets and pillows, which took a total of two days. We also prepared beds for ourselves. We were able to hang lamps here for the first time, put a washed-up cup next to each bed, as well as spittoons, and shirts and underpants could be stored in cupboards.

My father-in-law stayed in Kozani for a while so that we could share meals with him, who was housed in a building half an hour away from us. Andrea and his brothers had to leave again to support the Greek troops.

We heard that the Turks had been pushed out of Kailar. Victory had been achieved on October twenty-sixth, but as there had been heavy fighting, we now had to prepare for the arrival of the wounded. So we dressed again in our nurses' uniforms, all slept for half an hour and shortly afterwards a total of one hundred and seventy-five wounded arrived at intervals, all of whom needed new bandages and their wounds examined. We were on our feet all night. We rushed through the rooms until six o'clock in the morning, treating one after the other. About one hundred and sixty soldiers who arrived afterwards were ill and were kept in another part of the hospital, separate from the other wounded.

After allowing myself at least an hour and a half of sleep, I went straight back to work, changing the bandages and feeding the wounded who couldn't eat for themselves.

One of my worst experiences during the war came on our last afternoon in Kozani. I had to help with the amputation of a leg. The patient had to be given the chloroform at a certain Mamaent, and he had to be prevented from biting his tongue immediately afterwards. At the same time, I also had to administer swabs, a bowl and other things. My surgeon carried out this amputation in a small room, away from the other wounded, for which a screen had been erected. Once I had overcome the nausea I was feeling, I concentrated on the rather interesting way in which the surgeon amputated the leg. When the operation was over, the leg was still on the floor, as I realized shortly afterwards. It had simply been left there and I pointed it out to Madame Agyropoulo and asked if someone could remove it, because I couldn't touch it. I just couldn't get over my disgust. She understood, but picked it up herself, wrapped it in some cloths, simply tucked it under her arm and left the hospital to bury it somewhere outside. So she went out and the cloths shifted as she carried it so that you could now take a look at the bloody, uncovered piece of flesh. As the lady was elderly and suffered from severe hearing loss, I called out to her to be careful, but she couldn't hear me. She just kept walking and everyone who passed her stopped and stared at the leg under her arm. It was only when a soldier came up to me, became aware of the grotesque scene and started to laugh that my tension eased and I couldn't help but laugh too, as he

humorously remarked that she had a third leg.
More wounded arrived that evening, by midnight everyone had been treated and I went to bed, getting a little more sleep than usual. The next morning, eight doctors and three nurses arrived in Kozani, working for the Athenian Red Cross, and the two ladies from Elassona who had already been working for the Red Cross. That was the end of my work in Kozani and I was able to travel on to Verria, where I arrived on the first of November to receive the wounded. After first aid, however, they could be taken to Thessaloniki, which was nearby, and across the sea to Piraeus.
I stayed in Verria for four days. My father-in-law had traveled with me, but we were accommodated in really poor conditions in a small dwelling. What's more, it rained every day and all night long.
The Greek army was still on its way to Monastir, but then had to change direction and reached Salonika on the seventh of November, just a few hours before the Bulgarian forces marched in.
As I learned later, Constantine had to lead his men over a narrow mountain pass. Then he had some of them advance further over the mountains, and a troop unit was sent to cut off the path of the advancing Ottoman soldiers in the valley. In Verria, I was able to observe the fighting through binoculars, and even though I couldn't hear the gunshots, others told me that there were many of them.
In the meantime, the rain had turned to snow and it had become bitterly cold. The rapid onset of the cold gave me neuralgia, severe nerve pain in my neck and face, but a doctor gave me aspirin and within half an hour the pain became bearable. Apart from that, I felt quite well, but had lost weight and told my mother that I was now just as thin as Louise - flat as a board. I said she would certainly not recognize me. Although I had lost so much weight, I was still blessed with the same appetite as before the war and my work as a nurse, enjoying meals when there were any. But it was probably also due to the work, because I was on my feet a lot, had to be quick and spent most of my time running back and forth between the wounded. So I couldn't put on any more weight, I could only lose it.
The twenty-six thousand Ottoman soldiers in Salonika quickly surrendered to the Bulgarian and Greek troops and were allowed to withdraw unmolested after the final conquest of the city on the ninth of November. However, there were minor clashes between our troops and the Bulgarian troops. The soldiers all saw themselves as victors, but everyone wanted to be the real winner.
After this victory in Salonika, the first wounded soon arrived in Verria and I was able to receive them there in a small hospital that had already been set up.
It was not only the Greek troops who achieved successes, so it amazed me

how every fighting party in this war was so insistent on claiming victory for itself. They fought together against the Turks and it was only through unity that great battles could be won. But there were always disputes about who had been best when and where, with the best strategy, and it was something I didn't understand.

The Serbian forces had defeated the Turks in Kumanovo in Macedonia on the third and fourth of November. They entered Üsküb, now Skopje, just two days later, took the Prilep region in mid-November and then Monastir on November twenty-ninth.

The Bulgarian troops also defeated the Ottoman troops on October one and twenty-two in Kirk Kilisse, near the border with Bulgaria, and at the end of October in a battle near Lüleburgaz. In this cruel battle, each side lost twenty thousand soldiers, who were wounded, killed or captured by the other force.

At times it was rumored that Uncle Nicky was considering intervening in the war to offer his military support to the Ottoman Empire, as the Bulgarian forces were becoming too vehement in their drive to conquer. Russia landed troops to prevent Bulgarian control of the straits on the Bosporus, but Uncle Nicky did not interfere in the war any further.

On the fourth and eighth of November, the Bulgarian troops then failed in their attempted conquest of Constantinople. On the twentieth of November, Bulgaria concluded a separate armistice with the Ottoman government. This was a solo effort, which was only intended to lull the Turks into a sense of security for a while, but was nevertheless high-handed and an affront to the other armed forces involved in the war.

I only found out after the war that my mother copied every letter I wrote and passed them on to the whole family. Georgie later confessed to me that he had never read anything so interesting before. And it filled him with immense admiration and pride to see how I had proved myself in bravery and endless efforts.

Sister Anna, the second nurse who had traveled from Darmstadt, arrived a little late, but she always had to telegraph a report to the *Alice Hospital* and she did not miss the opportunity to pass on many good things about me and my commitment.

On the eleventh of November, the king celebrated the victory in Salonika with us in his retinue. He awarded Nicholas the title of governor of the city, Constantine was *appointed* honorary general and set off with his troops for Monastir.

At the beginning of the war, I didn't have many helpers. Nona had immediately offered to come from England as a volunteer. I then sent her a telegram advising her against it. But when she read in my first letter to Mama what tasks I had set myself, she threw my objection overboard. I didn't really want her to come or feel compelled to, but it was her free decision. A nurse called Miss Boase, who had trained at Charing Cross Hospital in London and who knew Nona well, immediately agreed to travel with her. Mama sold some of her jewels and was able to give Nona one hundred pounds for the journey. She immediately set off for Athens with Miss Boase. From there she accompanied the Queen, a group of doctors and nurses to Salonika, where they arrived on November thirteenth.

My father-in-law, Andrea and I were able to move into a villa in Thessaloniki that had previously belonged to an old sultan who had now fled with his family.

We greeted Nona, my mother-in-law, Miss Boase, doctors and nurses as soon as they arrived. I thanked Nona very much for making the long journey, and Miss Boase too. She was amazed at how thin I had become. So she didn't believe me at first when I told her I was completely healthy and everything was fine. After talking to some of the people present, she said she had to tell Mama everything, how much everyone praised me for my commitment, from the doctors to the officers, everyone said I had worked miracles. It was a bit too much for me, because I had enjoyed doing it all.

Andrea offered me the chance to travel back to Athens so that I could be with the children again. But I flatly refused, even though I missed them very much. I made him understand that my place was now at his side and that I wanted to do something for the Greek troops, the troops of my home country. I felt that leaving for Athens would be cowardly and weak. My husband was aware of my strong will and knew it was impossible to discuss this with me. However, he insisted that I take a tonic before going to bed and drink a warm cocoa to regain my strength.

Everyone feared that the impressions I had gathered would soon affect my soul and that I was only suppressing them for the Mamaent. But I had long since come to terms with it all.

The hospitals in Thessaloniki had not been run well so far and so Nona and I set about curbing or even eliminating these shortcomings as best we could.

The people in the Jewish hospital had not had anything to eat for days and many of the seriously ill were in danger of starving to death. The sanitary conditions were terrible, so that typhus and dysentery spread among the patients. It was terrible how many sick people were dying. I sent for a rabbi to give the people some assistance. The dead had to be buried quickly and sprinkled with lime to prevent the contagious diseases from spreading.

Thirty Greek patients were examined and discharged as relatively healthy so that we could make room for others. These people were so upset that they even took on a five-kilometer walk to rush to the king and complain about me. Andrea thought that if they could walk that far, they were healthy. So my husband intercepted them on their way, sent them back to the hospital to pack up their things and leave.

Nona talked me into going back to Athens for at least a few days to see my children, so I finally agreed. On the twenty-third of November, I traveled to Athens with her to take some time off.

My girls were beside themselves with joy. They didn't want to let go of me when we saw each other again, and of course I was also happy to finally hold them in my arms again. But I only told them that their Papa was fine, that he was well and had fought bravely. They only heard a little about my work. They shouldn't be frightened.

Prime Minister Venizelos came to see me a few days later to thank me. He expressed his gratitude for himself, for all Greeks and Cretans and for the entire parliament. Everyone was deeply touched by my commitment and dedication. Out of pure tact, he also thanked the other princesses, but put me first in his speech.

He mentioned the fighting that was now beginning around the city of Ioannina, the capital of the Epirus region, and I immediately promised him that I would help the wounded again if he would organize horses and carts for me, which he immediately agreed to. My idea was to set up a hospital that was not in a fixed location, but to plan everything so that it could travel with the troops to provide better care directly on the battlefield, and Venizelos was so taken with this that he thanked me again. I told him that was enough, that I saw it as my duty.

I wanted to spend a few more days in Athens, also to help Konstantin's wife Sophie, who was pregnant. The baby was due in May of the following year. Her last birth, that of her daughter Irene, had been eight years ago and she was forty-two years old. A late pregnancy that no one had expected. The war, the separation from her husband and the pregnancy had taken their toll on her. However, I could no longer stay in Athens and on the sixth of December, Nona and I set off on a journey to Preveza in the Epirus region.

When we got there, it was pouring with rain and we were immediately told to look at makeshift hospitals in Filippiada nearby to inspect them. As I had developed hives on my face during the trip, I had to hide my face behind a veil.

When we returned to Athens, Sophie was already very upset to receive me. She was furious that I had sent nurses from Cairo, who were under her command, to Salonika without her permission, where they were urgently needed. I blamed it on her condition that she was so angry about my high-handedness, as I had not acted to hurt her in any way. But she probably wanted to make it clear to me what position I held in the royal family. She was the crown princess and I was just the princess. She was also involved, but at the Mamaent she could only manage and organize everything from her desk. The Prime Minister's effusive praise of me had more than offended her. There was no doubt about that. However, I didn't have time to dwell on such trivialities and traveled with Nona to Thessaloniki, where I inspected a reception camp for refugees to make sure that these homeless people were being provided with sufficient food.

We stayed in Thessaloniki, where we celebrated Christmas with the king on Christmas Eve and celebrated his sixty-sixth birthday. Afterwards, we returned to Athens.

Aunt Alix had sent me a brooch for Christmas, but I hadn't received a telegram or a card from Aunt Ella. We had been in occasional correspondence, but there had been no news from her since the war broke out. I put it down to the fact that she simply had too much to do at her convent. I also didn't have the time to answer letters.

I learned in a letter from Mama that my father had risen to a *First Sea Lord*, the highest rank in the Royal Navy, on the ninth of December. At the age of fifty-eight, my father had climbed the career ladder in the British Navy to the top rung and my mother wrote to tell me how proud she was of him, and Georgie and Dickie were now keen to get as far as my father. She also assured me that she was very proud of me, but longed for me, Andrea and the grandchildren. So she hoped, like everyone else, that the war in the Balkans would end soon.

Papa in his uniform as First Sea Lord, 1912

At the end of the year, Nona and I traveled to Salonika again, where the Turks deliberately delayed the signing of a ceasefire.
Andrea was waiting for us, and just a few days later our girls arrived accompanied by a nanny. Cäcilie had been ill on the journey, suffering from nausea, but she immediately ran towards Andrea like the others when she saw her father.
By this time, both my husband and I were a little worn out from the unsteadiness that had characterized our lives in recent months, the war itself. Andrea was suffering from the fact that he was not currently deployed in combat, because he hated nothing more than inactivity when everyone around him was at war, fighting for Greece. So he seemed a bit bored, depressed and annoyed. In the meantime, I was given injections of arsenic to strengthen me because I just wasn't putting on weight.

We celebrated New Year's Eve in a somewhat subdued mood, welcoming in the New Year and all longing for peace.

As a nurse with Andrea, 1913

in favor of his son Constantine. My father-in-law was a very people-oriented person, so he had never cared or cared too much about protection when he walked through the streets of a city, as he knew it from his vacations in France or from his usual walks through Athens. In his opinion, the effort Uncle Nicky made to protect him was too much of a fuss and completely unnecessary. In his view, it only alienated a monarch from his people.
So on the afternoon of March eighteenth, he set off on a leisurely stroll through Salonika, where he was still staying. He was accompanied only by an equerry and two policemen. However, he always insisted that these men walk a good distance behind him. As he passed the *White Tower*, the city's famous monument, he suddenly changed direction, took a few steps back, passed a café from which a disheveled person ran out and shot him in the back at close range. My father-in-law was killed instantly as the bullet had hit his heart, lungs and stomach. He was taken to a nearby hospital, but nothing more could be done for him there.
The assassin was arrested immediately, his name was Alexandros Schinas. He was forty-three years old, came from Volos near Thessaloniki and had worked for a time in New York as a waiter in the *Fifth Avenue Hotel*, where he had attracted attention through his fondness for socialist reading and his statements, from which it emerged that he abhorred the aristocracy and monarchy in the deepest way, and was also opposed to any kind of oppressive government.
At first it was believed that he was a Bulgarian or even a Turk who wanted to take revenge on the king for all the Ottoman soldiers who had died, but he was just a confused Greek. He had founded a school in Volos after the hotel in New York closed in 1908 and he had to return to Greece, where he spread his smear campaigns. This school was closed by the police, two of Schinas' followers were arrested and the others managed to escape. However, the school was later found to contain anti-monarchy literature and self-authored pamphlets against the king.
Shinas was asked why he had killed the king, but at first he refused to make a statement. Then he confessed that he was against any kind of oppressive government and that the king had refused to give him some money when he asked for it. The latter was a lie, because Schinas had simply shot at my father-in-law. There had been no exchange of words between them beforehand. Even when the policemen objected that he probably had no national pride because he had just shot the king, he said that none of this interested him. Due to his condition, he was classified as a drunkard and vagrant who did not appear to be particularly educated in the conversations with him.
They wanted to find out whether he had any accomplices. He was badly mistreated during the interrogations, but he proved to be a confused loner.

Schinas remained in custody, where he continued to be put under pressure. When he was taken to the prefecture in Thessaloniki on May 6 to be questioned again, he allegedly suddenly jumped up and threw himself out of the second-floor window. He fell nine meters and died instantly. It was said to have been suicide, but there were also rumors that he had been helped out and thrown out of the window. But none of that counted.
We received the news of my father-in-law's death in Athens. Andrea, Constantine's son George and I had to break the news to my mother-in-law gently. We were the only ones in the palace with her at the time. It was a very hard blow for all of us, but the hardest for the Queen, because she had lost her beloved husband. We all immediately traveled to Salonika to collect his body. Constantine had to come to Athens immediately, because he had to take the oath as the new King Constantine I of Greece.
After the assassination, Prime Minister Venizelos told the British ambassador that it was a gruesome murder, but fortunately the assassin was Greek. He probably feared even more unrest in the course of the war if Schinas had been a member of an allied war party or even the enemy. However, the press and Sir Francis Elliot, the British ambassador, no longer found fault with my father-in-law; instead, they said that he had been happy with the victories he had won recently and had consolidated his power in the end. His son, the crown prince, had been a victor on the battlefield, which had made him all the prouder.
We brought my father-in-law's body back to Athens on the yacht *Amphitrite* after all the honors, followed by ships of the Greek Navy. His coffin was kept for three days in the *Cathedral of the Annunciation*, which is in the center of Athens, so that the people could also bid farewell to their king. The Greek and Danish flags were draped over his coffin.
We then took the coffin to Tatoi and buried the king there. It was the second of April 1913 and I was wearing the Order of the Redeemer, which my father-in law had once awarded me. His sons threw bouquets of violets and earth into the open grave. It was a very sad but dignified funeral. We were also all very happy to see how many people had lined the streets of Thessaloniki, Athens and now Tatoi to pay their last respects to the king. I had held my father-in-law in high esteem as he had always been very good to me. It was a great loss for all of us.

The funeral of my father-in-law, Queen Olga is at the coffin in front, Sophie can be seen on the stairs second from the left, Minnie next to her, I am standing on the left, Konstantin can be seen in front next to my mother-in-law, April 1913

The people in the streets of Athens pay their last respects to their king, April 1913

On April thirteenth, my father-in-law's last will and testament regarding the country's policy was published. His words were received very positively by the people, because the king had encouraged his son Constantine to love his country with all his heart, to take into account the interests of the people, to give his children a good Greek education and also pointed out to him that in Greece he was dealing with southerners, a people who were quick to get excited, who said and did something at one Mamaent, but who settled and forgot an argument after just a few hours. For this reason, Constantine should never forget that as king he suffered more than his people.

My father-in-law's private will was not made public. It only concerned the family and everyone knew that the royal family had not been particularly rich. So he left a sum of eighty thousand English pounds, most of which went to Andrea and Christopher. My husband and I were promised an annual allowance of four thousand English pounds and we inherited Mon Repos on Corfu, including all the silver, linen and glass in it. It was to become our real home from then on.

The mother-in-law suffered in her grief. She was promised a place to live for life in the palace in Athens, but she no longer wanted to stay in Greece without her husband. Perhaps she simply needed some distance and so she decided to return to the country of her birth, Russia, to live with her brother, Grand Duke Konstantin Konstantinovich Romanov, in the Pavlovsk Palace in St.

Petersburg. Her brother was a very successful writer and wrote well-known plays and poems under the pseudonym *KR*.

A view of Mon Repos, around 1910

Mama learned from me in letters what was going on in Greece and she was horrified by the murder of the King. She informed me that Georgie had already graduated from Dartmouth Naval College on the fifteenth of January and had been promoted to a sub-lieutenant. We all knew that he too was destined for a brilliant career in the English Navy, for my brother was an excellent mathematician. Even when he traveled, he was always reading books on calculations and could do the most complicated calculations in his head just like that, and he was extremely fast.

Dickie as a cadet, left, with Papa as First Sea Lord and Georgie as Lieutenant, 1913

My younger brother Dickie was due to go to the Naval College at Osborne in May that year, again at his own request. He wasn't quite thirteen then, but because of Papa and Georgie he had a certain advantage as far as admission to the college was concerned.

Mama and Dickie in his uniform as a cadet, 1913

Dickie's life was completely determined by my mother until he entered college. She had the greater influence over him, organized his upbringing and education, and focused most of her maternal love on her youngest son. Since my father could only be present peripherally, as he was either traveling, busy in the Admiralty or had to attend to important state business, he rarely saw him. Just whenever he was ashore. Papa lived with Dickie at the *Burlington Hotel* in Dover, in Sheerness or took him on board his flagship in the Mediterranean, where my brother quickly became a favorite of the entire crew.
When Dickie entered college, his childhood was essentially over. At the naval school in Osborne on the Isle of Wight, he became Cadet Prince Louis of Battenberg, who, to avoid confusion, was called *Young Prince Louis*. But for my little brother, no other career was ever conceivable.
However, he quickly had to get used to a very hard life at Osborne. As a cadet, you were at the mercy of the bullying of the older pupils and the teachers also brought up the newcomers with a firm hand. Punishments were the order of the day. All this was allowed as long as it was kept within limits and was considered the perfect educational method to shape and harden the young people. Little Dickie, always friendly and polite, was immediately chosen by some as their victim and his nose was beaten bloody. But Papa and Georgie knew about these cruelties because they had experienced them themselves. So they warned him that he would be beaten up by his elders if he didn't put up a fight. Dickie first poured his heart out to Mama, but she couldn't do anything, comforted him, admonished him to be strong and shortly afterwards he had a fight with the son of an admiral, whom he knew from boarding school and who always bullied him. Dickie won. He proudly reported that the other boys had asked him to fight, and after he had emerged victorious, he was now a hero among them, because the other boy was a meanie and disliked by all the boys. But Dickie was also a nephew of the King, the son of the *First Sea Lord*, and sometimes he could only assert himself by being cheeky, which soon made him lonely among the boys. Many feared it would cost them dearly if they messed with him because of his status.
My little brother was very well educated, but he had a hard time learning because he didn't act or think quickly like Georgie, but carefully weighed everything up again and again.
Naval school meant getting up at six thirty, running naked to the cold shower, eating a less than spartan breakfast and then there were lessons that seemed endless to him. Mathematics, signaling, knot tying, navigation and sporting competitions. He was to long for the vacations in Heiligenberg more than once.
But Mama could no longer help her little boy. She hoped he would prove himself, but suspected that his muted eagerness to learn would make it harder

for him than Georgie.
The war in the Balkans was not yet over. After the siege of Adrianople on March twenty-sixth, the Bulgarian forces had finally conquered the city. Two Serbian divisions had come to their aid and sixty-five thousand Ottoman soldiers were taken prisoner of war by the Bulgarians. On the first of May 1913, the Ottomans finally reached another armistice with the Bulgarians.
The major European powers - Great Britain, Austria-Hungary, Germany, Italy, France and Russia - now acted as mediators in the war and the *Treaty of London* was concluded between the Ottoman Empire and its opponents on the thirtieth of May. This officially ended the war.
The Ottomans renounced all European territories, beginning west of the line between Midia on the Black Sea and Enez on the coast of the Aegean. The Ottoman Sultan *Mehmed V* formally renounced all claims to the island of Crete, but it was not until December 1913 that the Greek flag was raised there again in the presence of the king and the then Greek Prime Minister Venizelos. The Turks living on the island had to leave.
The states involved in the war founded the *Balkan League* as a kind of alliance of convenience to defend themselves against the Ottoman Empire.
This first Balkan war had the sad aftertaste of hundreds of thousands of Muslims fleeing eastwards from the Balkan peninsula. Furthermore, mosques were left to decay or converted into churches and Muslim clothing was banned. In just a few months, the centuries-long Ottoman rule on the Balkan Peninsula came to an end.
Albania had already declared its independence from the Ottoman Empire on November twenty-eighth, 1912. *The Treaty of London* also granted the country a larger territory. It now declared itself a principality.
Nevertheless, disputes arose over the conquered territories and there was another crisis, but for the time being all parties remained calm.

The new Greek king, Andrea's brother Constantine, had earned great respect during the Balkan War. But this was ruined by the fact that Tino had already begun an affair during the war with a lady who had worked in one of Ellen's hospitals. The whole military knew about it, but Sophie, his wife, didn't at first. In the meantime, I looked after her moods, because we all blamed them on her pregnancy.
On the fourth of May 1913, she gave birth to little Princess Katherine. Having a baby was actually a joyous occasion, but Sophie's happiness was soon overshadowed by the dark shadow of Tino's affair. And when he and the rest of us in the family confessed it, even appearing in public with the lady, he only feared that the affairs of state he had to attend to as king would keep him away from his new love. This distressed him more than his wife's grief or the

shame he brought on his children.
Wanda Paola Lottero was an Italian theater actress and had married Prince Hermann von Sachsen-Weimar-Eisenach in London in 1909. After his morganatic marriage, he had lost his claim to the title of the house and now called himself Count von Ostheim. Just two years later, the couple divorced, as the husband had already brought debts into the marriage due to his extravagant lifestyle, but could no longer hope for financial support from his family and so had been living off his wife's money. She filed for divorce because of this and also claimed that he had been unfaithful and violent towards her. But she was able to adorn herself with the title of Countess of Ostheim and had now turned Konstantin's head. She had an easy morality, as they say, not afraid to adorn herself with men who had money in order to secure a certain standard of living for herself and, as a girl from a simple Italian background, to achieve a certain, albeit dubious, prestige. Tino showered her with jewels, expensive clothes and precious silks and was not afraid to give her valuable ancient Greek finds such as vases that had once been discovered by famous explorers such as Schliemann. They wrote letters to each other and, unfortunately, even after Tino's death, this lady was to capitalize on these letters, pining for her with love, by publishing them in a book.
Sophie suffered in silence. She was now Queen of Greece, but although a Greek legend says that if a Sofia sits on the throne with a Constantine, this promises much wealth for the country, this good omen of her name did not help her. She was not particularly popular with the people as she was a German, sister of the Emperor of Prussia, so it was assumed that she was on very good terms with him, which was not true. Sophie was completely loyal to her homeland, Greece.

example, around forty-eight thousand Greek soldiers had lost their lives, one hundred and fifty-six thousand Bulgarians and one hundred thousand Ottomans, but ethnic violence had also broken out for the first time, with numerous civilians of the other peoples being murdered or expelled on all sides. In 1915 and 1916, however, the Ottomans were to take revenge on the Bulgarians in Eastern Thrace by murdering or expelling the Armenians living there, between three hundred thousand and over a million people, in a gruesome manner. An exact number was never known.

As king, Constantine was now commander-in-chief of the Greek army in the second war in the Balkans and once again led the troops victoriously against the Bulgarians. As a result of the two wars, Greece's territory increased by around ninety percent and the population grew from 2.6 to 4.7 million people. As a successful general and monarch, Andrea's brother now gained popularity among the people and soon had almost the same standing as Prime Minister Venizelos. At first, the two worked quite closely together, but they soon realized that they had very different views, especially with regard to foreign policy. Constantine was a descendant of a German house, Schleswig-Holstein-Sonderburg-Glücksburg. His ancestors were Greek-Danish, he was a brother-in-law of the German emperor and therefore pro-German. However, this outraged Venizelos, who was more oriented towards the English than the German Navy.

On the twenty-fourth of May 1913 there had been a great celebration in Berlin when Uncle Willy's daughter, Princess Viktoria Luise, married the Hereditary Prince Ernst August of Hanover, Hereditary Duke of Brunswick and Lüneburg. Guests came from all the noble houses of Europe, including Uncle Nicky, who traveled there alone, as Aunt Alix did not feel up to such a trip at the Mamaent and Alexei had not yet recovered sufficiently to be able to walk longer distances on his own. In addition, 1913 marked the three-hundredth anniversary of the Romanovs on the Tsar's throne. There was a lot of traveling through the country and so there would have been no opportunity to travel on to Hesse during the celebrations in Berlin.

But I longed to see my family again. In August, all the members of the Greek royal family were traveling again, so I persuaded Andrea to go with our girls. At first, my husband had reservations, fearing that another war might break out between Greece and Turkey, in which case he would have to return immediately. But this fear only seemed to weigh on him. It even went so far that he thought it would be nonsense to buy new clothes from his tailor for the trip or to go shopping for presents or anything similar. You never knew what was going to happen, but I insisted that we leave, partly for our own relaxation and to get some distance. So Andrea finally gave in.

First we went to England. In London, we stayed with my parents at *Mall*

House in *Spring Gardens* near Trafalgar Square. My father now had a great reputation as *First Sea Lord* and opposite him on the political side was the *First Lord of the Admiralty*, the later very famous Winston Churchill. My father had various tasks to accomplish, but as Commander-in-Chief of the Royal Navy, his main focus was on consolidating and improving the strength of the fleet and preparing it for possible deployment in war.
Mama was especially happy during our stay to present her grandchildren to her Uncle Arthur, the Duke of Connaugt and Strathearn. She was very effusive about it and told the girls he was their great-great-uncle. Uncle Arthur, now sixty-three years old, was amused, but a little shocked, because he immediately replied that Mama was making something like an antique artifact out of him.
Andrea visited King George V of England to return some of his father's English medals to him.
In September, we traveled with Mum to Darmstadt to visit Uncle Ernie and Aunt Onor and their two sons. We lived in Heiligenberg, but also spent a lot of time in Wolfsgarten.

The children had a lot of fun together and the girls got on very well with their Hessian cousins Lu and Don. After the chaos of the war, Andrea and I finally had time for our daughters again and made the most of every Mamaent to do something or play with them.
Uncle Ernie was very enthusiastic about technology and loved all kinds of progress. So he organized a trip in a zeppelin for us. On September 12th, we flew *in airship no. 1* from Frankfurt am Main via Friedrichshof, Wiesbaden, Mainz, Oppenheim, Darmstadt, Odenwald and Wolfsgarten. The flight ended back in Frankfurt. There was every comfort on board the airship, so we were served champagne and caviar.

It was a wonderful experience, as I had never flown before. This technology was still in its infancy at the time. But zeppelins were already a popular means of travel in Germany, so you could fly to Heligoland in them, for example. Uncle Ernie had often organized such sightseeing flights for Mum and Dickie. My younger brother was just as fascinated by technical innovations as his uncle and so he had once made it possible for his nephew to fly in *an Aeroplan*. It was still a fairly primitive seaplane where you sat astride the fuel tank and had to hold on to two tensioning ropes, but it made a great impression on Dickie. He had to talk about this experience over and over again.
My brother was also in Heiligenberg and Wolfsgarten this fall as he was on vacation from college. King George V presented him with a commemorative medal of his coronation, which Dickie now wore proudly on his uniform. He

still loved animals, who always traveled with him, some could be carried, others traveled in cages. Mama now had the task and burden of looking after them all with Louise when Dickie was at college.
We traveled back to England at the beginning of October as we were invited to the wedding of King George's niece Alexandra, a daughter of Louise, daughter of Uncle Bertie, on the fifteenth. Alexandra married her second uncle, Major General Arthur of Connaught, the only son of Mama's Uncle Arthur, at St. James's Palace. The bride was twenty-two years old, her husband eight years older. The last few years had been quite difficult for Alexandra, because in 1910 she had fallen in love with Andrea's brother Christo; it was rumored that it was a relationship that had a certain depth, but her parents rejected a relationship with a husband from a German-born family.
In December 1911, the family's ship capsized in Morocco on a trip to Egypt. Apparently no one was injured, but shortly afterwards her father fell ill with pleurisy and died at the beginning of 1912.
The bride was granted a happy marriage, which also brought with it the prestigious title of Duke of Fife for the groom, as Alexandra had inherited the title as the only surviving child of her family, but did not hold a seat in the *House of Lords* as a woman. This position could now be held by her husband.
She was due to give birth to a son in 1914 and she and her husband were both very involved in charity work.
Since Alexandra, like me, had also worked as a nurse to help the poor before her wedding, I felt very close to her and we got on well.
After the wedding, I visited the Greek Embassy as part of an official appointment, as well as *Charing Cross* and *London Hospital.*
Meanwhile, Andrea sat for a portrait of de László, which Mum had organized so that she could have one of me and one of him. Of course, I often kept my husband company, because it took a while to finish it.

Portrait of Andrea, 1913

After completing my husband's painting, Andrea and I took time for the children again. We took them on a bus trip to *St. Paul's Cathedral* and visited London Zoo, among other things.

King George V received me in early November to honor me for my services as a nurse during the Balkan wars and awarded me the *Order of the Royal English Red Cross*, which I was very pleased about. As my mother had copied the letters she had written during the war and passed them on to her relatives, everyone in the family knew about my commitment. I was a little embarrassed because I did it of my own free will, because I wanted to help, but of course I also found it very nice when relatives asked me about it and wanted to know more about what I was doing. But I never had the feeling that I had to prove myself to others because of my disability, because no one ever let me feel that I wasn't accepted because of it or that they didn't trust me to do everything like a hearing person.

whole month, I would soon beat her.
On the night of June twenty-fifth to twenty-sixth, I finally went into labor and gave birth to another daughter at six o'clock in the morning. My mother was a little disappointed that it was another girl, and shortly afterwards she also asked my brother Dickie to congratulate me on the birth, but doubted that I would ever give birth to a son. Andrea and I were very happy about the healthy baby and named her Sophie. But shortly after her birth, she was nicknamed *Tiny*, as she was *the* youngest of the girls.
Just two days after Sophie's birth, the Austrian heir to the throne, Archduke Franz Ferdinand of Austria-Este, and his wife, Sophie von Hohenberg, were shot dead in Sarajevo. When we received this terrible news, Mama was the first to suspect that our world would now be shaken. She remarked that she hoped there wouldn't be a war, but no one could have guessed how right she might be about her fears.

The assassination in Sarajevo was carried out by the nineteen-year-old student Gavrilo Princip, who belonged to the underground organization *Mlada Bosna*, *Young Bosnia*. This organization was anti-clerical, Serbian-nationalist in orientation and consisted of pupils and students who clearly represented revolutionary tendencies. It was founded in Mostar in 1893 and was associated with people from the later secret organization *Black Hand*, which planned assassinations from 1910 onwards. The members were predominantly Bosnian Serbs, but Croats and Bosniaks, also from Bosnia-Herzegovina, soon joined. The goals of these organizations were relatively simple to formulate - they wanted to strengthen Bosnian national consciousness, liberate Bosnia-Herzegovina from Austro-Hungarian rule by revolutionary means, end the union of the southern Slavic provinces of Austria-Hungary with Serbia and Montenegro, and dissolve the Ottoman *Sandzak Novi Pazar*, a district that included the southwest of Serbia, as well as the northeast of Montenegro and parts of Kosovo. By and large, they called for a united Yugoslavia. At the same time, however, the organizations also denounced social aspects such as the lack of education among the population, conservatism, the Jesuit school system in Austria-Hungary and they advocated equal rights for women. Some of their members were very talented writers, including the later writer and Nobel Prize winner Ivo Andrić.
The assassin Princip had wanted to fight in the Balkan War in 1912 to defend his homeland, but he was rejected as *unfit*. This led him to plan the assassination out of disappointment at being rejected by the military. Suffering from bone tuberculosis, he allowed himself to be arrested without resistance and immediately confessed to his crime. However, he regretted having killed Archduchess Sophie, as the couple left behind three children.

Princip could not be sentenced to death under Austrian law because he was not yet twenty years old, although the public prosecutor immediately demanded the death penalty. Instead, Princip was sentenced to twenty years of hard labor in the *Small Fortress of Theresienstadt*. Numerous members of his family were arrested, although many of them had known nothing about the crime.

In Theresienstadt, Princip was kept in solitary confinement, denied any visits and chained up for most of the day. In April 1918, he finally died of bone tuberculosis due to the poor prison conditions.

From my point of view, the punishment was very harsh, but quite justified, because he had robbed children of their parents, and even if it was about the heir to the throne of Austria-Hungary, the Archduke and his wife did not deserve such a death.

The aspirations for freedom of peoples, the rebellion against a monarchist rule was quite understandable, but it did not justify an assassination. But it made the *Old World* tremble and shook people.

Austria-Hungary had to act. On July twenty-third, 1914, Serbia was given an ultimatum limited to forty-eight hours. It demanded, among other things, that all actions and propaganda against the territorial integrity of the Austro-Hungarian government be suppressed immediately and that the assassination be investigated by Austro-Hungarian officials. This ultimatum was drafted in such a way that a sovereign state could not really accept it, as the actual aim of Austria-Hungary was now to render Serbia harmless through war. Count Leopold Berchtold, the Austro-Hungarian Foreign Minister, had drafted the ultimatum specifically so that the country would not be seen as threatening war, and therefore only threatened to break off diplomatic relations. Serbia complied with the deadline, but did not accept the ultimatum unconditionally. With Germany as an ally providing backing, Austria-Hungary declared war on Serbia on July twenty-eighth. The alliance obligations of the other great powers of Europe left them no choice but to enter the war. It was the beginning of the *First World War*.

Andrea's brother Tino had mixed feelings about the start of the war, as he thought it would be better for Greece to maintain a certain neutrality. First and foremost, as king he wanted to work for Greece's security and the prosperity of its people. A war should not become another burden for the population. In the early days of the war, Uncle Willy offered him the option of Greece fighting alongside Germany, but Tino feared that Germany could emerge from the war as the sole victor, as Uncle Willy was well prepared militarily. But then Greece would no longer have been neutral and would have been on the side of the Central Powers, which included Germany, Austria-Hungary, the Ottoman Empire and Bulgaria. In other words, the political

line with regard to the assassination in Sarajevo would also have been in line with Austria-Hungary. The Central Powers were opposed by the *Triple Entente*, an informal alliance between France, Great Britain and Russia.
When the war began, all parties still hoped that it would be over by the end of the year, at least that was the official line. And soldiers everywhere went to war rejoicing.
Kostantin's wife Sophie, as a German, seemed to side with her brother, Uncle Willy, but instead she was more pro-British like her father, due to her marriage to an English princess. Her mother, the Empress Friedrich, was still attached to her roots, even when she had been living in Germany for many years.
Tino did not want to jeopardize anything, as land had been gained in the Balkan wars. Prime Minister Venizelos was in favor of the *Entente*, as it had a very strong military Navy with England, which could be very helpful to Greece with its location on the Mediterranean. He was also firmly convinced that the German Kaiser was a warmonger and had only rearmed for the start of this war.
Constantine found himself in a certain predicament. On the one hand, he thought that the *Entente* might not support our country enough in the war, while on the other hand Germany could defeat and wipe us out.
My position was absolutely clear. I was loyal to Greece, although as a German princess I came from lower nobility, but I had also had great English influence on my life so far through Queen Victoria. It would soon be the same for me as for other nobles at that time, as I had relatives in different countries, but these became enemies during the war. My father was First Sea Lord, absolutely loyal to England and my parents and siblings lived mainly in England. My mother's cousin was the King of England and I had many friends and relatives in Windsor and Osborne, whom I had known since childhood. But I also had two aunts in Russia.
Aunt Irene was married to a brother of Uncle Willy. Uncle Heinrich was an admiral in the German Navy and, as he was an extremely successful sailor, he had made a name for himself at the annual regatta in Cowes and was in good contact with King George V of England. In December 1912 and July 1914, he had asked the King what England would do if Germany and Austria started a war against Russia. Uncle Willy was always known for only really reading what he *wanted to read*, i.e. what he liked. So Uncle Henry always gave him an embellished version of the King's words, which led the German Emperor to believe that England would assure Germany of its neutrality in such a case. Uncle Henry always told the story with a grin, as he believed that he had thus prevented a possible war. Uncle Willy's compulsion to arm his country for years and to wait for a war in which he could prove himself was

known everywhere.
I received the news from Germany that Uncle Ernie wanted to enlist in the war and was now in the German army.
My sisters-in-law were just as loyal to Greece as I was, even though Ellen was Russian by birth, Minnie was married to a Russian and George's wife Marie was French. It was no longer possible to speak my mind openly, I kept my private views on the opposing parties to myself and kept a neutral exterior, which would allow me to continue communicating with relatives, such as Aunt Onor. Mama and Papa could not do this because of Papa's position in the Royal Navy, which my mother regretted very much.
So Aunt Onor wrote me a letter in which she asked me to help her forward parcels that could guarantee a certain supply of special food for any German prisoners in need. I didn't refuse, but I promised her in a coded reply and hoped she would read it from my innocuous lines in which I told her about our quiet life on Corfu. My thoughts were always with her, because I had lived through two wars, felt for her and could imagine her worries.
We had to travel back to Athens shortly after this letter, as Andrea had to resume his military commitments. We had been on Corfu for four months, Dolla, Margarita and Cäcilie tanned from swimming in the water and playing on the beach. Tiny was developing beautifully and if it hadn't been for the war, our family life couldn't have been more harmonious.
My mother, Nona and Louise had traveled to Russia in the summer, where they first took a trip on the Volga to Yekaterinburg with Aunt Ella. Then they traveled on to St. Petersburg to visit Aunt Alix and her family. Papa had also planned to travel to Russia with Dickie in August. It was to be a semi-official diplomatic trip for him. England and Russia were about to conclude an alliance concerning their respective navies, as the Russian Navy had meanwhile recovered from its losses in the war with Japan and Uncle Nicky was in the process of modernizing and better equipping it. But this meant that Uncle Willy found himself in trouble in the Baltic Sea and the Turks in the Black Sea. Papa had already consulted Uncle Nicky and his foreign minister in writing and a solution could now be found, but the outbreak of war prevented the alliance and Papa's planned trip. My father telegraphed Mum that they should all return home immediately, while it was still possible. So they hastily packed their suitcases and Mum gave Aunt Alix her jewelry and jewels to keep for her until they met again, because my mother was afraid they might be confiscated on the trip. However, the return journey was not as easy as the journey there, as they first had to travel by train and steamer to Hapsal in Estonia and from there by ship to neutral Sweden. They could no longer use the money they had with them as payment, so they were forced to pay in gold, sacrificing some of the jewelry they still carried in small pouches attached to

lieutenant in the King's Royal Rifle Corps and was wounded by a shell fragment in Ypres in Belgium on October twenty-seventh. He died the same day. It was the first casualty of the war in our family and hit us all hard, as Leopold was only twenty-three years old.

But we were to be dealt another heavy blow, as my father had to resign from the Royal Navy as First Sea Lord on October twenty-ninth. He had been responsible for mobilizing the fleet before the start of the war and it was therefore well prepared for the outbreak of war. My father had always been very committed, had sacrificed himself for his work, his career, but the problem lay not in his duties, his performance, but in his opponent Winston Churchill and his German origins. As England was at war with Germany, the opinion soon prevailed, both in the Navy and publicly, that a German could not reliably command the British Navy or be in a position to represent its interests in an appropriate manner in good conscience.

The British press stirred up anti-German sentiment in the country and Lord Charles Beresford, an admiral, had enough influence to spread this sentiment in the Navy. Churchill, as First Lord of the Admiralty, increased this pressure on my father immensely.

They seized on every little detail of Papa's life to harm him, like our Heiligenberg Castle in Germany as a residence, my family's German servants. My poor father was even accused of spying for the German enemy. Papa had always been loyal to the English Navy and to England. For forty-six years this had been his purpose in life. Now, by his own admission, he felt like Jonas, forced overboard by the British government.

As early as 1912, when a new First Sea Lord had to be appointed, it was feared that a German was not really suitable for the post, and this was brought to the attention of Prime Minister H. H. Asquith, who was not happy with Papa's choice either. Although my father proved everyone wrong with his good work, Churchill, whom he regarded as a supporter, turned against him. This breach of trust hurt Papa all the more. Although he had been suffering from gout for some time, he had never missed a day's work and had given his all.

Churchill wanted to see Baron John Arbuthnot Fisher, who had been First Sea Lord from 1904 to 1910, reinstated to this post. Although he was now seventy-three years old, Fisher seemed to enjoy more prestige from Churchill's point of view and, as an Englishman, would be better able to stand up for the British Navy.

When the so-called *gentlemen's clubs* of the elite began to openly agitate against my father, he had to give in and tender his resignation. King George V opposed the resignation and did not want to see Fisher in my father's post, which he had worked hard to achieve. Papa was sympathetic, but he no longer felt physically or mentally able to continue his work under these conditions and the pressure. Politicians and members of the British Navy also publicly expressed their extreme dismay at Papa's decision. But my father showed dignity, asking Churchill to at least accept if King George offered to make him a member of the *Privy Council*. This so-called *Privy Council* is a political advisory body to the British monarchs. And the King promised him that he would be reinstated to his post immediately after the war.

My father no longer held a public post and could therefore consider himself a pensioner, guided by the hope of regaining his position after the war, as promised. He retired *to Kent House* on the Isle of Wight and began writing books about the British Navy. A three-volume work on military decorations would eventually become the standard work, which was at least a small success for my father.

My mother was, of course, beside herself. She was just as deeply disappointed in the people who had been trusted and considered friends and who were now turning against my father. To her, the king was a *buffoon* who couldn't really stand up for anyone.

My younger brother Dickie was in tears when he heard the news, because my father was his role model and now he said he had to do everything he could to clear Papa's name and restore his honor by pursuing his own career in the British Navy.

I thought it was terrible how someone whose lifeblood was in his work for the British Navy could be treated like that. Although my father devoted himself to writing, I think something was broken in him at the time that could not be repaired. Not even by putting him off by saying he would be back in his post later, which we all regarded as pure window-dressing. He was still formally a member of the Royal Navy, but only on paper.

On the second of November, Russia declared war on the Ottoman Empire. The Ottomans wanted to use the war to realize their expansionist aims, which were particularly focused on Central Asia and the Caucasus, but remained neutral for the time being, although they did speak of *armed neutrality*. The Ottoman Empire was not actually equipped for war, but for Austria-Hungary, Bulgaria and Germany, involvement meant that they could prevent maritime traffic between Russia and its allies.

On the fifth of November, England officially declared war and France joined a day later. Soon afterwards, a trench war broke out on *the Western Front* that was to last for years. The so-called Western Front stretched over seven hundred and fifty kilometers from the English Channel to the Swiss border, mainly affecting France and Belgium as well as a small German area of Alsace-Lorraine. In the north, the front was bordered by the North Sea on

Belgian territory, which was about sixty kilometers long.
My mother told me shortly afterwards that she had replaced her German maid Eugenie with Aunt Irene's English maid named Knight at her request. Perhaps she simply wanted to bring out the Britishness in her household again. But her German maid had relatives she wanted to be near. My mother fully understood this. However, none of these changes were due to any antipathy the ladies felt towards their employers as a result of the war.
I couldn't do that much in Greece. Most of the time I only heard about the plight of relatives and friends in writing. So I sold a dress made of fine Brussels lace to help Nona, who was working as a nurse in Rouen in Normandy, with the proceeds, because she had also been a great help to me during the war in the Balkans.
Uncle Franzjos and his wife Anna lived most of the time in the *Prinz-Emil-Schlösschen*, a small garden palace in Darmstadt-Bessungen. They had no children. When the war broke out, Uncle Ernie had asked them to leave Germany. Aunt Anna was a Montenegrin princess and Uncle Franzjos agreed. When Uncle Ernie offered him the chance to return a little later, Franzjos refused, as he felt the expulsion was an affront. The couple initially lived in Italy, as the country had declared itself neutral in the war. However, when Italy entered the war on the twenty-third of May 1915 on the side of England, Russia and France, the couple had to leave the country. They fled to neutral Switzerland and his uncle immersed himself in his beloved economic studies, but from then on they were constantly on the move from one exile to another. And as they were never particularly rich, they just got by. As Anna was extremely talented musically, she had been composing for a long time, but not under her real name, although she had some success with it and the couple lived off the sale of these compositions. Anna had even composed an opera in 1899 and received help from the famous Italian composer Pietro Mascagni when the couple were in Naples. In August 1916, the uncle was supposed to tell me that he was as good as broke, but I couldn't help him.
And Uncle Ernie, who actually detested the war just as much as Uncle Nicky, suffered from the situation of no longer being able to see his sisters in England and Russia and now having enemies in them, which he absolutely refused to accept. He was very musical, a nature-loving philosopher, an art enthusiast and had to join his soldiers at the front, although he told his mother how out of place he felt there. He admired the courage of the soldiers, their comradeship and their willingness to give their lives selflessly for their homeland, but he didn't share any of that. And the terrible things he had to see with his own eyes, such as the seriously injured and the dead, really affected him. Soon afterwards, he was suffering from depression because he didn't feel up to it all and missed his family, Aunt Onor and the boys too much.

On May 13, 1915, his banner as an *Extra Knight of the Garter*, the Order of the Garter, was removed from St. George's Chapel in London, as were those of Uncle Willy, Uncle Henry, Duke Carl Eduard of Saxe-Coburg and Gotha and other German noblemen. These banners had been awarded by Queen Victoria, but now during the war they were like memorials to the enemies of war. Uncle Ernie was not the only one who was more than saddened by this.
I felt sorry for some of my relatives, but there was nothing I could do for them. We couldn't visit each other anymore and that was very difficult, because we had always enjoyed the big family gatherings.
My mother always expressed her great regret in her letters, because she missed me, Andrea and her grandchildren terribly. As a fatalist, she was convinced that everything in life was predetermined, that you had a limited time on earth and that there was nothing you could do about it. From her point of view, it was because she had lost her little sister, little brother and mother so early, and also because of illnesses that simply took their loved ones with great severity. Now, in war, people had to die, nothing could be done about it and it was so pointless.
Mama was afraid for Georgie, who was actively serving in the British Navy, and for Dickie, who might yet have to do so the longer the war went on. She had to accept that fate could take Georgie from her at any time, but it was no comfort to her if he should fall for his country like Maurice. Papa's expulsion from the Navy and the worry for her sons weighed on her, yet she always tried to keep herself upright, especially for my father, so that he would not sink into his grief.
When it came to light that the Duke of Saxe-Coburg and Gotha was responsible for the banners being removed because he had sent his British medals and decorations back to England, the resentment among my relatives grew noticeably. Uncle Ernie had found out by chance. It had been a short-circuited action after England's declaration of war, a silent protest, but even King George V found it ridiculous, but complied with the advice of his cabinet. He saw the return of the pieces as a devaluation of England and they no longer had any connection with a once solemn bestowal by Queen Victoria.

As I said, we were still living carefree in Greece. Andrea had his military obligations, but for us the war was actually far away. Our family life was tranquil, everything went on as usual. We read the news in the newspapers and kept up to date with the war, but it didn't really affect us.

Of course, Dolla and Margarita in particular asked about their grandparents, their relatives, whom they all missed very much. I explained to them that we couldn't visit them at the Mamaent because of the war, and they wrote letters

As all the trains and ships were in military service, it would have been too dangerous to take the girls with me, but I wanted to be with my husband at least for a short time.
As there were mainly troops from England in Greece, I felt it was my duty to defend Constantine's attitude towards entering the war. So I asked the Earl of Granard for an interview. He was the secretary in the military service of the commander-in-chief of the British forces stationed in Salonika. I knew that my every word would be passed on to King George in England. I therefore assured the Earl that the King of Greece was in no way pro-German, but that he wanted to defend his country's interests in the best possible way and feared that by entering the war he would lose the territories he had conquered in the Balkan War. I pointed out that the King should turn to the Prime Minister, as was customary in a constitutional monarchy. Furthermore, in my view, the British ambassador Elliot Venizelos was also more inclined to Venizelos than the king and I made it clear how dangerous I considered the prime minister to be, as he was already almost more powerful than my brother-in-law. I wasn't trying to discredit Venizelos, but it was my opinion and that's how we all saw it in the royal family.

In the fall of that year, my brother Georgie had once again traveled to Russia by military means. He visited Aunt Alix and her family and he never told us whether he took this trip to perhaps ask for Tatyana's hand in marriage after all.
The Tsar's family had traveled to Romania in June 1914 to visit relatives there, where Crown Prince Carol and Olga were to be brought closer together. But my proud cousin protested against the marriage because she didn't like Carol and never wanted to leave Russia. My aunt and uncle had married for love themselves, so they accepted Olga's decision. But Carol soon traveled to Russia again herself and tried to win Olga over, but failed. He finally asked Marie to marry him, but as she was only sixteen years old at the time, Uncle Nicky refused. With the war, potential marriage candidates had become a distant memory. Many also refrained from courting my two cousins Olga and Tatyana because they knew about Alexei's illness. It was an open secret in the family. A wife who passed on haemophilia to an heir to the throne was not a good match.
Georgie never told us whether Uncle Nicky postponed a possible marriage until after the war or whether Tatjana refused to marry Georgie, which I doubted. Because they liked each other very much. Decisions are also *crucial* for the rest of your life, but nobody could have guessed what would happen in the years to come. My aunt and uncle would certainly have made different decisions if they could have seen into the future.

So Georgie met the Russian relatives, and when he said goodbye to them, he did not know that this was to be a farewell forever.
After his return to England, however, my brother began to court Nada de Torby more intensively when he didn't have to fulfill his military obligations in the Navy.

The Kingdom of Bulgaria entered the war on October 14th on the side of Austria-Hungary, Germany and the Ottoman Empire. Bulgaria was the strongest military power in the Balkans. The Entente had also wanted to win the country over to its side, but Bulgaria hoped to regain the lost Macedonia from Serbia with the help of the other powers. With Bulgaria, the Central Powers now controlled a contiguous territory stretching from the North Sea to the Red Sea. There were also exclaves in Cameroon and East Africa. Attempts were made to gain other states outside Europe as allies, such as Afghanistan and Abyssinia, but these failed. Many states remained neutral, like Greece.
Serbia, which was now being attacked by Bulgaria, was an ally of ours. Venizelos now insisted that Greece join the war, but Constantine made it clear that this was not a war in the Balkans that justified Greece's intervention as an ally, but a global war. England offered Constantine Cyprus, which they had annexed since 1914, in return for taking part in the war, but my brother-in-law continued to refuse.
Venizelos now had the Greek troops mobilized on his own authority, having already toyed for some time with the idea of stationing around one hundred and fifty thousand English and French soldiers in Salonika as a military force to help Serbia. Constantine had forbidden him to do so, as he saw this as an abuse of Greek territory. However, the prime minister took up this idea again and had the men landed in Salonika, also to ensure the defense of Serbia, which was not what the king wanted. My brother-in-law was so incensed by this unauthorized action that he removed Venizelos from office. At the same time, he publicly spoke out against the alliance with Serbia in this case.
Venizelos fled to Crete and Tino replaced him with Alexandros Zaimis, the son of a former Prime Minister of Greece, who had also been Minister of the Interior and Minister of Justice. But just one month later, Zaimis had to resign because his government did not receive a vote of confidence. Parliament still backed Venizelos.
And Constantine thought he had seen the last of this man, but Venizelos was not to be deterred. He began to set up a provisional government in Crete and waited like a spider in a web for his victim, my brother-in-law, to make a mistake, because he wanted to return to power at all costs.
Greece now found itself in a political crisis, which Tino tried to overcome

without giving up his neutrality.
I met a second time with the Earl of Granard to discuss with him at the Greek headquarters in Salonika that Constantine wanted to visit his troops officially to make his point. At our meeting I also raised the subject of the alliance with Serbia. I explained that the Serbs had not intervened two years ago when there had been a conflict between Greece and Bulgaria, which was fighting against Turkey. They had stayed out of it and so it was no longer possible to show any respect or loyalty to this country. The Earl was impressed by my political interest and listened patiently, promising to pass on my words to the King in England.
My husband knew about my verbal abuse and tolerated it because it was about his brother. He stood behind him and was just as shocked by Venizelo's influence and his ambitions for power.
Military camps had been set up around Salonika, fenced in with barbed wire and separated from each other by trenches. I wrote to Dickie saying how interesting I found it all, because fighting was predicted. And so we were expecting an attack. I quickly decided to stay in Thessaloniki so that my girls would have to celebrate Christmas without me in Athens, but I wrote to them about how important it was for me to be by their father's side.

Andrea and I on January 17, 1916 in Saloniki

In April 1916, the French Prime Minister Aristide Briand separated from his mistress Berthe Cerny and now Marie, George's wife, threw herself into a real affair with the Prime Minister, in which she was the driving force, as he wrote to her in a letter how much he regretted their affair, as he had once known George. This affair, which was to last until 1919, was not only a disgrace to the royal family. George became increasingly jealous as his pleasure-seeking wife lived out her love affair in public in Paris. There were also political consequences, as George tried to win over the Prime Minister to Constantine's view of Greek neutrality and was also able to convince him to send French forces to Salonika to defend Serbia against the Bulgarians. George and Marie were rarely in Greece. They only visited briefly in July 1915 and then returned to Paris as quickly as possible, although Marie made no secret of the fact that she longed for Aristide. But Briand was soon suspected of making his political decisions under Marie's influence.
The couple's two children were like strangers to us all, as they mostly lived in Paris. I had only seen little Peter briefly in 1912, when he was four years old. George also took the children to visit relatives in Denmark, but they never had much to do with their actual home.

We were still expecting an attack in Salonika, but nothing happened until May. There were rumors that Germany might be seeking a peace treaty, but it remained just a rumor.
At the beginning of July, a fire broke out in Tatoi, which was so devastating that it spread from the forest to the building. Eighteen people lost their lives in the fire, including Tino's wing adjutant. Tino and his wife were there at the time and managed to escape from the building, with Sophie running and running with little Katherine in her arms until they were finally caught up and calmed down.
It took forty-eight hours to extinguish the fire, but no cause was found. Tino was convinced that it was arson, deliberately committed by someone to harm him and his family. Of course, we all suspected who he had in mind, but even if Venizelos had been involved through henchmen, no one could be proven guilty.
Constantine decided to send Andrea to London and Paris in July 1916 so that he could make Greece's position in the war clear, on the one hand defending his brother's decision to remain neutral. Constantine also wanted him to dispel the rumors that Greece had a secret alliance with Germany and not with Bulgaria either. My brother-in-law made this diplomatic move independently of the Greek government. Andrea was happy to take on this task because he stood behind his brother.
He first traveled to London and had a conversation with King George V

forces on September 5, 1915. His ministers had strongly advised him not to do so, as his uncle, Grand Duke Nikolai Nikolayevich, was a strategist and militarist through and through. He had previously held this post, but conflicts had arisen between the two. Uncle Nicky was not born to be a commander, as my father pointed out, and this soon became apparent. There was one loss after another, the battles ended with thousands of dead Russian soldiers. The supply situation for both the troops and the people in the towns became increasingly catastrophic. The people soon suffered from hunger and the first protest marches against the government took place.
The uncle appointed General Michael Alexeyev as his new Chief of Staff, who was a militarist, but it can be said that Russia's position in the war was already shaky.
And to make matters worse, Aunt Alix was now interfering in the government through Rasputin, soon writing to her uncle about who he should appoint or dismiss because her friend had advised her to do so. So it was not only my mother-in-law who was soon of the opinion that the monk had to be removed once and for all and Aunt Alix freed from the clutches of this demon, as she put it. The vast majority of the Russian tsar's family shared this opinion.
So we were not only worried about Andrea's mother in faraway St. Petersburg, but also about Aunt Alix and her family. Revolutionaries, called Bolsheviks, came to power, there were strikes in the factories and soon the military also revolted because they no longer wanted to put up with the high casualty figures. The people demanded reforms, but Uncle Nicky spent most of his time at the military headquarters in Mogilev instead of in St. Petersburg, which was now called Petrograd, and only received reports on the situation from his ministers or his family.
But it was not only his position of power that was shaken. Things were also boiling in Greece.
The British ambassador Sir Francis Elliott approached Constantine once again and tried to persuade him to enter the war alongside England, France and Russia. Tino began to waver, but continued to insist on his neutrality. Elliott certainly saw Venizelos as a major threat to the king's position of power. But Tino remained stubborn. It could be said that he failed to recognize this danger.
Venizelos returned from Crete and installed a republican counter-government in Salonika in October 1916. British and French soldiers were still stationed there to put pressure on the Central Powers on their south-eastern front.
Constantine finally met with envoys from the French embassy in Athens, trying to reassure them that he never wanted to jeopardize the good relations with France, Russia and England and that he would avoid a war between the Entente and Greece at all costs. French reservists stormed into the garden of

the embassy during this meeting, shouting "*Long live the King*" and "*Down with France and England*". They fired shots from their revolvers, but then left the area again.
There were now two governments in Greece. On one side stood Constantine with the neutral government, on the other Venizelos with his republican government in Salonika. Rumors were spread by the republican government that Constantine had equipped Tatoi, which was in the process of being rebuilt, with troops, weapons and all sorts of defensive measures for fear of a civil war, in order to defend his castle against the revolting masses like a king in the Middle Ages. Of course, this was just a silly rumor. But we were all starting to get seriously worried now, and the first doubts about Constantine's perseverance began to arise in the royal family too.
When the protests in Athens increased, soldiers from the French and English ranks were sent into the city to maintain order as a kind of police force under the direction of England and France. This was a concession to Constantine, but he did not appreciate it. They wanted to avoid clashes between those loyal to the king and Venizelo's supporters, as they were now joined by Greek soldiers and other members of the military.
It was too late, my brother-in-law had lost all chances.

On November twenty-first, Emperor Franz Josef I of Austria-Hungary died at the age of eighty-six. His death marked the end of the era of an emperor in the Habsburg Empire, which was in the process of dissolving. He had not changed his will and had not named a successor, as his son, Crown Prince Rudolf, had taken his own life. The murder of Archduke Franz Ferdinand also ruled him out as a potential successor, so Archduke Charles, a son of one of the emperor's nephews, who was to reign as Emperor Charles I of Austria-Hungary for only two years, until 1918, was chosen.

My brother Georgie married Nada Torby at the Russian Embassy in London on November fifteenth, 1916, and I was very sorry that I could not attend the wedding. Mama wrote to tell me about the small celebration and I congratulated my brother and his wife by telegram. After the wedding they moved to *Lynden Manor*, also called *Bray*, near Holyport in Berkshire.

Georgie and Nada on their wedding day, 1916

My younger brother Dickie had already served on the battlecruiser *HMS Lion* in July, when the ship was involved in fighting, he was transferred to *HMS Queen Elizabeth* where he unfortunately broke his leg during his service. The healing process took a long time, and by the end of the year he had to take his final exams from his sickbed. He was very upset that he was no longer able to attend the battles as a result of the accident.

The young cadets were usually spared this, but in war this was not always possible when a ship was needed for defense. Dickie, however, felt it was his duty, since Papa was suspended from duty, to fight for him for England, so to speak. He was only fifteen years old, but restoring Papa's good name by being as dutiful as he once was was very important to him even then.

On the first of December, English and French warships bombarded Athens in order to take control of the city. Many shells came down on the palace like a deadly rain. The soldiers in the city started firing their guns, I even saw a large round machine gun, like the ones used on the battlefield, in the streets. I had just finished working at the needlework school when chaos broke out. People in the streets were running around in a wild panic, some of them fell to the ground after being hit, and when I heard that the palace was also under fire, I rushed home out of concern for my children. I ran through a hail of bullets, saw dead and injured people in the streets, the bullets whistled around me, but I ignored everything, I only had my children on my mind and luckily I didn't hear the people screaming, the shots. It was a Mamaent in which I thanked God for my disability. Nevertheless, I couldn't help but notice the people's faces widened in horror, the aggression in the soldiers' expressions. At the palace, I saw Sophie, who, like the others, was on her way down to the cellar. She already had my girls in tow and so I followed them downstairs. There I hugged my crying children, who pressed up against me. I looked into their fearful faces, those of the others, stroked my daughters' heads and reassured them that everything would be all right. But out of the corner of my eye, I also noticed Sophie holding little Katherine in her arms, cradling her gently. Her lips moved and I noticed how she verbally condemned her husband for letting it come to this.
When the unrest subsided and we were finally able to leave the cellar after many anxious hours, Margarita told me that she wished she couldn't hear like I could, because then she wouldn't have been so scared. I replied that it was a certain advantage not to be able to hear gunshots or bombs, but I still wanted nothing more than to hear the voices of my children, my husband, my parents and all my dear relatives. Margarita was already an adult for her eleven years and understood what I meant. But the situation, the war, was new for the children, because it wasn't like the wars in the Balkans. It wasn't happening far away from them, but right in front of their eyes.
During the war, of course, we heard about what was going on in the world and explained things to the older children, but there is a difference between just reading about it and experiencing it directly. And then there was the fact that Konstantin was not entirely innocent in all of this.
But I have to admit how much I felt like a Greek even in those days, I considered the country my home and would never have given a thought to leaving it.
The crisis worsened rapidly in Athens and spread to the whole country. There were supply shortages, people were soon suffering from hunger here too, they were exhausted by the general situation, hopeless.
Sophie and I were soon working in soup kitchens, mainly to save

malnourished children from starvation.
Deep in my heart, I wished for peace, especially for my own children, so that we could all find peace again.

On the seventeenth of December, Prince Felix Yusopov, who was married to Irina, the daughter of Uncle Nicky's sister Xenia, and Dmitri, Aunt Ella's foster son, murdered Rasputin together with two other men. Felix invited him to his palace on a pretext, where they initially wanted to poison him. But as he didn't eat any of the poisoned wine and cakes because he had been suffering from stomach problems since an assassination attempt by an offended admirer with a knife and could no longer eat or drink anything, they began to torture him with kicks and blows. When he was still alive, they shot him and threw his seemingly lifeless body into the ice-cold Neva. But the monk was tough, he was still alive, had only been unconscious, but was now drowning in the river.
My aunt Alix's world collapsed when she was informed that the body had been found. Her only support, the only person she felt could help her son, had been murdered by her own relatives. She insisted on an autopsy and had the monk buried near the palace in Tsarskoye Selo. It was only a small funeral, which she and her two eldest daughters attended, but she demanded that Felix and Dmitri be punished. They had both betrayed her and her family, even though Rasputin's influence on my aunt had become irrefutably too great.
Some relatives got together and signed a petition to ask for mercy for Dmitri. My mother-in-law Olga signed it too, because it was about her grandson. She had already fallen out of favor with Aunt Alix because she had spoken out against Rasputin in her presence and warned my aunt not to listen to this man so much all the time. But now Aunt Alix avoided any contact with her.
Uncle Nicky knew how much his wife wanted satisfaction for the murder; after all, it had been a brutal murder that had to be punished. So his uncle rejected the petition and banished Dmitri to the Persian front, which would later save his life.
Yusopov, Dmitri and their co-conspirators had publicly confessed to the murder, but this earned them support among the people of St. Petersburg. Aunt Alix had demanded the execution of the murderers, but the St. Petersburg authorities did not want to enforce this drastic measure, as the majority were behind the perpetrators. They were not arrested, but they were given a court hearing. Yusopov was banished by Uncle Nicky to the family estate in Rakitnoye near Kursk. The co-conspirators escaped unpunished and went into hiding.
My mother was relieved that her sister was no longer under Rasputin's spell, but she also feared that she could now fall into even deeper depression, which

would then be reflected in her psychosomatic illnesses. In other words, her suffering would worsen and there would be no help. And then there was the worry about Alexei.
And a political upheaval was looming in Russia, which made my mother fear for her sisters. Nevertheless, she hoped that everything would turn out well. Perhaps, she remarked in a letter, her sister Alix would come to her senses now that the monk was dead.
She was also very concerned about us in Greece and asked me to report news whenever I could, which I was happy to do.

Despite the war, we tried to offer our girls a halfway normal everyday life. At carnival, they were allowed to dress up for a small children's party and invite some of their friends' children and cousins. It was supposed to be a little distraction for them all.

Tiny, left, Dolla, Margarita in the middle and Cäcilie, right, February 1917

At the beginning of 1917, the situation in Russia escalated. More and more people took to the streets of Petrograd and protested in so-called hunger marches. There were also strikes by workers in the factories and demonstrations by Bolsheviks. Uncle Nicky rejected the demand of Duma President Mikhail Rodsyanko to appoint a government with a majority in the Duma. The bourgeois parties in the Duma then formed a committee under Prince Lvov, from which a provisional government was to emerge. At the same time, the convinced communist and revolutionary Vladimir Ilyich Lenin arrived in Petrograd from exile in Switzerland. He had already turned against the Russian monarchy once before and now saw his chance to overthrow Uncle Nicky.

My uncle remained at the military headquarters in Mogilev, he misjudged the explosive nature of the situation and had the Duma dissolved. He also issued an order to shoot at the rebels on March 11, which led to even more protests and unrest because of the casualties it caused, many of whom were civilians who had been demonstrating peacefully. The police and military were soon unable to maintain order. Instead, many mutinied, refused to obey orders and defected to the demonstrators. The regiments renounced my uncle's service and also joined the insurgents. We received more and more reports in the newspapers about the revolution that was now beginning in Russia.

Aunt Alix wrote to Mama about it, but she was not only very worried about her husband, but also about her children, who were all suffering from measles. Her loyal friend and lady-in-waiting Anna Wyrubowa was also ill.

When Uncle Nicky wanted to take the imperial train home to Petrograd, the train was diverted to Pskov, where the generals convinced my uncle that it was better to abdicate. This was a very difficult step for my poor uncle, who saw his power as God-given. He wanted to abdicate in Alexei's name, but his personal physician, Dr. Botkin, advised him not to do so because, in his opinion, Alexei would not live very long due to hemophilia. Moreover, this illness would not be beneficial for a tsar to be able to perform his duties adequately. So his uncle turned to his brother Mikhail, but he refused because he did not feel able to take control of the situation in Russia. Thus, on the fifteenth of March 1917, the three-hundred-year reign of the Romanovs came to an end with a single signature under the abdication document.

My uncle was allowed to return to his family in Petrograd, but from then on they were under house arrest in their own palace, controlled by the provisional government under Alexander Kerensky, a Russian politician. In Tsarskoye Selo, they were now guarded by the once loyal soldiers, who were gradually replaced. Nevertheless, Aunt Alix wrote to Mama that Uncle Nicky seemed somehow liberated, as if a great burden had been lifted from him, and at least they were all together. They very much hoped that my uncle would not be put on trial in Moscow, but that they would all be allowed to go into exile abroad or perhaps to the Crimea. Fortunately, Uncle Nicky had already sent his mother there before the revolution broke out. She was living in Ai-Todor Palace with her daughter Xenia, her daughter Olga, her husband and their young son. They were safe.

We were also worried about Aunt Ella. But she soon wrote to Mama in England that riots were also the order of the day in Moscow. Criminals who were insane or psychologically impaired had been freed from prisons and asylums and were now loitering in the streets, ambushing people, injuring or even killing them, which was never punished. Revolutionaries and armed soldiers drove around in trucks, seizing passers-by at random, forcing them to climb onto the open loading area and taking them away. No one ever saw these people again. They were at the mercy of the insurgents. The provisional government advised Aunt Ella to retreat to the interior of the Kremlin, i.e. to St. Nicholas Palace, but she refused. After all, she had not left the palace in order to flee back in through a revolution. It belonged to a life that she had discarded. Written communication was extremely difficult in Russia at that time, so although she learned of her brother-in-law's abdication, she accepted it as God-given, but she was not told about the house arrest of Aunt Alix's family until much later. Letters and telegrams did not reach her at first and those she did write were returned as undeliverable.

Even Uncle Willy sent a Swedish minister to tell her that her uncle wanted to take her in and offer her asylum in Germany, but Aunt Ella, who knew how in love he had once been with her, which she never reciprocated, refused this too. Life in her convent was to continue as it had been before the revolution and she did not want to leave Russia, where she had been living for thirty years, at any price. Her sisters in the convent also needed her and she would share any fate that awaited them without hesitation.

My aunt was very sure that nothing could happen to her because, although she was still a Romanov, she did so much good for the poor and the sick that, in her view, her good reputation was a protection for her. She did not play a political role, she thought, and she had also expressly spoken out against Rasputin's influence at court. So she threw herself back into her work. Shortly afterwards, when everything had to be boiled or boiled off due to a lack of hygiene and the poor supply situation, this precautionary measure even had to be applied to lettuce. But my aunt also looked after people who were suffering from typhoid fever as a result of this poor situation. Whether she caught it there or was infected through water or food could no longer be determined, but she fell ill herself. Nevertheless, she wanted to continue working and used a face mask, but when she became weaker and weaker, a doctor was called in. Even then, however, she insisted on lying on a thin mattress near the sick person for only a few hours a day. Her foster daughter Maria visited her and was surprised at how robust her aunt was. Even lying on the mattress with an elevated temperature, she refused a blanket, never remained quiet in her costume with shoes on her feet, but listened attentively to everyone who came, gave advice and instructions, and when she was told that she needed rest, she was very upset. Because she had made a promise to God to help, and no illness in the world could stop her.

Nevertheless, I had to think of my great-grandmother Queen Victoria, who had tried to prevent both Aunt Ella and Aunt Alix from marrying into Russia. If she had been able to witness all this, she would certainly have said that she had known. I am not referring to the abdication of the Tsar, because she would certainly never have expected such a thing. But that fate would not be kind to her two granddaughters there.

With the onset of the revolution in Russia, it also ceased to be a significant warring party. Tino had hoped for this country as an ally, because he was now in the process of reconsidering, as public opinion was increasingly turning against him.

He had wanted to protect Greece from war, which was a perfectly honorable goal, but now he had to admit defeat.

In April, the idea first arose that Tino and the entire Greek royal family should leave the country. Monsieur Ricaud, the head officer of the French secret service, expressed the suspicion that if just one more shot was fired in Athens, the palace would be bombed and destroyed.

On the second of May, Tino told Sir Francis Elliot for the first time that he was considering going into exile with his family in neutral Switzerland.

The newly formed government of Tinos under Zaimis, who was still officially in office, tried to maintain order. But at a meeting in the military club, which Andrea also attended, he was supposed to convey Tinos' wish that people should behave in a generally disciplined manner and continue to recognize the authorities. My brother-in-law feared that the military would revolt against the monarchy in the same way as in Russia. But Andrea didn't sense any negative vibes there, as he put it. It was more the case that many people could not understand the situation in Russia, that is, such an escalation of conditions.

Mama told me that the British government, and therefore the king, had offered Uncle Nicky and his family political asylum in England. However, this offer was withdrawn shortly afterwards, as the king feared for his popularity and that protests might arise among the people if someone like the tsar, who was notorious in England as a strict ruler and inveterate autocrat, was

accepted. George V believed that my uncle's presence would also lead to a revolution in England.
Mama was very angry about this, because Uncle Nicky was a cousin of the king and it was also about the children. But Aunt Alix would never have left Russia without her husband, as she wrote to my mother. Separation was out of the question for her, not even from the children. And like Uncle Nicky, she saw herself as Russian. Despite everything, leaving the country would have been wrong and cowardly for both of them. Perhaps, Mama thought, her uncle was under the illusion that he would be reinstated if the revolution failed and the new provisional government did not achieve what the people and the military had hoped for.

In June, the Greek Navy fired on French sailors who had landed their ship in Piraeus without orders. This prompted England and France to call on Tino to abdicate, even though he had not given the order to fire. The French occupied Salonika and Monsieur Jonnart, the chief commissioner of the French and English troops in the city, traveled to Athens. Jonnart presented Zaimis with an ultimatum demanding that Tino abdicate in favor of one of his sons. The prime minister drew up a document stating that one of his sons was to act as viceroy until the end of the war. Konstanin's son George was ruled out as a candidate, as he had received his military training as a young man in Berlin. The decision was therefore made in favor of Tino's second-born son Alexander. He was almost twenty-four years old and was sworn in as King Alexander I of Greece in the palace in Athens shortly afterwards. It was only a small formal swearing-in ceremony and no one from the royal family attended.
We had all taken refuge in the palace, but we were all very upset by Tino's abdication. Although this development had been foreseeable, nobody expected it. For Tino, the only satisfaction was that the monarchy continued to exist in Greece and that one of his sons was now leading it into what he hoped would be better times. It can also be said that my brother-in-law was simply not born to rule and was too fickle. But a king had to be able to make decisions and not hesitate. Especially not in a war, where it was important whose side you were fighting on or whose side you were on.
When the people of Athens realized that the king was leaving the country, public opinion of him changed in a positive direction. A large crowd of reservists gathered in front of the palace to prevent him from leaving. Some of the people were arrested. However, Tino and his family were unable to leave as planned on the night of June 12th.
It was not until five o'clock the next day afternoon that the gathering dispersed and Tino, Sophie, their children, the former Crown Prince George, Paul, Helene, Irene and little Katherine traveled to Tatoi with an entourage. There

were forty-five people in all who left the palace.
They had to wait two days in Tatoi before they were able to leave for Switzerland on June 14th from the port of Oropos on two Greek ships escorted by French destroyers.
Andrea and I were firmly convinced that we would be allowed to stay in Greece under his nephew's government. My husband remarked that he and his brothers were now playing the role of *bad uncles* after their nephew came to power. They still stood for the regency of Tinos, who in reality had achieved nothing for the country, had not been able to hold his own against Venizelos and had ultimately been dethroned by other powers. Under the young King Alexandros I, as he was known in Greece, everything was to improve. Alexander had only completed his training at the Athens military academy *Scholi Evilpidon* in 1912 and was involved in the Balkan wars as an artillery officer. It was hoped that he would bring a breath of fresh air to the regency. Nevertheless, the influence of my husband and his brothers had now dwindled. That's why the government more or less politely asked them all to leave the country until the crisis was over.

An antique picture postcard of the time

Andrea's brother George was in Denmark and France, and Nicholas had also fled to Switzerland with Ellen, the children and Christo shortly after Tino's departure.

My father wrote to us that he firmly believed we would be allowed to stay in Greece. Venizelos would become the country's new prime minister, he respected Andrea. But from my Papa's point of view, the new king would only be a side note in history, who could receive helpful advice from my husband as the only prince still present in the country. Andrea should prove himself as his advisor and thus make himself and Venizelos irreplaceable, so to speak. Papa also remarked that Andrea should have been made king, as he had shown great commitment in explaining Tinos' reluctance to go to war to the other powers, supporting them but remaining neutral in his own opinion. This was a very advantageous attitude for a king's advisor. Alexander had never been prepared for a regency, as he was the second-born son. Andrea was now able to prove himself here.
Papa was certainly right. He also held a post as advisor to the king, but this was really only pro forma. However, my father was distinguished by the fact that he had learned how to deal with authority during his service in the Navy. But these had mostly been long-established admirals and officers. In Greece, a young man had been put on the throne who had to learn his role as regent from scratch, and he was also used in war and in times of crisis.
I saw an appropriate role for my husband in Greece if he was given the opportunity. However, Andrea had already resigned his command in the army under pressure from the new government and even though we both never wanted to leave Greece, the pressure on us was increasing.
Alexander was assured that his uncles would only be taking a short break out of the country and that they could all return with their families after a month, but in reality the government was reluctant to allow this. They also feared that there might be people who could take advantage of Andreas' presence to harm us through rumors. So we had to give in.
We left Greece with our children and traveled to St. Moritz in Switzerland. As my husband had saved some money, we would be able to live quite well there, but the pain of separation was still deep in all of us. We had to leave our beloved Mon Repos, our home country. With the help of his wingman Metaxas, my husband had sold the cars that were exclusively in our possession shortly before our departure. Metaxas accompanied us into exile. Soon we were all living together in a hotel, which wasn't too expensive.
The Greek royal family was now scattered to the four winds. Andrea's sister Maria, the Greek Minnie, who had been more than unhappy in her marriage to the Russian Grand Duke Georgei, had been living separately from him outside Russia for a long time, which she justified with the health of her children Nina and Xenija. When the war broke out, she was in England and had no intention of returning to Russia. Her husband was serving as a general in the Russian army and all we knew was that the two girls were suffering

terribly from the separation from their father and were very homesick for Russia. But the revolution prevented them from returning once and for all. Maria lived in Harrogate in North Yorkshire, financed three military hospitals during the war and was also involved there. Contact with her was not particularly close.

Christo had already become engaged to the wealthy American Nonnie May Leeds, who was called *Nancy*, on Capri in 1914. But the whole thing had not become official, and the war had made marriage a distant prospect, but the two were very much in love with each other. Nancy's first marriage had only lasted four years, then she married the millionaire William Bateman Leeds, and when he died in 1908, she inherited his considerable fortune, took her then six-year-old son from this marriage and traveled through Europe. She belonged to high society in Biarritz and was a very good match for Christo. Nancy was ten years older than my brother-in-law, but no one in the family was bothered by this or her two previous marriages. Everyone just wanted to see Christo happy.

Andrea's mother Olga was still in Russia. After her relatives fled abroad in February during the revolution, she remained in the Pavlovsk Palace with a servant named Anna Egorova. They only lived on a little bread, which they dipped in oil, otherwise the supply situation was very poor. However, my mother-in-law still refused to leave Russia and believed that things would soon calm down once a new government had been installed and gained a foothold. She felt that the tsar's abdication was completely justified, as he was no longer in control of the situation. She didn't really understand why her son had lost his throne in favor of his son, because in her view Tino had behaved correctly, thinking only of his country. However, she did not go into any further detail in her letters. The only thing that shocked her and us was the fact that former supporters of Tino were now being arrested and executed in Greece.

Alexander, who was now the only member of the royal family in Athens, became more and more of a puppet as king. The once loyal servants in the palace were replaced by those who were loyal to Venizelos, including former enemies of Tinos, and Alexander was separated from people who were well-disposed towards him as the new king. They were transferred or arrested. Soon he was completely isolated. Even pictures of the royal family were removed from public buildings, destroyed in public and Alexander's ministers were not afraid to call him the *son of a traitor* in front of parliament.

On June twenty-sixth, Alexander Venizelos was forced into office as the new Prime Minister of Greece. So my Papa's hunch came true. And the rest of us never doubted that Venizelos would return to the position of power he had held under Tino until the latter deposed him. Zaimis, whom Tino appointed, had to announce his resignation. When Alexander, who was not favorably disposed towards his new prime minister, openly expressed this to him, Venizelos threatened him that he had the means and the power to have him deposed and install his brother Paul. However, as he was still a minor, they would have to work with a government councillor at his side. Poor Alexander reported this to the British ambassador and the Entente warned Venizelos to rein himself in, but the new king was soon a prisoner in his own palace. His instructions were ignored and Venizelos' spies followed everything he did at every turn, passing everything on immediately to the prime minister. At least he managed to get the British ambassador to allow him to read documents carefully before he had to sign them. He was also allowed to travel to the front to give moral support to the troops, but otherwise his position was that of a henchman. Andrea described it even more correctly by calling his nephew a servant of Venizelo.

King George in England was increasingly confronted with the growing anti-German sentiment among the people the longer the war went on, and so he decided to banish everything German from his name as well. The British royal family had to recreate itself for the sake of popularity and so he changed the surname of the royal family of *Saxe-Coburg and Gotha* to *Windsor* after Windsor Castle. This was publicly announced on July seventeenth, 1917 and was well received everywhere.
The King suggested to my father that he change his surname to *Battenhills*, but Papa felt this was a corruption of his rather noble-sounding surname and so, after careful consideration, he agreed to the Anglicized form *Mountbatten*. With this change of name, he also received the title of *first Marquess of Milford Haven*, making my mother a *Marchioness* and Louise a *Lady*. Papa also received the subordinate titles of *Earl of Medina* after the river on the Isle of Wight and *Viscout Alderney* after the Channel Island. In each case, the eldest son, in this case my brother Georgie, would now also hold the title of *Earl of Medina* as a courtesy title.
Like the King, my father renounced all German naming rights and titles. Even the Queen's German relatives from the House of Teck were now given British titles of nobility. Aunt Beatrice, who had previously called herself *Princess Henry of Battenberg* in public after her late husband, simply changed her name to *Her Royal Highness Princess Beatrice*. Her eldest son was given the title *Sir Alexander Mountbatten* with the addition of *Marquess of Carisbrooke*. Her youngest son was also given the title *Lord Leopold Mountbatten*. He received the hereditary title of *Marquess of Carisbrooke*, but was only allowed to use it if his elder brother died before him. As I was already married, I was the only one of our family to still have the name of a *born Princess*

of Battenberg. And Uncle Franzjos, who was not resident in England, also carried on the surname and title of Prince of Battenberg.

At the beginning of August, Aunt Alix and her family had to leave Tsarskoye Selo because they were allegedly afraid for their safety. As my aunt told us, she had initially hoped that they would all be allowed to travel to the Crimea, where it was warm and the climate was good for her and her son, but they only found out on their departure that they were going to Tobolsk in Siberia. On the twelfth of August, they were accommodated in the house of the former governor of the town. News was slow to reach us, mostly to Mama, whose address had remained the same. She then passed the news on to me. It was hard for my Aunt Alix to have to leave her home, but she was reunited with her family, there had been no trial against Uncle Nicky and so she tried to accept her fate. They were now only Romanov citizens, no longer imperial highnesses, but some servants were allowed to travel with them and they were so loyal to them that they did not hesitate to accompany the family, like the French teacher Pierre Gillard. Although they were not allowed to live in the same house, they lived opposite and were allowed to visit the family. The soldiers were still quite friendly, life was cramped, but they made themselves at home. There were a few animals such as chickens and turkeys that you could look after, Uncle Nicky chopped wood or worked in the garden, which you were allowed to enter at certain times and where there was also a swing for the children that the soldiers had set up. You had to limit yourself, but Uncle Nicky described it as quite a pleasant life, because he always loved physical activity and was literally absorbed in chopping wood for the winter or teaching his children geography.
Tobolsk was a long way from Petrograd. The people were of course aware of the Tsar's abdication, but when the family was allowed to visit the local public church, many still fell to their knees. As the guards soon became uncomfortable with this, they stopped these church visits and services were only held in the house.
Mama was still very worried because she didn't think this was the end of the road for her sister and she hadn't heard from Aunt Ella in Moscow.
I wanted to finally see my mother again, as well as my father, and thought long and hard about whether I could ask for permission to visit them on the Isle of Wight. Christo had been refused permission to enter England by the Secretary of the British Foreign Office because Tino's brothers were considered supporters of his neutrality in the war. No Greek prince should be given permission to enter the country. However, this did not apply to me and King George personally wrote to me to allow me to visit my parents.
So I traveled from St. Moritz to Paris, where I met Andrea's brother George.

I didn't want to confront him about his wife's affair. George enjoyed very good diplomatic contacts and saw his role during Tino's reign as an unofficial Greek ambassador. I didn't meet his wife or children. Nor was he particularly positive about Alexander's reign. He regarded him, as we all did, as a mere puppet that Venizelos could order around at will.

I had booked into the *Hotel Lotti*, where I met Papa shortly afterwards, who had come for me to accompany me on the trip to the Isle of Wight. He was very sorry that the girls weren't with me, but in these times and after what we had been through, they needed to get some rest in Switzerland.

On the fifth of September, we took the boat via Southampton to the Isle of Wight. My parents felt at home in Kent House, a gray stone building that belonged to my mother's Aunt Louise. She had gladly left it to them. It was situated between Osborne and the town of Cowes, where the annual regatta always took place.

I hadn't seen my parents since the beginning of the war. I had my father show me the work he was doing on his books about the orders of the English Navy. In addition to his writing, he was also treasurer of a branch of the English Red Cross on the Isle of Wight. Mama spent her days working in the rather generous garden, which in good weather could take many hours a day, as Papa explained to me, or doing charity work. In his opinion, she took on too much, but it also distracted her from the many thoughts she had about all the family members. She was particularly worried about the fate of her sisters in Russia and the uncertainty of what would become of them. As news or even letters rarely came through, Mum brooded day and night, waiting for some small piece of news. Because she just had to be sure that they were all right. Of course, she was also very sad about the fact that the girls hadn't come with us. So I had to tell her everything, how big they had grown, what they liked and disliked, whether they were good pupils and much more. Just the things that interest a grandmother.

No worry or burden in the world could stop my mother from talking. She was still, as they say in English, *talkative*. In other words, extremely talkative.

My parents were both in excellent health, but my mother had become thin, her hair slightly graying, only her face hadn't changed. When I remarked on this to her, she just said that I looked pretty good, that Switzerland and the distance from Greece seemed to take the edge off my nerves, but that I looked like I had a slight anemia and should have it checked soon because I was so pale.

I hadn't meant to offend her, but she didn't take it that way either. She was almost fifty-four years old and my father was sixty-three. She said that signs of age were inevitable.

My parents in 1917 in front of Kent House on the Isle of Wight

The only thing that really annoyed my mother was the fact that they had to change their surname at the king's behest. It was true that they now also had a nice title, but even if she could understand the king's basic idea, you don't just change a German Schmidt to Smith like that. She told me that she had written to Nona that her old friends would no longer be visiting her, but a pair of crumpled English aristocrats whose good names had been changed. The war had brought so many changes, she remarked, it had become a world that was always upside down, an eternal back and forth that she no longer really wanted to follow. But she had never expected the change of name to bother her so much. And Uncle Franzjos and Aunt Anna were still allowed to be called Battenberg because they didn't live in England.

Mama also had to tell me that Nada was pregnant. The baby was due in December and she was really looking forward to having another grandchild. Unfortunately, I didn't get the chance to see Georgie and his wife, and I also missed Dickie very much. But I was only planning to stay with my parents for ten days.
Louise came from Rouen to the Isle of Wight for a few days. My mother had already asked me to have a positive influence on my sister regarding the problem with her lover Shakespeare. When Louise and I went to London for two days, I had the opportunity to meet Alexander Stuart-Hill in person. I found him very eccentric, but also very friendly. But even though he was a real charmer towards my sister, there was something off-putting about his character. Maybe you could say I felt how much he liked Louise, and there was certainly some love involved, but more from her side than from his. Because to me, he seemed more attracted to men than women. But I didn't say it openly to her, because she had become so exuberant, so strong in character through her work at the hospital. It was extremely difficult to express any doubt, as Louise had also waited two years to confess to my parents that she saw the young man as a suitable husband and wanted to marry him. And he certainly had a good future ahead of him as an artist, because he was very talented. But it wasn't just me and my parents who were worried about this, because the life of an artist was also very unsteady for the most part.
Louise and Alexander informed me that they had secretly got engaged and would tell Mama and Papa gently, but wanted to wait until the war was over before getting married. That's why they didn't announce the engagement publicly. At the time, only Georgie, Nona, Dickie and I knew about it. But I knew how my parents would react. It wouldn't suit them if you wanted to dress it up in words like that.
At times, Alexander even seemed a little too affected to me, exaggerated in his compliments towards my sister, for whom the sky was literally full of violins.
I wrote this news to Aunt Onor straight away so that she was in the picture. And I spoke to Louise, trying to be gentle, she was open to my objections, but it was her life.
My father had even offered to take Louise on a short trip to the West Indies, to America and Canada. On this voyage, which he was planning for the winter, she would get some distance from Alexander and my father also wanted to show her some of the places he had been to as a young sea cadet. My father's invitation sounded generous to my sister, she confirmed this to me several times, but it would sadden her too much to be separated from her Shakespeare for so long.
He had been at Kent House from the twenty-seventh to the thirty-first of July

to get to know our parents better, Louise reported, but she had only hinted at an engagement with him, quickly adding that they both had to save up enough money for a wedding first. This statement had made my parents even less positive.

Louise insisted that she had waited her whole life for this man, he shared many of her views, including on marriage, and it was her unconditional desire to become his wife. She didn't base it solely on her deep love for him, as she had seen too many marriages fail because of this often confusing fact. In a marriage, everyday life would return at some point, but she knew that both of them would master it. She supported his art and was enthusiastic about it. In their marriage, she would also be his support, just as Mama had always been for Papa.

Alexander was financially dependent on his father, and while he was still alive, marriage was out of the question under these circumstances, as Louise wanted to be independent. But shortly before she came to England from Rouen, her father had died. During his lifetime, she suddenly explained, Alexander had had to support himself by selling his paintings and had received no money from him. She contradicted herself.

Now he had about four hundred pounds a year at his disposal. They would be able to get by on that, because everyone predicted that he would have a great career as a painter. The sale of the paintings would secure their future together. Before the war, he had even saved a thousand pounds, exhibited in small galleries and in the fall of 1914 he was supposed to organize a larger exhibition with his works, for which he drew them in Italy. But the outbreak of war had prevented the exhibition. We believed Louise, but the doubts about her choice remained.

We finally had the opportunity to visit Georgie and Nada in Edinburgh, Scotland. So Louise and I went there, we stayed for five days and I got to know my sister-in-law for the first time. She was very nice, polite, tactful and a real beauty. Nada spoke very highly of my parents, which was mutual. My brother and she were very excited about their first child. She was undoubtedly a good match, as she received two thousand pounds a year from her father, extra money for travel, the purchase of cars and jewelry. But she also had a not exactly small sum to fall back on, as her father had already set aside and saved money for each of his children when they were born. Her older sister Anastasia, who was called *Zia*, had recently married one of the richest bachelors in England. Sir Harold Wernher had become wealthy through the acquisition of some profitable mines in South Africa and he owned a wonderful estate called *Luton Hoo* in Bedfordshire. The couple lived there in splendor.

But for my brother, who was aiming for a brilliant career in the British Navy himself, it wasn't Nada's money or that of her family that counted. He was

overjoyed with his beautiful and educated wife.
After Scotland, I visited Uncle Bertie's widow Aunt Alix in Sandringham. She was of course also very worried about her sister, Uncle Nicky's mother, as well as the other relatives in Russia. From my point of view she was still a beauty, but she was going deaf, and she suffered terribly from the worry, even remarking that she was afraid she would go mad over it. It was obvious how Aunt Alix was suffering and she would certainly never get over it if anything happened to her sister, as well as the rest of the family. I was almost too sorry to leave her again, but she still had her daughter Toria, who always stood by her side.
I traveled on to Cambridge to visit Nona and her husband Dick. As she was also very involved in charity work, I gave her some money to support her work, which she was very happy about. She and her husband were also very happy together. It was nice for me to see our faithful soul like this.
I wasn't back in Switzerland until October. I had been on the road for eight weeks, which was also due to the fact that traveling was not so easy in wartime. So I was correspondingly exhausted afterwards.

Unfortunately, my trip had a diplomatic aftermath. Rumor had it that I had met with the king in England and that after a long conversation with me he had agreed to support the reinstatement of Tino as king. The British Consul General in Zurich had allegedly received this highly explosive information from an important supporter of Venizelo. As I had not met the king in England, but only his mother, Aunt Alexandra, she must have mentioned something, as she had been very outraged by the removal of her nephew. In our conversation, however, we had actually talked more about our Russian relatives and it would never have occurred to me to openly express my opinion about Tino's dismissal to my aunt. In these times, it was best to keep your true opinion to yourself, and your aunt was more concerned about her sister in Russia and also about Aunt Alix and her family. We almost only talked about that. Apart from that, she asked about my children, Mama and Papa - those things that relatives exchange when they see each other again after a long time.
The rumors had been started and reached the British Foreign Office. Espionage was the order of the day, and every little thoughtless utterance had its way.
The King's private secretary, Lord Stamfordham, publicly stated that there had never been a meeting between me and the King. He also refuted any attempts by the King to restore Tino to the throne in Greece.
But we had other things to worry about than these silly rumors, because on the seventh of November 1917, the *October Revolution took* place in Russia.

According to the Julian calendar, which still prevailed there, it was October twenty-fifth. The Bolsheviks, led by Lenin, stormed buildings, vandalized them, arbitrarily arrested people and overthrew the provisional government by storming the Winter Palace where it was based. Just a few days later, revolutionaries also stormed the Pavlovsk Palace. My mother-in-law was now literally trapped here. While they looted, ransacked and even stole private belongings, she was not physically attacked, but verbally. She was allowed to stay in the palace, but was subjected to constant harassment by the Bolsheviks, who simply came in whenever it suited them, insulted her and damaged objects. My mother-in-law now realized that it was better to leave Russia. But no help was possible from Greece for the time being, as everything was in upheaval there too. So we tried to ask various embassies from our side, such as those of England and Germany, who could help her get out of Russia, which was very difficult in wartime. My mother-in-law had to stay there for better or worse and we hoped that she would not be harmed. The Bolsheviks didn't want to let her leave for the time being either. We assumed that they saw her as a bargaining chip, but that was pure speculation.

Mama wrote to me in November that she had received a letter from Aunt Alix in Tobolsk. She thanked her for the congratulations on her birthday on June sixth, which had reached her in a roundabout way. Some mail was probably sent to them after a very long delay, but Aunt Alix remarked that it was difficult to write to her or the other members of the family as she was not sure she would receive this mail. Otherwise, her letter was rather formal. She only hinted at how emotionally stressful the whole situation was for her and that Olga was receiving arsenic injections because she was suffering a lot. My aunt Alix and her eldest daughter had always been very similar in their melancholy and capacity for suffering. Olga, like my aunt, had also not been able to work as a nurse for long because it was too much of a strain on her. Even though Aunt Alix was worried about her husband, she noticed that he struggled with the overall situation in Russia, but had come to terms with his fate of no longer being Tsar rather more than she had.

It was to be the only news of the family that ever reached my mother after the October Revolution.

Shortly afterwards, however, Mama was summoned to London, where a lady she did not know arrived from Russia and sent her news of Ella. This lady, obviously from the aristocracy, did not want to give her name, was on her way to exile in France and preferred anonymity because of her escape from Russia. She told Mama that Aunt Ella was doing well, that she was still working at the convent, but was very sad about what would become of her homeland. With all the chaos and anarchy around her, she saw the old world crumbling and still didn't want to leave the country. She refused all offers to get

her out of there. She thought she was safe and was still firmly convinced that she would be left alone because of her work.
And the rumors about my trip to England took on more and more bizarre forms. Lord Granville, who was in Athens, informed us that the Greek Minister of Foreign Affairs, Nikolaos Politis, had received a delegation who assured him that it would not be long before Tino would be reinstated as king. With the exception of France, all the other powers viewed this development with great concern and, on my return to Switzerland, I would have publicly announced everywhere that the English king was behind the whole thing. It would also be his express wish to see Tino back on the throne and Venizelos deposed. Granville dismissed it as rumors that he didn't believe, and objected that Politis also knew that these rumors were basically null and void. But they had become public knowledge. Andrea didn't blame me for my trip to England, and neither did the other relatives. Because everyone knew the real reason. I had only wanted to visit my parents. Everything else had just happened, but there was never any political motivation behind it and I knew how explosive it was in these times. Besides, I would never have interfered and Andrea described everything as pure harassment to further damage the royal family. We were already deprived of our home, sitting in our exile and didn't know how much longer it would last. My husband became increasingly depressed as he felt condemned to inactivity. And Tino was just a shadow of his former self. He lived apathetically into each new day or thought about how he could take action against Venizelos, and the doctors found that he drank and smoked too much. He also continued his affair with the Countess of Ostheim and his poor wife Sophie now not only suffered from the fact that her husband was no longer king and they had to live in exile, but he also took refuge in his grief in the arms of the other woman, showing himself in public with her. For the children, it was a reason to turn away from their father and stick by their mother, because they too had to live with the humiliation.
I never encouraged my husband to talk to his brother about it because it wasn't my place to interfere. But Andrea probably didn't see any way of having a positive influence on his brother either. And he was struggling with himself and fate. So I was also busy being a support to my own husband so that he didn't slip into the same apathy as his brother.
There was at least one small ray of hope when Mama wrote to tell me that Nada had given birth to a baby daughter on the sixteenth of December. Georgie had insisted on naming the little one after our cousin and so the girl was called Lady Tatjana Elizabeth Mountbatten. She was also the first Mountbatten *to be born.*

All the upheaval and worries left their mark on me. I tried to hold myself up, to be strong for my family, but I often found it very difficult. I started reading a lot to find distraction. A few years ago, I had already started to take an interest in things beyond our perception. In 1912, Christo and I had done some séances. It was called *automatic writing*, a kind of contact with a spirituality that then guides the hand on the paper. I was also no stranger to glass moving. I didn't see anything wrong with it, because I had always believed that there were things outside our normal world that could influence people. There was so much energy in a person, it couldn't just disappear after death, and I firmly believed in the souls that still walked the earth. But a belief in the occult and the spiritual was nothing special at that time. However, it was more *fashionable* at the turn of the century to make contact with spirits. Even my aunt Alix had not been averse to it, ever since a fortune teller in London once prophesied to her as a young girl that she would one day be one of the most powerful women in the world, but would fall very low.

I came across a book by Édouard Schuré by chance. It was called *Les Grands Initiés*, *The Great Initiates*, and I bought it in a store in St. Moritz in 1917. The author was a French writer and theosophist. The book was first published in 1889, in which the author attempted to present an esoteric secret teaching behind various philosophies and religions in human history. He had also written dramas, novels and philosophical treatises, but this book was the best known. However, it was more philosophical than doctrinal. But I always enjoyed questioning things rather than taking them for granted.
Schuré was a friend of Richard Wagner, as he was very moved by his music, and he was also acquainted with Friedrich Nietzsche. It was through him that I came across Nietzsche, as well as the Russian occultist Helena Petrovna Blavatsky. Unfortunately, she had already died in 1891, but her works were still very popular among interested people, as she had studied various forms of occultism on numerous trips around the world, such as the *voodoo cult* in New Orleans in the USA.
Schuré impressed me very much. In *The Great Initiates*, he took up the old esoteric idea of the transmission of original wisdom by initiates. In his work, he dealt with the lives and teachings of Jesus, Rama, Krishna, Hermes, Moses, Orpheus, Pythagoras and Plato, in whom he saw the true initiates. Behind the philosophies and religions they founded, he suspected a kind of continuously handed-down secret teaching. The difference to older ideas of this theory was that the author transferred the beginning of the chain of tradition from Persia to India, i.e. to Rama. Blavatsky had also shared this view in her works. According to Schuré, the wise initiates guided the history of mankind. Furthermore, he demanded evidence for the religions, the lives of the initiates, because otherwise, according to him, no religion would be worth anything in

itself. Religion appealed to people's hearts, science to their minds. In his view, however, the two were not in harmony. I soon tried to delve deeper into this subject, read books about the various religions and tried to understand them. When I told my mother about it, she said it would only confuse me and that I shouldn't let the supernatural in particular get to me because it could have a very negative effect on a person's spirit. It's too easy to get caught up in spirits that you call up and can't get rid of. She was very skeptical as to whether my studies would be positive for me, because she herself was very down-to-earth and believed in fate, but also in God. She wasn't interested in anything else. Especially not occultism.
Andrea accepted it because he saw it as a pure distraction for me and I didn't let him in on the things that were on my mind after reading. However, I shared them with Christo, who was very interested, but unfortunately lacked the necessary intellect to get to grips with them.

I bought a book by Rudolf Steiner, the esotericist, about Christianity as a mystical fact and the mysteries of antiquity, which also fascinated me very much.
Christo had met an American woman who conducted spiritual sessions. I only heard about it and didn't take part in her sessions, because I learned that this lady was probably already in the process of no longer being able to free herself from the world she was immersed in. It was only shortly afterwards that she could no longer get rid of the spirits. Christo told me that she had been admitted to a sanatorium because she had gone mad.
I was already involved in these things, but I also saw it as a mere pastime because there was so little to do in exile. Sure, I had my girls, took care of their education, organized teachers for them so that they could continue to receive a good education, but otherwise life consisted more of idleness.
So for myself, I felt it was okay to contact the other world when I had to make a difficult decision, and I continued to practice automatic writing whenever I was unsure. And it's fair to say that I was a very superstitious person. That's why I also practiced card reading during this time, from which I drew strength and hoped for help. I delved deeper into the matter, but didn't see myself getting caught up in it. It was a difficult time for everyone, the war, the social upheavals. Everyone tried to deal with it in their own way. But I did these things on my own, never tried to convince my husband or children to join me and share them. Christo was the only one I could talk to about it and who understood me because he believed in the spiritual as much as I did.

In April 1918, Aunt Ella was arrested in her convent in Moscow by the new Soviet secret police, the *Cheka*, at Lenin's behest. Her former chambermaid, who also lived and worked with her as a sister in the convent, Varvara Alexeyevna Yakovleva, who was called Sister Barbara, was allowed to accompany her. The faithful soul did not want to leave her aunt alone.

When a separate peace was concluded between the newly formed Soviet Union and Germany in Brest-Litovsk on March third, the government had offered Ella to leave the country, and Uncle Willy twice sent his ambassador Count Mirbach to see her at the Convention to persuade her after all. The Emperor's offer was welcome to the government, but as Aunt Ella refused, they could no longer tolerate her presence in Moscow. She was still a Romanov, she stood for the old world, the old days, she was the focus of the so-called *White Army*, the tsarist loyalists who were fighting the Bolsheviks, and everything that stood for the former monarchy had to be eliminated.

It was the twenty-seventh of April when Aunt Ella was arrested and placed under arrest. She was given half an hour to pack up her things. *Varvi*, as she called Sister Barbara, and also Sister Catherine Yanisheva, asked to accompany her, although no one knew what awaited all three of them. The patients, orphans and other sisters cried when Ella said goodbye to them, and no one can guess what she was feeling at that Mamaent.

They were taken to a convent in Perm. However, it was decided that they should not stay there and they were taken to Ekaterinburg, where they were housed in the Novotikhvinsky Convent. Three of Konstantin Konstantinovich's sons, Grand Princes Ioann, Konstantin and Igor, Grand Prince Sergei Mikhailovich, the brother-in-law of Grand Duchess Xenia, Uncle Nicky's eldest sister, and Prince Valdimir Pavlovich Paley, a son from the second marriage of Grand Prince Paul, the father of Ella's foster daughter Maria, were already there. They were all under arrest there, just like Aunt Ella.

She must have been doing relatively well there, because my aunt was able to send an Easter package to her sister and her family with coffee, eggs and chocolate.

Aunt Alix, Uncle Nicky and my cousin Marie had already arrived in Ekaterinburg on April thirtieth. They were now living in the same house of the factory owner Ipatiev that Mama had passed on her journey in 1914.

As Alexei had been injured again in Tobolsk by the high-spirited ride down the stairs on a sledge and had to recover from a severe attack of hemophilia, Uncle Nicky and Aunt Alix decided to take Marie with them and leave the other daughters with their sick brother until they should follow them after his recovery. My Aunt Alix had heard about her sister's arrest in Moscow from the newspaper and was very sorry, but was surprised that they had all been banished to the same province. Aunt Ella had not known where her sister was, she had assumed she was in Tobolsk. However, her parcel had been forwarded as it had been addressed to Aunt Alix. She received a thank-you letter

from Marie with the address of the Iaptiev House in Yekaterinburg. It must have been all the more painful for both sisters that they were so close to each other and yet so far away. They were not allowed to visit or meet each other. On the twenty-third of May, Uncle Nicky, Aunt Alix and their children were all reunited in Ekaterinburg, but they had been separated from almost all their servants, such as the children's French teacher Pierre Gilliard. They were left with Dr. Botkin, the personal physician, Trupp, Uncle Nicky's valet, and the maid Demidova. All the others were no longer allowed to see the family and were themselves under arrest. It was probably hoped that they could reveal intimate details of the tsar's family life during interrogations, which could then be used to harm my aunt and uncle even more. But they had already sunk too low.
As the government had now gathered a large number of Romanovs in one place, to put it succinctly, it was decided that it would be better to break up this concentration before the *White Army* could attempt to liberate them. So the prisoners around Aunt Ella had to pack their things on the twentieth of May. Now they were taken to Alapajevsk, north-east of Yekaterinburg, deeper into the Urals. They were accommodated in a small school, the so-called *Napolnaya School*, which translated meant *school in the field* and was located outside the city. Aunt Ella soon began planting vegetables such as cabbage and lettuce, making a cross over the plants every time she watered them. Otherwise, she passed the time with embroidery and other handicrafts. It must have been quite a relaxed life under the given conditions.
Grand Duke Ioann Konstantinovich was married to Princess Helen of Serbia, who had a special status because, although she was married to a Romanov, she was protected by her foreign citizenship. She had been arrested with her husband and followed him into exile, but in Alapajevsk she and Ioann decided that if she was offered the opportunity to leave, she would take it, as she had her two young children in the care of her mother-in law, who had fled to Norway. Helen took the opportunity and was allowed to travel to her children after several interrogations and a short detention in Perm prison and then in the Kremlin. She developed psychoneurosis as a result of the torturous conditions in prison. But by leaving the country, she was able to give us some information about how Aunt Ella was doing.
Shortly afterwards, my aunt was separated from the two sisters and taken back to Yekaterinburg. Two of the Grand Duke's servants also had to leave there. The two sisters were offered their freedom, but Vivi wanted to return to Aunt Ella and asked the Cheka to let her travel back. She was informed that she would then have to share whatever fate awaited my aunt. But Vivi had been faithful to her all these years and would not be dissuaded. So she traveled back to Alapajevsk.

My uncle Nicky believed his brother Mikhail and his wife Natlya, called *Natasha*, were safe because they lived unmolested on their estate in Gatchina even after his abdication. Their seven-year-old son Georgei and Nicholas Johnson, Mikhail's secretary, were with them. But on August twenty-first, 1917, they were placed under arrest on the estate. Mikhail probably sensed the imminent danger from the new rulers and drew up a document in which he had the Bolsheviks confirm that nothing would happen to him and his family. Although he was assured of this, they were nevertheless all arrested and taken to Perm in the Urals. They were put up in a hotel, they were closely guarded and Mikhail asked his wife to leave with their son when she was offered the chance. Natasha was able to flee to England with their son, but Mikhail and his secretary were arrested by armed men on the night of June 12th to 13th, driven into the forest in a carriage and shot there. Their bodies were burned. At first, the news spread that they had both been able to escape, but no one really believed this. For the Bolsheviks, the only reason for the murder was the fact that Admiral Kolchak was nearby with the *White Army*, the tsarist loyalists, who wanted to overthrow the Bolsheviks and could have freed Mikhail and Johnson.

But my uncle Nicky certainly didn't find out about his brother's death, because he and his family were already completely cut off from outside news in the summer of 1918.

The events in Russia now came thick and fast. On the night of the sixteenth to seventeenth of July 1918, Uncle Nicky, his family and the servants were taken to the cellar of the Ipatiev house under the pretext that there were riots in the town, where they were all shot. Their bodies were transported to a nearby forest and buried in an unknown location.

And after that fateful night, on July seventeenth, the local Cheka told the prisoners around Aunt Ella in Alapajevsk that an attack by the *White Guard* was imminent and that they all wanted to be freed, so they all had to be housed outside the city in a forest until the attack was over. They were urged to leave quickly, although Aunt Ella was cooking dinner and asked to be allowed to eat at least then, which they had to do in a hurry. They were supposedly given time after all, so they could go to sleep. Then they were woken up at night, told to get dressed, blindfolded and their hands tied. They were taken in carriages to a forest far outside the city.

At an old mine shaft that had filled up with water, they all got out, took off their bandages and shackles and led them to the shaft at gunpoint. Aunt Ella was the first to jump. She asked to be allowed to say a short prayer, but afterwards she didn't want to jump in without pulling her cape over her head so that she wouldn't have to see the dark depths. Her last words were: *Lord, forgive them, for they know not what they do.* Then she jumped into the shaft,

but it was not deep and so she landed in the water, but was able to help Sister Vivi, who had to jump in after her, out and began to pray with her. The grand dukes were now supposed to follow the two women, but Sergei Mikhailovich refused. So he was shot in the head and thrown into the pit. When they were all in the pit, they could be heard talking, Aunt Ella and Vivi sang Christian songs. The soldiers had to silence them and threw a grenade into the depths, but the singing didn't stop. They threw in a second one, planks, branches from the forest and set everything on fire. But for many, many hours - there was talk later of three whole days - the singing and prayers could still be heard. When they finally stopped, the shaft was filled with earth. But we only found out about all this later.
On July twenty-fourth, Mama received the news of the murder of Aunt Alix and her family in Yekaterinburg. Only a few days after the murder, the *White Guards* had reached the city, but they were too late to save the family, finding the house devastated, personal belongings and Alexei's dog *Joy* running half-starved through the rooms, which one of the soldiers took care of. In the cellar, however, there were bullet holes in the walls, blood on the floor and someone had written on the wall *that Belshazzar had been* killed *by his servants that night.* It was obvious what had happened to the family and their loyal servants, but the bodies were not found. In addition, a telegram was received informing Lenin that the family had shared the same fate as the tsar. We all suspected that the murder had been planned long in advance. Especially after Uncle Nicky's brother had also been murdered. But no bodies of our relatives were found in Ekaterinburg either.
Now we feared for Aunt Ella, because it was said that she and the others had managed to escape. This false report was spread, but it gave us hope in order to reassure those loyal to the tsar. But it was no longer credible in these times. Soon the news of the death of the Tsar's family went around the world and for my poor mother it was a shock that cannot be put into words. The rest of us couldn't understand how they could just kill them all. My poor cousins, the fragile yet cheerful Alexei, Uncle Nicky, my Aunt Alix ... It was unbelievable.
On the second of September, Princess Marie-Louise of Schleswig-Holstein-Sonderburg-Augustenburg visited Mama and Papa on the Isle of Wight. She was a daughter of Aunt Lenchen and my father drove her to Kent House in Dickie's automobile, which he gave them when he was on naval duty. She handed him a letter from Buckingham Palace, which she asked him to read at once. It was a letter from the secret service, in which a British member of it, who had been under General Poole in Murmansk, confirmed from a reliable source the death of the entire Tsar's family. There was no doubt about this source and so this tragic information was vouched for. My father now knew

that all hope was in vain, but he could not give the letter to my mother until after lunch, so much did he fear for her reaction. It intensified her grief, but she said she was certain that her sister had gone to her death with all her deep trust in God. She couldn't say any more, she didn't have the words.

I found out from Papa in Lucerne and immediately wrote to Uncle Ernie in Darmstadt. Until then, I hadn't dared to write to my mother because I knew how much she was suffering. Uncle Ernie too, of course. I had seen the siblings all together so often, remembered the lovely family reunions and yet we dared to hope that the news of our relatives' deaths would be spread just like that, that perhaps they really had been able to escape. But every time we hoped in the time that followed, the cruel reality was confirmed. It was like a bad dream that you couldn't wake up from. We clung to the hope that at least Aunt Ella was still alive and well. But even this hope was shattered when the *White Guard* captured Alapajevsk on September twenty-eighth and began searching for Ella and the others. The bodies were finally found between the ninth and eleventh of October. An autopsy was carried out and it was discovered that Aunt Ella and the others had suffered terribly, with the exception of Mikhail, who died quickly after being shot in the head.

On the first of November, Aunt Ella and the others were given a formal funeral in which they were all buried in the crypt of the church in Alapajevsk as *martyrs of Alapajevsk*. A small requiem was held for them, which was also attended by the local population. People were very saddened, especially about the death of my aunt and Vivi, as they had both been in the service of the church.

Of course, the losses of the Russian relatives hit me hard, but the one that affected me the most was that of Aunt Ella, because she had given up all her worldly possessions and devoted herself entirely to helping the poor and the sick. I found it more than shocking how this woman, who had given so much of herself for others, could be executed so cruelly. It's not a slight on Aunt Alix's family, because I think it's generally reprehensible to kill other people because they have a certain status due to their birth. My mother and Uncle Ernie, the other relatives, saw it the same way. Perhaps the murder of Uncle Nicky during the revolution could have been understood by the Bolsheviks and from their sick point of view in these times of turmoil, but not by Aunt Alix and the children. We were robbed of our relatives and the whereabouts of the bodies were unknown. For this reason, even shortly after the murder, charlatans were able to exploit our grief by claiming to be Alexei, Olga, Tatyana or Anastasia, like the lady who later achieved dubious fame under the name Anna Anderson, but whom I never believed to be my cousin. That's why I don't want to go into detail about this person. We had to accept that our loved ones had been buried somewhere like garbage. And my mother told me that her only consolation was the certainty that they had all been together when they had to face death.

I would never forget them all. Uncle Nicky, a man who, like Aunt Alix, was deeply connected in his belief in his rule by the grace of God, but who as a person was a family man through and through, loved his wife dearly, his children just as much and had a big heart. My aunt Alix, always tormented by her psychosomatic ailments caused by fear for her son, got lost in Rasputin's confused words but, like her uncle, was always there for her family. Often quiet and rather thoughtful, she could also be humorous, played with her children and us, and was also uninhibited. But just like her husband, she was not up to the emerging problems in Russia. And my cousins, with whom I would never be able to talk or spend time again - Tatyana, who was called the *governess* because she was always concerned about her siblings, Olga, who was very similar to Aunt Alix in that she brooded a lot, but also questioned things that were happening in the world, and in this respect was more like her father. Maria, the dreamer who had to be lured out of her proverbial shell, and Anastasia, the eternal goblin who couldn't let anything spoil her mood and who always made everyone laugh with her jokes. And Alexei, the fragile boy with an ailment that could always threaten his life. But that was precisely why he understood other people's ailments and illnesses and was so compassionate that he usually no longer seemed like a child, but like an adult.
Revolutions are always cruel and my mother remembered the picture of Marie Antoinette and her children, once painted by Lebrun, hanging in Aunt Alix's palace. Perhaps my aunt had often looked at it during the hard times and feared she would share the fate of the Queen of France.
The murder of our Russian relatives suddenly left a huge gap in our family that would never be filled again.

The war had now become a minor matter for us, even if this may sound strange. For a few months, reports had been circulating about the *Spanish flu* that was ravaging people. People hoped they wouldn't catch it anywhere.
By the sixth of April 1917, the USA had already declared war on Germany and the fabric of the Old World in which I had grown up was slowly crumbling. Bulgaria surrendered on September twenty-ninth, 1918, the Ottoman Empire on October thirtieth and Austria-Hungary on November third. On the eleventh of the month, the *armistice of Compiègne* was concluded, with which Germany also capitulated. This officially ended the First World War. The Prussian Empire collapsed and there had been unrest in Germany for some time, as people were tired of the war, starving and demanding the abdication of the Kaiser. In November, a republic was proclaimed and on the

twenty-eighth of November, just nineteen days later, Uncle Willy abdicated and fled into exile to Doorn in the Netherlands, where his wife, the Crown Prince and his family followed him. They found exile in Wieringen.
The war had claimed almost ten million casualties among the soldiers, around twenty million had been wounded and many of them had to live on as war invalids. Among the civilian population, around seven million people had fallen victim to this war and it was not only the casualty figures that were terrible, but also the fact that everything was now in a state of upheaval. The former rulers, such as Uncle Nicky and Uncle Willy, had been wiped off the map of history and people's resentment was now generally directed against the nobility and their former power.
After Uncle Willy's abdication, the Danish embassy in Russia issued my mother-in-law with a passport, which she was finally able to use to leave the country in November. She arrived in Switzerland via Germany and was finally reunited with us. The last few months had left their mark on her and, at the age of sixty-seven, the strain was clear to see. Nevertheless, she was glad to have escaped unscathed after everything that had happened to her relatives in Russia.
Tino had fallen ill with *Spanish flu* a few days before her arrival. He was happy about his mother's arrival, but shortly afterwards he was struggling with death. Seeing her son suffering like this, who had already suffered enough for her from his abdication, made her almost despair, and we all hoped that he would recover. But the illness dragged on for a long time, he was in a very bad way for weeks, one more worry that put an additional burden on us. When he finally recovered, his convalescence took a very long time. And even during his illness, his mistress came to support him. My mother-in-law, who was only now really realizing the affair, as she had been unaware of it during her time in Russia, was shocked at how her son was exposing his wife and children. But she could only support her daughter-in-law Sophie, she couldn't convince her son to come to his senses and end the relationship.
That November, Aunt Irene and Uncle Heinrich also had to flee Hemmelmark. Their two sons had served in the German navy, as had Uncle Heinrich, who was also a brother of the Kaiser, and although they were not asked to leave the country, the uncle did not want to take the chance. So they left Kiel in a car. They were accompanied by two sailors, one of whom was shot when they crossed the Dutch border.
In December, they were in Amsterdam, where Uncle Henry drew up a document in which he declared that he would stand behind his brother and never want to harm him. In the following months, he concentrated on lobbying King George in England to restore his brother to the throne, as he believed that he

had tried everything to prevent a war, but the general public saw things differently. Uncle Henry even compiled papers to prove that England was provoking a war, but his efforts were unsuccessful. As he was not seen as a threat and his statements, which he made publicly, were ignored, he and Aunt Irene were left alone. They soon returned to Hemmelmark, where they lived unmolested. For the new rulers in Germany, he belonged to an old regime that was no longer listened to.

In November, Uncle Ernie and Aunt Onor were confronted by an angry mob who wanted to storm the New Palace where they were staying. The people chanted *"Down with the Grand Duke!"* and *"Kill the Grand Duke!"*. A State Council had been formed in Hesse and shortly afterwards a *People's Council for the Republic of Hesse*. The latter was to represent all classes of the people. A delegation from these councils now came to the palace. Uncle Ernie and Aunt Onor could have got into a waiting car and fled, but my uncle let the people in and waited for them in the so-called Throne Room, his wife beside him. As they rushed towards them, the people suddenly paused, looking embarrassed because they had been politely let in. My uncle addressed them in a loud voice, saying that they were not wearing Hessian uniforms, but that they should form a small delegation and tell him what they wanted him to do. And in the meantime, since no one had ever come to the palace without being properly entertained, Aunt Onor would make them tea.

The people's demands were actually obvious. Uncle Ernie should resign and they wanted to declare a republic and formally secede from Prussia. My uncle didn't take a stand at first, because he didn't see the point in abdicating. So a committee was formed, which placed them under house arrest. Uncle Ernie's chamberlain Count von Hardenberg and Aunt Onor's lady-in-waiting Georgeina von Rotsmann were with them and remained under arrest with them throughout the winter.

SAYS CZAR AND FAMILY ARE IN NEUTRAL LAND

Nephew of Skoropadski Asserts Their Whereabouts Is Known to Allied Government.

WARSAW, Dec. 24, (Associated Press.)—"There is no doubt that the Czar and his entire family are alive. I am positive of this," was the declaration made to the correspondent today by Michael de Tchihatchef, a nephew of General Skoropadski, who has just escaped from the Ukraine after a recent trip to Petrograd, Dvinsk, Vilna, and Rovno.

"I cannot reveal where the Czar is because he does not wish it," he added. "He does not care to be bothered and he wants to be left alone.

"His whereabouts is known to an allied government. It is in a neutral country. Accounts of his murder at Ekaterinburg were manufactured by Trotzky and Lenine for propaganda purposes.

"It took much money and time and also the lives of many officers to accomplish his escape. Among the officers killed was Count Tatichev, the Czar's former personal military attaché, who was shot instead of the Czar. Documents describing the Czar's escape were in the hands of German Consul Koenig at Petrograd, who forwarded them to Berlin."

In mid-December, the *New York Times* spread the news that Aunt Alix and her family were still alive and had managed to escape. False reports were soon to make the rounds in newspapers and magazines all over the world, spreading the news that my cousin Tatyana was living with a family in Russia disguised as a maid, that the family was living in hiding in the Urals and much more. But there were people who wanted to clarify the fate of our relatives on the spot. And although only a few months later you could read in the headlines that remains had been found and that the murderers had boasted about the crime, the speculation did not stop. Every few weeks, another one of our cousins, Alexei or even Aunt Alix, was discovered somewhere in Europe. It was very painful, because we all had a tiny bit of hope in our hearts and my mother put it best when she said that the press was playing with our feelings just to increase circulation.

Mama at least had some variety in the visits from Nada, Georgie and her little granddaughter Tatjana. Nada surprised my parents at Christmas with the news that she was pregnant again and that they were expecting the baby in May next year.

At the end of December, my sister Louise broke off her engagement to her *Shakespeare*. In the summer, her fiancé had visited my parents and Louise at Kent House from the twenty-third to the twenty-fourth of June, but after this stay my father decided to talk to Louise when the opportunity arose, to make it clear to her that her fiancé was not a suitable match for her. In the fall, after she still wanted to marry Alexander, my father took her aside and told her that she could not marry this man, because it was obvious to which sex he was really attracted. Louise, who was really very sexually inexperienced and had never come into contact with the subject of homosexuality before, was distraught. She had never been educated about it by my parents and couldn't for the life of her imagine a man being intimate with another man. Perhaps you could say she had grown up too sheltered, a little naive and in her really deep love for this man she had never noticed his actual inclination. So I wrote to Aunt Onor about how much Louise was suffering, but had realized it. This marriage would not have been a happy one for her. But my poor sister was now enriched by a shocking experience.
My parents were absolutely right in their decision to advise Louise against Alexander as a marriage candidate, because only a short time later *Shakespeare* opened a small backyard gallery, if you want to call it that, but never really made a big success of it. He spent his free time doing needlework, was very skilled at embroidery and took over an hour to get dressed up, put on make-up and dressed very eccentrically. We learned this from London acquaintances, but none of us were really surprised.
In January 1919, my uncle registered as a candidate for upcoming elections. However, his candidacy was ignored and in July of that year, Hesse was declared a republic, thus seceding from Prussia. My uncle never officially abdicated, but he was now only a Grand Duke in title. Some of his property was confiscated and he literally left politics and the military to one side, becoming involved in cultural activities for the people of Darmstadt. He thus devoted himself to what he was actually more interested in: organizing exhibitions of art, promoting science, philosophy and architecture. His patronage was soon widespread, as this commitment was appreciated. And soon he was even organizing performances by important artists for the opera in Darmstadt.
You could say that what started with my father losing his position in the British Navy continued with the loss of my other relatives' positions. Andrea put it like this: 'The war had taken its toll.
On January thirtieth, Andrea's former brother-in-law, Grand Duke Paul

Alexandrovich, Minnie's husband, Grand Duke Georgei Mikhailovich, his cousin Grand Duke Dmitry Konstantinovich and Grand Duke Nikolai Mikhailovich were shot in the *Peter and Paul Fortress* in Petrograd. They were arrested, maltreated in custody and their bodies were buried in a mass grave near the fortress. Only that of Dmitri Konstantinovich was allowed to be collected by his former adjutant wrapped in a carpet and buried in the garden of his private house. All attempts to save the men, even in exchange for money, including from the writer Maxim Gorky, were stopped and rejected by the government.
I doubt whether our *Greek Minnie* was really grieving for her husband, as the marriage had not been a happy one and the couple had been separated for a long time. She also made no attempt to save her husband. Even if it sounds harsh, his death rather relieved her of an unpleasant connection. But as we had no real contact with her and she didn't want any, we went our separate ways. I only felt sorry for my mother-in-law, who didn't get to see her grandchildren.

My poor Papa had already received the news at the end of 1918 that he would not be reinstated to his post in the British Navy as promised. It was with a heavy heart that he officially resigned his commission on January 1st, 1919 and officially retired, which he had actually been doing for years. After a career that had lasted almost fifty years, he had never really assumed deep down that they would keep their word and reinstate him, but there may still have been a spark of hope in him, because my mother wrote to me that he was suffering greatly from the fact that he had basically been lied to. The new situation meant a change for my parents, as they now had to live on a lower income. Papa had invested a lot of money in a platinum mine over the years before the revolution in Russia, but now it was all lost when the Bolsheviks came to power. My parents couldn't keep Kent House either and they had no choice but to sell it. Furthermore, after careful consideration, it was no longer possible for them to maintain Heiligenberg Castle. Finding a buyer for the castle where my father spent his youth, his childhood home if you want to call it that, was even harder for him. We all associated wonderful times with Heiligenberg, family reunions, we children spent our summers there, wonderful days and weeks at our grandparents' side. But maintaining the castle would have been a huge burden for my parents. Unfortunately, it was not so easy to find a buyer. So soon after the war, people had to sort themselves out. It wasn't until 1920 that my father found two investors who bought it. They were Privy Councillor Dr. Theodor Görges from Berlin and his son-in-law Prince Heinrich von Hohenleuben, who used the castle for private purposes. My father received a purchase price of around one hundred and fifty thousand

US dollars for the castle, but due to the inflation of the German mark, the proceeds were reduced again. This left my parents with only his small halved income, which he still received monthly from the British Navy.
After my parents sold Kent House, Nona offered them to live in *Fishponds*, a house in her grounds of *Netley Castle* in Hampshire. The castle was actually a castle near the village of *Netley*, built in its foundations in the sixteenth century, first used as a fort and then extended over the centuries. In 1881, the castle was bought by the Chrichton family and further extended. It was quite a handsome building with a beautiful, large park, orchards, gardens, a pond and a boathouse. The latter was designed like a small cottage and now served as accommodation for my parents for a small rent. As my mother was always ready to adapt quickly to new circumstances and never set great store by a sumptuous home, it was perfectly acceptable to her. What's more, it was very generous of Nona and Dick to offer my parents this opportunity in the first place. And my mother could get back to gardening while my father finished his books at his typewriter with a view of the lake.
King George V awarded my father an honorary *Military Grand Cross of the Order of the Bath*, the so-called *Most Honorable Order of the Bath*, and he was also allowed to wear the title *Admiral of the Fleet*. But this was only a small compensation for my father.

It was only in April 1919 that Uncle Nicky's mother and her other relatives in the Crimea were able to flee from there because her sister, Aunt Alexandra, sent them a ship from England. In the spring of 1918, the Bolsheviks had arrived in Crimea to shoot all the Romanovs living there, which a sailor was only able to prevent by protesting that there was no such order from Moscow. And when the Germans took Crimea during the war, the Romanovs there were relatively safe.
All the other Romanovs, such as Marie, Aunt Ella's foster daughter, had already fled and were now mainly in France, where they lived in exile.
Uncle Nicky's mother spent some time with her sister, but behaved very eccentrically there, just as she was used to as a former tsar's mother, and broke up with her sister and moved to Hvidore in Denmark with her daughters. She firmly believed that her son and his family were still alive and would reappear at some point.

I couldn't get over my aunt's cruel death and was never really able to overcome my grief for her. But this was due to the fact that she had been a true saint in my eyes.

On the twelfth of May, Georgie and Nada had a little son, whom they named

David. We were all very happy for them. My mother acknowledged the birth by saying that some had gone, but new ones had been born, alluding to the loss of the Russian relatives.

In 1919, we moved to the *Grand Hotel* in Lucerne and it became our real home. We often commuted between Lucerne and the *Hotel Rigi-First* in Rigi Kaltbad, where we took short boat trips with the children on Lake Lucerne, later Lake Lucerne, organized picnics and enjoyed nature. From time to time we traveled to Zurich, where we stayed at the elegant *Grand Hotel Dolder*. There was an opportunity for the children to ride donkeys nearby, which they really enjoyed.

In Lucerne, we stayed in a hotel with Tino and his family and his mother-in-law. The children enjoyed the constant company, but the exile was also a burden for all of us, as we didn't know what would happen next.

My brother Dickie was very saddened by the death of his beloved cousin Marie. Mama told me how she had to break the news to him very gently, but Dickie couldn't stop crying afterwards. When my mother pointed out to him that the whole family around Aunt Alix and Aunt Ella were dead, so he had to mourn them all, he told her he would miss them all, cry for them all, but for Marie most of all. Then he confessed to Mama that he had always wanted with all his heart to marry her one day. He put a small picture of her on his bedside table and would always treasure it. Even in later years, it was always on his bedside table.

Dickie visited us a few times in the spring, went skiing and ice skating with us all, before studying engineering at *Christ's College*, Cambridge University for two semesters. They had set up this course especially for veterans of the British Navy.

Margarita told him that she loved the summers in Switzerland more than the winters, but that she missed the sea because the lakes in Switzerland were all too small for her. It was difficult for the girls to live in this constant uncertainty as to when they would be able to return to Greece or whether we would have to live in Switzerland forever. Dolla and Margarita in particular, who were always together, often asked what we were going to do now, but we couldn't answer them. We just tried to make their stay in Switzerland as pleasant as possible. The two younger ones, Tiny and Cäcilie, took it for granted, they didn't question many things yet. They also spent their time together and were very close. Dolla, Margarita and Cäcilie all had lessons and I made sure that we didn't let them slip, because despite all the adversities that time brought with it, a good general education was very important. Everyone was a hard-working student and enjoyed learning. Perhaps also because it distracted them from thinking about everything we had experienced in the last

few months. I had long conversations with my two older daughters in which we shared our grief for the Russian relatives. They had known them well and didn't understand why they all had to die. But it was also difficult to explain the many changes to them and to make them understand this transition from the old world to a new one. We adults also had to adjust to the new circumstances first.
Andrea suffered greatly from the boredom that soon set in for him, as there was nothing really for him to do. But we knew that he, like his brothers, was always being watched by diplomats in Greece, Switzerland and Italy. Even though we could move around freely in Switzerland, we were still under surveillance. So you always had to be careful what you said in public, think carefully about who you met or where you went. There were still fears in Greece that Tino might try to retake the throne.
It was soon discovered that my brother-in-law George in Paris was serving as an intermediary for messages between Tino and his son Alexander in Greece. They used an extensive network of couriers who carried messages in briefcases via Rome and Tino also used a slow, reliable *channel* via Alexandria to contact his son. Only part of this network was exposed, but it didn't help our efforts to return to Greece in the foreseeable future. Andrea submitted a petition to the Foreign Office asking that we be allowed to live in Corfu again, but there was simply no response. We received no response, although my husband was told by Venizelos from Greece that he had no objections. He wanted to speak out in favor, but this also came to nothing.
Papa and Louise visited us in Lucerne in June. Louise would stay with us for a month, my father for a shorter time as he didn't want to leave my mother alone for so long. Both Louise and Papa told me how my mother was really doing, which I couldn't make out from her letters as she always kept her composure. Physically she was fine, she had a blessed appetite, according to my father, and worked long hours in the garden, but mentally she was at the end of her tether. Her nerves were literally shattered by the grief for her sisters, Aunt Alix's family. She simply couldn't accept how cruelly they all had to die, but didn't feel able to broach the subject either. That's why she turned down an invitation to Lucerne. Papa confessed to me that it wasn't possible to talk to her about it at home either. Her pain was simply too great. He argued that we were all suffering, but it was her sisters and she didn't want to talk about it with her brother either, which is why she completely left the subject out of her letters to Uncle Ernie. When my mother heard about the death of the Russian relatives, Papa said, she went into the garden without saying a word and threw herself into work. She worked there for many hours. But what was most disconcerting was the fact that she didn't speak as much as before. She had literally lost the desire to talk and my father had never known his

wife to be so taciturn and often silent.
He himself had also had to suffer a lot in the last few years, but new things always came up, he said, and even when he was invited to committees and made a patron of charitable organizations relating to the British navy, he turned down every invitation. My parents' life was now very secluded.
In London, Mama had met Sophie von Buxhoeveden, the former lady-in-waiting and friend of Aunt Alix. She had gone into exile with the family to Tobolsk, but was then separated from them in Yekaterinburg and arrested. Sophie was able to flee to Omsk with the help of the Russian *White Army* and, as Omsk was under the protection of the British military, was able to leave Russia. Her next stops were Vladivostok, China, Japan, Hawaii and San Francisco, until she reached her father in Copenhagen, stayed there for a while and was then allowed to move to England through the mediation of her father, who turned to Uncle Heinrich. The lady-in-waiting must have been a close friend of Aunt Alix, whom she called *Isa.* I remembered her well. But there were still doubts about her loyalty to the family, because she was accused of knowing about the jewels sewn into the girls' corsets and Alexei's shirt. My aunt had hidden a few pieces of jewelry because she hoped that she might be able to use them to pay for her family's escape if the opportunity arose. These sewn-in pearls and jewels made the murderers' bullets bounce off my cousins, but they were later found on the bodies. Now there was a rumor that Isa had revealed this secret after her arrest in Yekaterinburg. It was not until many years after the murder, when one of the murderers revealed himself, that the gruesome details of the night of the murder came to light, but this contradicted the rumor. For if the murderers had known about the pearls and jewels in the corsets and the shirt, the girls and Alexei would certainly have been killed immediately with shots to the head and their bodies would not have been shot first. And the former lady-in-waiting could certainly not be blamed if she had told some very intimate details about the family's life during the rather rude interrogation.
Isa was later to publish three books describing her time at Aunt Alix's side and later her escape from Russia. It should be mentioned that her book about my aunt reveals nothing against her, but is rather a requiem for her, showing her as a loving mother, a faithful wife and a tsarina who loved her country.
So we never believed the rumors about Isa. It was also Isa who unmasked the false Anastasia as just that, and immediately said at a meeting that she wasn't our cousin.
But now, so soon after the death of Aunt Alix and her family, Mama Isa's comments about the last few months had really hit home. Papa thought it was a good thing that my mother found out about this, but it only made things worse for her to know how her sister had despaired during this time, clinging

to her faith, always hoping that they could all escape their fate. And the more Mama burdened herself with this, the more she grew to hate King George, who refused the family political asylum in England, which he must have regretted greatly, but for my mother, forgiveness in this regard was never possible. It was more than a mistake from her point of view. It was a betrayal of his cousin Nicky and his family. My father openly admitted how Mama also blamed the king for her death. For her, the relationship with him was destroyed once and for all.

I would have loved to have my mother with us in Lucerne, but I understood if she didn't feel up to it at the Mamaent. Perhaps she was afraid that the subject of Aunt Ella and Aunt Alix would somehow come up. We were all aware of the sensitivity of this issue and avoided even reminiscing about happy times with our Russian relatives because it hurt too much. When you are grieving yourself, it is difficult to offer someone support in this. You can share it, but the grief can still overwhelm you.

My father nevertheless gained something very positive from this trip, as he made contact with his brother, Uncle Franzjos, and his wife, Aunt Anna. They commuted between Lausanne and Thun or lived south of Bern in a small town. My father would pay them a visit and kept in touch during his stay with us. Even though there had never been an argument between them, they made up, as Papa explained to me, and he was happy to keep in touch because he was, after all, his brother.

Uncle Ernie and Aunt Onor informed us that they were traveling to the Engadin with their sons to stay at *Tarasp Castle* for a while in mid-July. The castle is situated on a conical rocky hill in the southwest of the municipality of Scuol in the canton of Graubünden. The very imposing castle is considered a landmark of the Lower Engadine. It had been owned by the Dresden patron and industrialist Karl August Lingner since 1900, who bought it for twenty thousand francs after a stay at a health resort in the area. Lingner was known for the antiseptic mouthwash *Odol*, which he developed with inventor Richard Seifert and launched on the market in 1892.

After his death in 1916, Lingner bequeathed the castle to King Friedrich August III of Saxony in his will. However, he showed no interest in it, as it was allegedly stipulated in the will that he would have to live there for some time each year. However, this clause did not exist. It was rumored that the king was more concerned about the upcoming maintenance costs for the castle. However, as Uncle Ernie was the second heir, should the king refuse, the castle became my uncle's property. Aunt Onor and Uncle Ernie had known Lingner as a charitable benefactor for maternal and infant care long before his death and were in constant contact with him. They also both knew Count Kuno von Hardenberg, who had been Lingner's artistic advisor and designed

the interior of the palace. In 1917, after Lingner's death, von Hardenberg became Uncle Ernie's last court marshal and grand ducal property manager.
In 1919, however, the republic had been proclaimed in Hesse and my uncle was no longer officially Grand Duke, but the new *People's State of Hesse* agreed with him that Tarasp would become his private property as a so-called *Schatullgut*. Uncle Ernie could thus dispose of the castle freely and pass it on within the family. But it also had to be maintained. He therefore decided to offer guided tours of Tarasp when he was not there with his family.
After my father's visit, I actually wanted to relax with Louise and my family in Vulpera, a small settlement after Tarasp, as there are mineral springs there that are said to have healing properties. We were already booked into the Hotel Waldhaus, but Uncle Ernie invited us all to Tarasp. Without further ado, we decided to have a family reunion, the first since the war, and traveled to the castle. My uncle had hoped that my mother would also like to come, he had sent her an invitation, but she hadn't replied. Not wanting to burden my uncle too much, I turned to Aunt Onor and explained to her Mama's emotional state when we arrived there on the seventeenth of July. Maybe next summer she would be strong enough to meet up with all of us again. I knew Mama dreaded meeting her brother the most, because Uncle Ernie was very squeamish. Even as a child he was, as they say, built very close to the water. But you could also call him sensitive, which is rather rare in a man, but also very pleasant if he can relate to his wife's grief, for example. But my mother was too afraid that we would talk about the sisters and my uncle would no longer be able to enjoy the vacation as a break. Everyone was carrying a heavy burden at that time, because they had been stripped of their power and that also affected them.
During these times, I often felt like a ship in rough seas. New waves kept hitting my bow, tossing me to and fro, and there seemed to be no sun in the sky, no calming of the sea. I wanted to stand by everyone and help them, but I found it difficult. So I tried to enjoy the days in Tarasp and distract myself. It was a shame that Papa was leaving again and didn't want to follow us. Nevertheless, for the sake of the grandchildren, he promised me that he would persuade Mama to come to Tarasp for at least a few days. And he was successful. My mother agreed to come to us, but she hurt her brother and aunt a little by not wanting to stay at the castle as their guest and instead taking a room at the Villa Maria guesthouse in Vulpera, which was nearby. She insisted that we should move in with her so as not to burden her brother, who shook his head when we also moved into the guesthouse.
My Aunt Onor didn't have the heart to tell my uncle how Aunt Ella had died. And certainly not the meagre details about the murder of Aunt Alix and her family. She asked us not to tell Uncle about it in all its horrible detail, and so

Louise and I were in two minds as to whether Mum's stay was really such a good idea because, as we discovered, she felt the need to talk about it. At the same time, she also wondered whether it might break her brother. So the stay turned out to be a bit difficult because you always had to be careful what became a topic of conversation. So the girls, Andrea, Louise, Mama and I, spent most of the day together. Our children enjoyed the warm summer sun and were soon tanned. They enjoyed the company of their cousins Lu and Don, the presence of their grandmother and seemed very relaxed.
We all met every day for tea in the castle, then went on little excursions or for a walk and in the evening we all had dinner together.
It wasn't easy not to spend too much time with Uncle Ernie avoiding *the one subject.* So we mostly talked about the children, their development, the upheavals caused by the war or other rather terse things.
This vacation with us was also very welcome for my sister in order to come to terms with her engagement to Alexander, which had taken its toll on her. On long walks with me and Andrea, she poured her heart out to us, confessing that she had been stupid because she hadn't recognized his tendency in her deep love for him. Love had blinded her and that annoyed her greatly. Even though she looked like a naive little girl who had heard about homosexuality for the first time in front of my father, she was so ashamed of it. Louise also feared that she had made a mockery of herself among her relatives and would end up as an old maid. I saw no danger of that, because she had learned from this unpleasant story and I assured her that she had many qualities, because although she was very slender and fragile, she was very pretty and very helpful. She should just forget about it, tick it off as a mistake in her life. Everyone would make them.
Mama was tempted after a few days to confront Uncle Ernie with what she knew about the death of our relatives, but avoided it when Aunt Onor asked her to wait until there was more peace in all our lives.

After our family reunion, Mama traveled back to England and we returned to the Grand Hotel in Lucerne, where Tino and his family were also based again after short trips within Switzerland.
On her return to England, my mother decided to sell some of the shares that she and Papa had as a nest egg. This raised 3200 English pounds. Mama now gave each of her children eight hundred pounds, which was mainly to provide financial help for us in exile, for which I was very grateful. She didn't announce her plan to us, she wanted it to be a surprise. She succeeded, of course, because I would never have expected something like this.

Tino was at odds with himself and the world, because he was not satisfied with what had been decided for Greece at the *Paris Peace Conference* after the end of the war, which was to last until 1920. Although the main part of Thrace, which had been under Bulgarian and Turkish rule before the war, islands in the Aegean such as Imbros and Tenedos and the Smyrna region (now Izmir) in Iona in western Anatolia now belonged to Greece or, like the latter, were under Greek mandate, he did not agree with this. Our homeland had now grown by a third in terms of area, but Tino still demanded more land. He did not consider the territorial claims to be satisfied and openly stated that Constantinople should be taken.

However, his dissatisfaction was compounded by a second one, as his son Alexander was in love with a woman. He had already informed his parents of his relationship with Aspasia Manos in 1917. She was the daughter of the Greek general and head of the royal navy, Petros Manos, and Alexander knew her as a childhood playmate. Aspasia already belonged to a distinguished family, but was not fit to be the bride of a king and Tino asked his son to wait until the end of the war before deciding to marry or make his relationship public. Alexander asked his parents several times to agree to a marriage.

In March 1918, Mama's uncle Arthur had traveled to Athens to present Alexander with the honorary *Order of the Bath* on behalf of the King. He suggested the young Princess Mary, the King's daughter, as a marriage candidate, but met Aspasia and was so taken with her that he said that if he were a few years younger, he would want to marry her too. Alexander committed himself to her and rejected any other marriage candidate outright. The young king also believed that wooing Mary could be misinterpreted. It did not seem right to him, as it could appear as if he was only trying to curry favour with the English king in order to improve relations between England and Greece.

Alexander was isolated from us, because even letters to his parents were confiscated or simply not delivered, by which I mean they were *lost* in the palace as soon as they were written. So he soon only had Aspasia to support him.

Although Prime Minister Venizelos, who was re-elected in 1917, was a good friend of General Manos, he and the Greek government did not want the king to marry a commoner. They also saw the danger in such a marriage that the general could literally be used as a secret means of communication between Alexander and his parents.

Venizelos tried to convince Alexander of how unpopular such a marriage could make him among the people.

In England, it was feared that the king would abdicate in order to marry Aspasia. This would give Venizelos the opportunity to proclaim a republic in Greece and then French influence could quickly gain the upper hand.

Alexander had been allowed to visit Paris at the end of 1918, but had been under constant observation there, but his parents were increasingly hopeful that he would change his mind and break away from Aspasia after all. Sophie in particular, who was absolutely opposed to the marriage, had tried to reach her son by telephone in the Paris hotel where he was staying. However, a minister answered the call and rudely turned her away, explaining that the king had no time. It later emerged that Alexander had not even been informed of his mother's call.

By 1919, Aspasia and Alexander had tried three times in vain to marry in secret. With the help of Christo Zalocostas, Aspasia's brother-in-law, they finally managed to get married secretly on the evening of November 17th in front of the royal chaplain, Archimandrite Zacharistas, at the palace in Athens. The chaplain was asked to remain silent, but he confessed everything to the Archbishop of Athens, Melitios Metaxakis. However, according to the Greek constitution, members of the royal family were only allowed to marry with the consent of the king and the Greek Orthodox Church. Alexander's marriage caused a scandal, as the archbishop felt that his consent to the marriage had been ignored. He had not been asked, because then he would not have given his consent, which was due to the circumstances.

Although the prime minister was not happy with the marriage and was still against it, he agreed to let Aspasia and her mother move into the palace if the marriage was kept secret. The bride was dubbed *Madame Manos* and refused to be addressed as queen.

As with all things that should remain hidden from the public, information nevertheless leaked out and the marriage became public knowledge. To prevent the scandal from making waves in Greece, Venizelos asked Aspasia to leave the country to avoid humiliation. Fearing negative headlines in the press, the bride fled to Rome with her mother, to Naples and then to Paris, where Alexander was only allowed to meet her six months later. However, they were forbidden from appearing in public and accepting invitations that could have a negative impact. It was the couple's honeymoon, if you want to call it that, but they had to enjoy it together in secret.

And Tino and Sophie were both beside themselves when they found out their son was getting married. But their hands were tied far away in Switzerland. They had to live with their son's decision.

Alexander and the beautiful Aspasia

The marriage of Alexander and Aspasia had not been under a good star and, unfortunately, their future life together was not to be a happy one either.
Meanwhile, new conflicts were brewing in Greece. After the *Paris Peace Conference* and the incipient collapse of the Ottoman Empire as a result of the First World War, Venizelos and the government refocused on *the Megali Idea*, the *Great Idea*, as part of Greek nationalism. The main aim was to expand the territory by reintegrating the Greeks who had settled on the coast of Asia Minor since ancient times. Some areas had already been granted to them, but this could also be used politically to turn Greeks back into real Greeks. There were still Greek-populated European territories in Turkey, including the capital Istanbul.
But first Venizelos had to get the scandal surrounding the king's marriage under control. Since his re-election in 1917, he had always tried to prevent contact between Alexander and his parents because he feared for public opinion and that of other states. Lord Granville had come to Athens in October 1917 as British ambassador and found that the king was being isolated too much from his family, which he confirmed. He deeply regretted the exile of his parents and uncles, as he could not turn to them for advice. Alexander's reputation had been badly damaged that year when it emerged that his father and Uncle Willy had been in contact via secret telegrams. These were discovered and made public. It was obvious once and for all that Tino was pro-German in times of war. Now he could no longer deny it. And Tino was accused of having deceived everyone, including the Greek ministers, his

generals and the Entente. Alexander immediately made it clear that he did not believe in a German victory, but compromising letters were found in his possession, written to him by his father in invisible ink. Tino disappointed us all greatly with this behavior, as it also jeopardized our return to Greece. The dust settled slightly, but even in 1919 it was still hovering over us and was repeatedly picked up and exploited by the press.

Christo was still in love with the rich American widow Nancy Stewart Worthington Leeds. Until now, however, the laws of the royal household had prevented him from marrying her, as she had been divorced once, was now a widow and absolutely not befitting her station. After several discussions with Venizelos and the Greek government, the latter finally agreed. On the first of February 1920, the two married in Vevey according to the Orthodox rite. Four days later, Nancy converted to the Greek Orthodox faith for Christo and took the first name *Anastasia*. She was now officially given the title Princess Anastasia of Greece. Christo was overjoyed with his beautiful bride, who was also blessed with sufficient financial means to keep us all afloat. She did not hesitate to offer this openly. Her fortune was said to be around thirty-five million dollars, which she also invested in art and valuable antique furniture. She had been a regular customer at *Cartier* in Paris for years and even had her own room where she was shown pieces. Despite her immense wealth, she was still a loving mother to her son, an extremely helpful woman and a loving wife. Her son was now eighteen years old and was well received by all of us in the family, but his affections quickly turned to my niece, Grand Duchess Xenia, the daughter of the Greek Minnie, whom he met in Paris. The relationship between the two was soon to become closer.
Shortly after their marriage, however, Nancy was diagnosed with breast cancer. She was just forty-two years old and the diagnosis came as a shock to the couple. Margarita hit the nail on the head when she said that Anastasia had everything she could wish for, enough money, a nice husband, a good son, but unfortunately she couldn't buy health with all her money. My eldest was very sad, as we all were, but Nancy hoped that her financial means would help her by contacting the best doctors and specialists.
But Nancy's fortune had another advantage for all of us, because since she was generous with it, Andrea and his brothers could now use it to silence the press once and for all with their speculation and rumors about Tino.

At the beginning of 1920, I came down with a severe flu and infected both Andrea and the two little ones. We were slow to recover. Nevertheless, I soon felt well enough to ask Venizelos and the Greek government for permission to leave for Italy so that I could meet my parents in Rome, where they were

spending a few days with Louise. They then wanted to travel on to Corfu, but I couldn't get permission to visit them in Italy or even see them in Greece. So I left Margarita and Dolla in the care of my mother-in-law and took Andrea, Cäcilie and Tiny to Lugano so that they could all recover from the flu. Fortunately, my parents and Louise decided to cut their travel plans short and came to visit us in Lugano. I was finally able to thank my mother in person for her financial support.
As soon as my family had recovered and I thought everyone was well again, Cäcilie fell ill with scarlet fever. My little daughter was very sad because she wanted to spend time with her grandparents and Louise, but now she had to stay in bed.

In May 1920, Venizelos allowed Alexander to travel to Paris, initially describing it as a well-deserved vacation for the king, but rumours of the secret marriage had spread. And by the time Alexander traveled to France to meet Aspasia, the marriage was already on everyone's lips. Nevertheless, as mentioned, the two had to hide from the public. We learned in July that Alexander had returned to Greece and that Aspasia was pregnant. The young king resumed his duties, but as we learned in a roundabout way, he still felt like a puppet in Venizelos' hands.
In July, the Prime Minister and the government lifted the state of emergency in Greece. The opposition now called for Tinos to be reinstated as the rightful king, but the British government immediately argued that they were absolutely opposed to this. Tino's behavior during the war ruled him out as king once and for all. We did not have high hopes in this respect either.
However, Tino and Sophie seemed to be at least a little happy for their son when they heard the news of Aspasia's pregnancy. They also finally allowed her to return to Greece, but she had to stay at her sister's house in Athens. It was only after a few weeks that both Alexander and his wife were allowed to live in Tatoi again for a while. Aspasia was a support for him, as he was still not allowed to keep in touch with any of us.
On August 10, 1920, the *Treaties of Sèvres*, a suburb of Paris, were concluded between the Entente and the Ottoman Empire. This treaty was a dictated peace that would have meant the loss of many areas and territories for the Ottoman Empire if it had been ratified. The terms of the treaty were positive for Greece, as Eastern Thrace, with the exception of Istanbul and its immediate surroundings, was to be ceded to Greece. All Greeks living there were to be reunited in one state.
Bulgaria had already had to cede Western Thrace to Greece, and treaties were to come into force with England and France to protect the minorities in this area in particular. Smyrna and its surroundings were to be placed under Greek

administration and occupation and given a local parliament. After a transitional period of five years, this same parliament would then vote by referendum on whether the area should join Greece.
This would all have been acceptable to Venizelos within the framework of Greek nationalism and expansionist policy, but there were of course other conditions to this treaty, which the Sultan Mehmed VI accepted, and its signing was to degenerate into a political upheaval in his empire. His prestige and authority were shaken, as the Ottoman nationalists in Ankara rejected the treaty outright and soon declared themselves the legitimate government. However, the sultan's government in Istanbul continued to exist, even though on August 19th the nationalists declared the signatories of the treaty to be traitors to the fatherland, punishable by death. This revolutionary countermovement was led by the popular General Mustafa Kemal, who later called himself *Atatürk*. They now began to form a military force to oppose the Entente. The situation threatened to escalate and we all feared another armed conflict.
Venizelos almost fell victim to an assassination attempt carried out by two Greeks after signing the treaty in Paris. He was only slightly injured, but was unable to return to Greece as quickly as planned. Supporters of the Prime Minister rioted in Athens in July when they learned of the assassination attempt.
Shortly afterwards, men from a security battalion assassinated the anti-Venizelos politician Ion Dragoumis in mid-August, which contributed to Venizelos' reputation among the people sinking noticeably. Their policy of repression, including against the young king, caused the popularity of the royalists to rise again. Added to this was the fact that the people were *tired of the war*. The people were tired of uprisings and unrest after four years of war. They wanted peace and quiet in the country. And the royalists represented the old traditional values of the monarchy, in which many people still saw stability. The deposed King Constantine I was reintegrated into the political struggle of these very royalists in order to promote values that had not yet been banished from people's minds.

During his time in exile, Tino had of course not just sat around idly and struggled with life. Like all of us, he was able to move around freely, had couriers who carried news for him outside Switzerland, and he had recently started publishing a weekly journal in which he also took a stand on political issues. His journalistic activities soon convinced the Greek government that he was plotting against them and Venizelos. It was even suspected that Tino might be planning an assassination attempt on the prime minister, which of course never occurred to him. Efforts were made to prevent him from publishing his

journal, but these interventions from outside, i.e. from Greece, were usually not very effective and only short-lived. Nevertheless, they continued to undermine his contacts with people who were loyal to him.
Christo and Andrea traveled to Rome at the end of September. It was an ordinary little vacation trip, but rumors suddenly began to circulate that they wanted to intercede with the Italian government on behalf of their brother Tino and create a mood for him that was clearly pro-Constantine. The British government in particular had this spread by its Foreign Office, but of course this was *not* true. There were reports circulating that were supposed to substantiate the rumors. This weighed heavily on all of us because they were still trying to harm all members of the Greek royal family. It was simply impossible for these people to believe that we were living normally, without any ambitions or aspirations to bring Tino back to power.
The Italian government was finally forced to inform the British government that Tino would never be allowed to enter Italy. In October, the rumors were still circulating, but they were overshadowed by a tragedy that we all never expected.
On the second of October that year, Alexander was walking his sheepdog Fritz in Tatoi when he was attacked by the tame Barbary macaque belonging to the manager of the palace vineyards. When Alexander tried to separate the animals, a wild Barbary macaque that had come along attacked him. This monkey bit him on the leg below the hip and in the stomach. Servants rushed over, chased the monkeys away and helped the king to treat his wounds. However, the wounds were not disinfected. Alexander did not attach much importance to the incident and asked that it not be made public.
But that evening he felt unwell and developed a fever. Blood poisoning developed, which reached its full extent five days later. His fever rose to forty degrees Celsius, he fell into a delirium, woke up again, but his temperature only dropped by one degree Celsius. Aspasia was by his side, fearing for his life. The doctors did everything in their power, even considering amputating his leg, but none of them wanted to perform such a risky operation, as they feared he might not survive it and would be physically limited. For a king, this was unthinkable from the doctors' point of view. So they waited, administered medication to combat the fever and scraped out the wounds in a minor operation on the tenth of October, but by the nineteenth his body was so weakened that there was hardly any hope left. Aspasia nursed her husband devotedly, which was all the more tragic because she was expecting his child. Fearing for the king's life, a report on his condition was published in the Greek press, but the question immediately arose as to who would occupy the throne again if the king died.
It was a shame that Sophie was refused entry to Greece by the government,

as her son's life was at stake. However, my mother-in-law was allowed to travel to her grandson, which she did willingly and set off for Athens immediately. However, the sea was stormy and her journey took longer than planned.
Alexander was now suffering from meningitis due to the infection and was in a deep delirium from which he would not wake up. Shortly after sixteen o'clock on October twenty-fifth, he died in the presence of his wife. My mother-in-law arrived in Athens twelve hours later. She immediately had all the other family members informed of Alexander's death by telegram.
Sophie broke down because she couldn't be with her son, Tino and the other children were equally devastated by the news of his death. And it got worse, because they were also refused to attend the funeral. No one from the royal family, who was in exile in Switzerland, was allowed to enter Greece, so only the mother-in-law, who was there, was able to carry her grandson to his grave.
Alexander was first laid to rest in the Athens Cathedral so that the people could bid farewell to their king. He was buried on October twenty-ninth after a ceremony in the cathedral and the transfer to Tatoi. A small group of people attended the funeral. The mother-in-law supported the grieving widow Aspasia, Crown Prince Alexander of Serbia was present, his sister, my sister-in-law Ellen, Crown Prince Gustav Adolf of Sweden, his uncle, Prince Eugene, members of the Athens diplomatic corps as well as Rear Admiral Sir George Hope from England and Rear Admiral Dumesnil from France.
The Crown Prince of Sweden understood Aspasia's pain, as he had lost his wife, whom we all called Daisy, on the first of May. She had been suffering from an earache but had ignored it. However, it was a middle ear infection that she carried over and so she had to be operated on, even though she was eight months pregnant and expecting the couple's sixth child. Like Alexander, she died of blood poisoning shortly after the operation and the baby could not be saved. Now the crown prince had to care for his five children, the three youngest of whom were just ten, eight and four years old. Just as Aspasia now had to raise her child alone.

With the king's death, there was now the problem of succession in Greece, as there was no direct successor from Alexander's line, as his marriage had not been in keeping with his rank. The Greek government demanded that Tino and his son, Crown Prince George, be generally excluded from the succession, but still wanted to offer the throne to a member of the royal family.
So a minister was sent to Bern to offer the throne to Tino's son Paul on behalf of the Greek government on October twenty-ninth. But Paul refused the crown, as he could not really legally wear it because his elder brother and his father were still alive and both had never renounced the throne of their own

free will, but had to abdicate.
So the succession to the throne remained unresolved when elections for parliament were held in Greece on November 1, 1920, and this time the opposition won more votes and the supporters of Tinos returned to power. Venizelos was ousted from his post and Dimitrios Rallis became the new Prime Minister of Greece. He and his monarchist party were absolutely loyal to the royal family.
After the election, it was rumored that Christo and his wife had been involved and had invested a lot of money in a fund that supported the election campaigns of the monarchists in order to weaken Venizelos. But this could not be proven and we didn't really care. Nancy had a lot of money, was helpful and gave generously when it could be used for something. But we suspected that people were *fed up with* Venizelos, to put it succinctly. People wanted a stable monarchy again, back to the old values.
Venizelos felt defeated by the conservatives and disappointed by the Greek people. He decided to leave the country voluntarily and chose to live in exile in Paris.
Rallis, the new prime minister, now asked my mother-in-law to take over the regency until Tino and his family had returned to Athens from exile. My brother-in-law saw it as the will of the people that they wanted to see him back on the throne and he publicly stood by his stance that he would be a good ally to the British when he was king again. It was in the hands of the Greek government, even if the allies like England did not want to see him back on the throne and refused to recognize his regency in advance.
It all began when the British minister in Greece, Lord Granville, refused to accept an invitation from my mother-in-law, as she only held the regency in the name of her son Constantine. He feared that he might be resented in England for accepting such an invitation or that it might even jeopardize his position.

We were still very happy that we would all be traveling home again. Especially as I was pregnant again. It had surprised me to be expecting another child after Sophie's birth six years ago. But Andrea and the girls were beside themselves with joy, and we all hoped that this time it might be a boy. The baby was due to be born in June of the following year, so it was a great stroke of luck to experience the birth in Greece. Because, Andrea said, the child would then be a genuine Greek and not a Swiss exile, which I agreed with. We seemed to be heading for better times again.
On November twenty-second, Andrea and Christo arrived back in Corfu on a Lloyds steamer. The people gave them a warm welcome. Shortly afterwards, however, they traveled on to Athens, where they were greeted just as

joyfully by the people the next day. They drove from the port of Phaleron to the city in an automobile, and even on the way there the people surrounded the car so that they could only drive at walking pace. They came to the windows, which they rolled down, held out their hands, cheered and almost seemed to want to pull them out of the car with enthusiasm. Andrea and Christo let the cars stop at some point, got out and were immediately lifted onto their shoulders by people, dancing and laughing. When they were finally able to drive on and arrived at the palace, it was already surrounded by crowds of people, the men were throwing up their hats, the women and children were waving Greek flags. Andrea had to give a short speech on the balcony in which he assured the people how pleased he was about the warm welcome and how happy he was to be returning home. When he told me about it later, you could still see the joy in his face. And it made him all the happier that he was able to take up his post in the Greek army again.
The children, Christo's wife and I arrived in Corfu a few days later on the steamer *Triestino*. However, we also traveled on to Athens first and were received just as enthusiastically everywhere we went.

Despite the people's joy at our return, the French did not agree that Tino should be reinstated as king. However, the British government was open about this, with Lord Curzon, the English Secretary for Foreign Affairs in England, publicly stating that the English government would accept this new and, in their view, unacceptable situation, but would continue to oppose it. After several diplomatic disputes, the government in England decided to keep Lord Granville in his post as minister in Greece, but he was given official instructions to literally stay out of Tino's way and avoid any contact with the king.
This weighed heavily on Tino, but when he returned to Athens on the nineteenth of December, the cheers of the crowds spoke for him as King of Greece. It was even mentioned in the English *Times* how enthusiastically he had been received. The people sang hymns of praise to him, sang well-known folk songs, paid homage to him by decorating the railings of the balconies in the city's houses with olive branches and garlands of the same, the Greek national flag hung in the windows, people waved it back and forth. It was a truly royal reception. Nevertheless, shortly afterwards the Venezilists published a caricature in a Greek newspaper in which Tino emerged from a coffin as a king, while Venizelos and his ministers stood trembling next to him.
But to see Tino that day on his arrival in Athens, in the uniform of a general, relaxed and at ease, a smiling wife beside him, waving to the people, was proof that he had risen from the ashes like a phoenix. And in his speech, which he gave from the balcony of the palace, he spoke out in favor of good

transporting the coffins from Beijing via Shanghai, Hong Kong and Bombay to Port Said, a port city in northern Egypt. Father Serafim and the two novices accompanied them without question.

The coffins arrived in Port Said in December 1920. Mama and Papa had traveled there to receive them and the travelers. They then all had to travel together from Suez to Jerusalem, where, thanks to Mum's organizational skills, a gathering of British diplomats, Greek and Russian Orthodox church representatives awaited them at the train station. Members of the Russian community living there, exiled Russians, had also come, as well as citizens of the city. The coffins were first placed on a platform, a memorial service was held and they were then taken to two cars decorated with green ribbons. The procession set off, driving through the town, where people took off their hats in reverence, as the arrival of the coffins had been mentioned in the press. Pilgrims, simple Russian women, then agreed to carry the two coffins up the Mount of Olives to the church. Papa later told me how these bearers were united in their weeping and sobbing, carrying heavy loads because the road was stony, but nevertheless everyone wanted to contribute something, to touch the coffins.

When the coffins were in the church, they were placed on a raised platform, people gathered around them and the honorable head of the *Church of Zion*, also known as *the Church of the Apostles on Mount Zion*, Patriarch Damian, held a funeral service before the coffins were laid to rest in the church's small crypt. Mama said it was very dignified and in Ella's spirit, also that Vivi lay next to her in a coffin.

My parents only traveled back to England in February 1921 as they wanted to enjoy their time in Jerusalem. On their return journey, they received my letter informing them that I was pregnant again and that we were expecting the birth at the end of June. My mother immediately said it would be wonderful if it was finally a boy this time. She remarked that she was only a year younger than me when she gave birth to Dickie and that the age difference between the new baby and Tiny would be just as great as between Dickie and Georgie. But first and foremost she was happy that I was doing well.

Crown Prince George married Princess Elisabeth of Romania on February twenty-seventh and her sister Helen married Crown Prince Carol of Romania on March tenth in Athens. I was able to attend the latter wedding with Andrea. I had to give up attending the former due to my pregnancy, as I didn't want to travel any further away in my condition.

Life in Mon Repos was very tranquil. The house was surrounded by cypress and eucalyptus trees and you could see across the Ionian Sea to Albania and northern Greece. But after we had been away for three years, having lived in hotels and guesthouses, we noticed how sparsely furnished the house was and

how it lacked any modern comforts. There was still no electricity, no gas or hot water from the mains and certainly no central heating. It wasn't really a place to bring a baby into the world, but after everything we had experienced, this sparseness didn't bother us too much. I had a Greek cook, a Greek cleaning lady, an English couple who acted as janitors and also took care of other matters. The nanny, Miss Roose, who had also looked after me as a child, had been at our side in exile and now also in Mon Repos. Although she was a little older, she was so excited about the baby that she ordered pretty clothes and baby food, such as cookies, from England. I had to slow her down a bit because she really wanted everything to be there and was a bit too eager. She firmly assumed that it would be a boy, so she ordered clothes that were suitable for a boy.
Andrea had initially remained in Athens, as he hoped that the military authorities would deploy him in an impending conflict with Turkey. He asked for a command, but was initially refused. So he traveled to Mon Repos and spent some time with us. But he was determined to serve in the Greek military again. After the many, many months in exile, during which he was condemned to inactivity, he longed for a task again. Nevertheless, he suspected why he was denied a command, as there were prejudices against the officers who were dismissed from the Greek army in 1917, and Andrea was a member of the royal family. He was eventually given the rank of major general and put in charge of a cavalry brigade, but his influence there was very limited. Moreover, it was a task that did not really fulfill him. Nevertheless, he accepted it in order to be able to work in the Greek military again.
On the twenty-fifth of March, Aspasia gave birth to a baby daughter, whom she named Alexandra after her late husband. But the little girl was not a Greek princess, as her parents' marriage had not been in keeping with their status. It was not until July 1922, after many months of intercession by her mother-in-law Sophie, that a law was passed that retroactively recognized the marriage of members of the Greek royal family, even if they were not in accordance with their status. However, with the exception that these persons were not in the position of ruler. It was presented as an exception for King Alexander, but even with the passing of this law, a king or crown prince was never allowed to marry a commoner. But little Alexandra became *a royal highness* and *Princess of Greece*. Sophie had not agreed to her son's marriage, but had now got to know Aspasia and respected her as her daughter-in-law, although no close relationship developed between the two. Nevertheless, little Alexandra was a lasting memory for Sophie of her son and her first grandchild. This literally softened her heart.

Sophie and little Alexandra, 1921

The Greek royal family in 1921, from left to right: Sophie's daughter, Princess Irene, Sophie, Tino, her daughter, Helen, now Princess of Romania, Crown Prince Carol of Romania, her husband and Sophie and Tino's son Paul

But Sophie still had another grandchild to look forward to, as her daughter Helen was already pregnant when she left for Romania with her husband on May 8th after their honeymoon on Tatoi.

Andrea and I in the spring of 1921 with a new Mercedes automobile, which he bought for us in January

Andrea next to the Mercedes, spring 1921

Since the *Treaty of Sèvres*, the territories in this area, such as Western Thrace and Smyrna, remained with Turkey under international law. After Greece formally took over the administration of the territories in 1919 with the arrival of Greek troops in Izmir, Mustafa Kemal still refused to recognize the treaty. Since then, partisans have repeatedly attacked the Greek soldiers. This also included war-like actions, such as attacks of a military nature, which also affected many civilians. Russia supplied weapons to these partisans, which prompted the Greek troops to take action against the partisans with so-called punitive expeditions. In the summer of 1920, Greece expanded its military operations in order to finally suppress the recurring attacks by Kemal's troops and strengthen the Greek administration.

Since the treaty stipulated that after five years, the people in the affected areas were to decide by referendum which country they wanted to live in, either Greece or Turkey, Kemal's military government feared that the 1.8 million people living there might choose Greece.

The Entente was not pleased about the conflict, but the powers were rather weary of war after the First World War and were reluctant to participate in mediation between the two parties. Great Britain initially strengthened our government, but did not tolerate the reinstatement of Tino, as he was still considered pro-German. Italy supported the Young Turks around Kemal with arms supplies and war material.

During the 1920 election campaign, the opposition to Venizelos had campaigned in Greece with the slogan "*Homeward*" and assured the people that

troops would be withdrawn from all theaters of conflict, as they were also tired of the war. However, when the government came to power, it changed its mind about the conflict with Turkey. Military operations were extended into the hinterland of Asia Minor, which is why this campaign was soon referred to as *the Asia Minor Campaign*. Although the supply of troops was always assured, it soon proved difficult far from the coast.
In the summer of 1921, Greek troops advanced on Ankara and were repulsed by Turkish troops at the *Battle of Sakarya*. This military conflict was accompanied by ethnic hatred on both sides of the conflict.
Kemal wanted to create a modern nation state that was limited to the core regions of the Turkish-populated areas in the Ottoman Empire, but also renounced imperial territorial claims in Arabia, the Caucasus and the Balkans. Nevertheless, these core regions also included Greek Orthodox populations living there.
In February 1921, a peace conference in London had failed. And a conflict between the Sultan and Kemal was also smouldering in Turkey. Sultan Mehmed VI wanted to preserve the dynasty at all costs and thus responded to every demand made by the major powers after the First World War. In the meantime, he was accused of treason, as he was seen as a mere executive organ of the great powers.
At the *San Remo Conference* in April 1920, its negotiators accepted the territorial reorganization of the Middle East, which reduced the Ottoman Empire to Anatolia. Among other things, Greece was granted territories on the west coast of Anatolia, the Arabian Peninsula became independent, Great Britain was given the mandate administration over Mesopotamia and Palestine, France over Lebanon and Syria. This was a thorn in the side of the Young Turks under Kemal, because in their view it deprived the Ottoman Empire of its territorial integrity and national sovereignty.
In 1921, Kemal appointed himself President of the National Assembly in Ankara and assumed supreme command of the Turkish troops. There were always new conflicts, battles for cities, uprisings. And we were all still really worn out from the First World War, we longed for peace, but Tino led the Greek soldiers into another war.
However, this new military conflict was positive for my husband, as he was finally able to prove himself again. In June 1921, Tino gave him command of the XII. Division and Second Army in Thrace.
Of course, I was reluctant to let him go, as the birth of our fifth child was imminent, but I knew how much his heart was set on the military and that he needed this job to boost his self-confidence and to stand up for his country again. I also knew about his safety, so I was not shocked by the news in the newspapers on the sixth of April that year reporting his death. He had been

killed in the battles for Asia Minor, but I knew better and wasn't worried. It had rather been a report to harm the royal family, to attack me emotionally, but it was impossible to determine who had brought it about. And I immediately had to write to my mother to reassure her, who doubted the news, because I would have told her something like that immediately by telegram, and who was rather outraged at how such a shock could be given to an expectant mother.

On the tenth of June, I went into labor in the early hours of the morning and the doctor who had been called from Corfu recommended the kitchen table as the best place in the house to give birth to my child. At ten o'clock in the morning I gave birth to a son. In agreement with Andrea, he was given the name Philippos and was registered under this name in the city of Corfu. Andrea himself could not be present at the birth as he had had to leave Athens for Smyrna the day before the birth. He and his troops followed Tino, who was now himself in command of the Greek army. Many months were to pass before Andrea was finally able to hold his son in her arms. However, we wrote letters to each other in which he told me how warmly he and Tino had been received by the people in Smyrna, but a few days later he remarked that the Greek troops he was leading were poorly equipped and had little experience in battle. Nevertheless, he believed deeply and firmly in a Greek victory over the Ottoman Empire.

His joy at having a son, even though he was only the sixth in line to the Greek throne, made him overjoyed and spurred him on even more to do his best for his country. In any case, when I read his letters, I had the feeling that an even greater euphoria of victory flooded through him.

I spent the next few weeks after the birth mostly lying in the sun on a chaise longue on the terrace. We called our little one Philip and his sisters were terribly proud of him. It had been an easy birth for me. So I was soon able to answer the many telegrams with congratulations, mostly dictated to Dolla or Margarita. Our housekeeper couldn't get enough of Philip, she was delighted with his healthy appetite and what a cute, adorable baby he was.

As an Englishwoman, she really disliked Greek cuisine, which she also found insufficient for a baby. She therefore soon insisted on feeding Philip rice milk as well. When he began to eat solid food, she cooked him rice and tapioca puddings and highly nutritious Scottish porridge as a matter of course. Philip quickly won everyone's hearts as he was the baby of the family. Tiny, now deprived of this position, did not resent the little bundle of joy; she loved looking after him as much as her sisters did.

My parents, especially my father, were very happy about the birth of a second grandson. He was looking forward to the Mamaent when he could finally see the little one for himself, and I promised my parents that I would visit them soon, of course, so that they could meet Philip. Little did I know that fate would not allow my father to fulfill this wish.

Andrea told me that his troop consisted of men from the new provinces. They were recruits from Thrace, Eastern Macedonia and Asia Minor. The vast majority of these men did not even know how to handle a rifle properly. And many officers were uneducated, they could neither read nor write. This made it very difficult to pass on orders in writing. They were all determined to fight, but Andrea found it a very difficult task to train the men while they were all already in combat. He would still have to serve until the end of September, he wrote to me. And he didn't know exactly whether it would take any longer. However, my husband became increasingly aware that this conflict could now cost the lives of thousands of Greeks, as there had already been numerous attacks on civilians.
Moreover, Andrea had already written to the commander-in-chief, General Papoulas, asking for a brigade equipped with artillery for military battles in the mountains. There was a division that could be sent, but everything was so disorganized and not even the general knew where these men were. Andrea gave instructions that were simply ignored at the top. So he and his men in Alpanos found themselves facing eight thousand Turkish soldiers. The fighting lasted six hours, but they could only rely on four artillery units with guns, which was not enough. The untrained men under my husband's command fired on their own soldiers at one point. Incidents like this, which were not allowed to happen, caused Andreas' euphoria to slowly ebb away in each of his subsequent letters. And now I also began to worry whether the incompetence of his men would not outweigh his own military skills. I was worried about his life, but tried to keep my spirits up for my children and wrote to my parents that I believed Andrea would not lose his life in this conflict because he was strong. He knew how to protect his life, even if he was standing up for his men.

The summer of 1921 was something special for my father. Although he had started to take it easy at the age of sixty-seven, he was full of plans.
On February eighteenth, Arthur Lee, 1st Baron Lee of Fareham had been appointed *First Lord of the Admiralty of the British Navy.* He was a quiet admirer of my father, had great respect for his long career and was very sorry to see him virtually dumped. Now he invited him to a Navy *Club dinner* on July twenty-first. My father had so far stayed away from these meetings because he was too offended by his involuntary retirement, but now Mark Kerr, Nona's brother, persuaded him to accept the invitation after all, precisely

because Lee was such an admirer of his. Papa overcame himself. Hundreds of members of the British Navy were present at the dinner, and when they began a toast to his health, initiated by Lee, my father was deeply moved. He made a small speech thanking them and the gentlemen in attendance gave him a five-minute toast so that he could hardly speak. He was so moved by the evening that he told me in a letter, and I was delighted that he could be proud of his career again.

It was Lee who approached the King after that evening to confer the rank of honorary retired Admiral of the Fleet on Papa. It was the highest rank an officer in the British Navy could hold. The King agreed immediately, Lee had the news delivered to Papa in a letter on the fourth of August when he was in London, and my father went straight to his office. My father was even more touched by what Lee had done for him, and he sat down on a sofa there with tears in his eyes. Without further ado, he confessed to Lee that this was the greatest Mamaent of his life. It would mean everything to him in terms of his career in the Royal Navy.

Of course, my mother was also delighted that all this had rehabilitated my father. She was only too happy to see him happy and exuberant.

At the time, Dickie was serving as a *junior officer* on the battleship *Repulse* in Scotland. My brother spoke to the captain of the ship about the possibility of making Papa happy by inviting him to spend a week on the ship. Dickie wanted to celebrate Papa's appointment and the captain agreed. My father enjoyed the time with Dickie, the time on a ship where the crew members looked up to him, asked him about his career, his travels. He blossomed again, as Dickie told my mother in writing. They docked in Invergordon and there was even a little party for Papa in the castle there.

My father felt so good that he even planned to accompany Georgie, who was serving on the cruiser *Cardiff* in the Mediterranean, for a few days.

But towards the end of the trip, my father caught a cold and shortly afterwards developed a fever, which quickly rose to thirty-eight degrees Celsius. To make matters worse, he also got lumbago, which the doctor on the ship treated with back massages. But my father had to stay in bed. After two days he seemed to recover, he left the ship, said goodbye to Dickie and thanked the crew and the captain and traveled back to London. He met Mama and Nona there at the *Naval and Military Club*, reported on the voyage, completely overwhelmed, they exchanged family news and Mama pointed out to him that Dickie had told her about his illness in writing. He was well again, he assured her, but he was more worried about me and my family in Greece. When he said he was tired, they all went to *Club Annexe* in *Half Moon Street*, where Mama and Nona had booked a suite. The next morning, Papa was very pale and felt weak, so she sent for a doctor, to which he immediately protested, saying he was an old man and just tired from the trip. When the doctor examined him, he said it was nothing to worry about. He prescribed him some medicine. It was September 11th. Louise had also arrived and Papa was happy to see her. Mama and my sister took the afternoon tea with Papa, then they both went to a pharmacy in St. James's Street to get the medicine. The janitor brought my father some soup and toast at Mama's request, and he ate a little of both.

When Mama and Louise had been gone for a while, a maid knocked on the door to collect the dishes and tray. No one answered, so she entered cautiously. She thought my father was asleep on the bed, but as she approached, she noticed how peaceful he seemed and he wasn't breathing. She quickly sent for the janitor and they both eventually realized that my father was dead. Now when my mother returned with my sister, they encountered crying members of the house staff, of which the maid stepped forward and told Mama how sorry she was, but the admiral had passed away in her absence.

My mother broke down, Louise couldn't understand it either. He had been so full of ambition and had finally come back to life. It was a huge shock for all of us. At the autopsy, it was discovered that my father had died of a heart attack caused by the flu.

Louise immediately telegraphed me to Greece and also informed Dickie and Georgie. Without thinking twice, I decided to travel with Philip to England for my father's funeral. The girls stayed on Mon Repos. They were very upset about their grandfather's death, but I told them to remember him as he had been and there was no need for them to join me on the trip as I didn't want to stay long. It was better if they stayed on Corfu in case their father did arrive when he could take a break from his duties. Andrea had been given command of a second army corps at the beginning of August. The military authorities and Tino were firmly convinced that they could now advance on Ankara like a parade. In other words, it would be easy to take the city.

Andrea was skeptical, believing rather in a *Pyrrhic victory* in which the victor emerged from the war as weakened as the vanquished and was unable to build on it. He had crossed the *Anatolian salt desert*, the *Tuz Gölü*, with his troops. After Lake Van, it is the second largest in Anatolia and one of the saltiest in the world. The salt lake is located in the dry highlands between Ankara, Konya and Aksaray. He and his troops then won the battle for the Kale Grotto region. But after this battle they had little ammunition, little food and the division's horses were starving as there was nothing left for them to eat. There wasn't even any wood to make firewood so that the cook could process the little food they had. By now it was clear that the enemy knew their terrain better. The losses of Greek soldiers outweighed those of Ottoman soldiers, the Turkish soldiers took many prisoners and suffered hardly any material

losses. But the Greek troops did not receive any supplies. Andrea soon realized that none of the military plans of Major General Stratigos, his superior, made sense. He considered them to be completely counterproductive. So he decided on an alternative maneuver at his own discretion instead of following the instructions of the military headquarters.
On August twenty-third, the Greek troops attacked the Ottoman troops on the *Sakarya River* near *Polatli*, a town in the province of Ankara. The fighting in the vastness of the river was to last for three weeks. Tino wanted to advance with the troops as far as Ankara, but Andrea realized that the supply situation would get worse and worse the further they advanced into the area, as they were still a good eighty kilometers from Ankara and there were frontal attacks, retreats and surprise attacks. The landscape was barren, rocky and hilly in the area. This was supposed to be difficult for the animals, the machines and the transportation of heavy artillery. An important railroad line was captured along with the front, but the military authorities and Tino continued to press for an advance to Ankara in order to defeat Kemal once and for all. When the king gave the order to attack the Turkish lines on the tenth of August, they first had to march for nine days to even come into contact with the enemy. As the troops were split up and some of them, like Andreas, took the route via the area of the salt lake, he was unable to prevent his and other soldiers from plundering Turkish villages along the way, as they soon suffered from hunger. And at the *Sakarya River*, communication broke down for several days, so that no more supplies of food, weapons or ammunition were available. Tino was temporarily captured by a Turkish patrol, but was freed shortly afterwards, and Andrea saw little point in all of this. He therefore decided not to carry out an order to attack in order to spare the lives of the soldiers under his command, and had to report to General Papoulas for disobeying orders. He pointed out to him that he alone gave orders that a man had to carry out, as he was the commander-in-chief. Andrea asked to be allowed to leave the service, which the general refused. As a member of the royal family, Andrea had a duty to defend his country.
But soon afterwards my husband wrote to me to say that word was getting around about his decision not to fight and that Papoulas was now considering taking him out of his command for three months, literally sending him home. Andrea assumed that he would soon be back on Corfu, which made him very happy, as he finally wanted to see his son.
My father's death also hit him hard and he advised me to travel to England for the funeral.
I made the journey, which took a few days, so I was not present when the coffin with my father was taken in a large military procession from the private chapel at Buckingham Palace, where the coffin had been laid out for a few

days, to Westminster Abbey. Seven Admirals and a Major General of the Navy acted as pallbearers to pay their last respects to my father. After a memorial service, the coffin was taken on a special train to Portsmouth, then by ship to the Isle of Wight. My father was laid to rest in St. Mildred's Churchyard in Whippingham.

I arrived in Paris on September twenty-second, traveled on to Hampshire and arrived in Fishponds after the funeral. For my mother, Louise and my brothers, my sister-in-law Nada and her two young children, Philip provided a small distraction from the grief.

The British press also paid their last respects to my father, paying tribute to his career and his services to the British Navy. And King George had insisted on a funeral with full honors, because he also paid tribute to my father, having served under him on a ship as a young man.

Mama, Louise, Dickie, Philip and I traveled to London a few days later, where Christo's wife made *Spencer House*, an almost palatial mansion in the upscale St. James's district, available to me and rented it for us. It was in the immediate vicinity of St. James's Palace and *Green Park*. She even organized a cook and servants for us. We received condolences there and were still able to share our grief together.

Mama had my father's will opened, according to which I inherited over six thousand English pounds of his property in England, half a million rubles that he still had deposited in a bank, and over seven hundred thousand German marks from the sale of Heiligenberg Castle. His jewelry, paintings, books, prints and other works of art were divided equally between us four siblings, unless my mother wanted to keep an item. But she was already considering leaving Fishponds because there was too much there to remind her of my father. She mourned my father very much, but was not a woman to give up on herself because of it, and told us straight away that she would now have to look for new tasks, because her main task had been my father, her life had revolved around him as well as us children. But Georgie and I were married and already had children of our own, and in her eyes Dickie could pursue his bachelorhood for as long as he wanted. Only Louise's future worried her. My sister was now thirty-two years old and there was still no suitable marriage candidate in sight from my mother's point of view. There were no more balls or parties in the old pre-war tradition, most of the once young men were now married. Dickie hadn't been able to attend Papa's funeral either, as he was spending a weekend with the Duke and Duchess of Sutherland at *Dunrobin Castle* in Scotland when my father died. It was a short break from his duties on the *Repulse*, and when the news reached him by telegram on the afternoon of September twelfth, there was no train to London. The six hundred miles to London would have been too far by car and the journey would have taken too

balls to give Edwina her debut in society.

Dickie felt a bond with this young woman with the big sad blue eyes and reddish hair. They met several times in June and July 1921, then for *Cowes Week* in August.

Mrs. Vanderbilt, who was vacationing with her husband on the posh yacht *Atlantic*, noticed something developing between Dickie and Edwina. Without further ado, she invited Edwina and then Dickie to join her and her husband on a trip to Le Touché and other ports along the French coast. Mrs. Vanderbilt felt compelled to move things forward, but even though Dickie was more than impressed by how athletic Edwina was, swam in the sea like a fish and obviously soon felt more for him, he didn't dare ask her to marry him. After the story with Poppy, and since he would be traveling to India with the Prince of Wales in the fall, he hesitated to leave a possible fiancée lonely, who might also make a monkey out of him by dumping him just like Poppy. Nevertheless, he wanted to introduce her to our parents and asked them to accompany him to Fishponds. And Edwina was immediately taken with our father and he with her. Mama also thought she was very nice and an excellent match, as Edwina would bring the stately Broadlands estate and the castle in Scotland into the marriage as a dowry. Moreover, Dickie and she would never have money worries, but my mother initially feared that this very carefree attitude might lead to her son trading a career in the British Navy for an unsound lifestyle of leisure, as he would no longer have to work for a living. But this career meant a great deal to my brother, even more so after the death of my father, whose good reputation in the Navy he wanted to maintain as much as Georgie did. They wanted to give him a worthy reputation, if you like, by being as involved in it as he was. And Edwina, who was absolutely behind Dickie, who supported his career, would not, she assured Mama, put any obstacles in his way. Furthermore, she immediately saw something in Mama's motherliness that attracted her. She saw in her the mother she had lost so many years ago. They got on very well straight away.

At that time, nobody suspected that not only my father would soon die, but also Edwina's grandfather, who had developed chronic bronchitis. He was advised to travel to France, where Edwina had accompanied him, because of the warm climate, but he died on September twenty-first, 1921. Death united them both, if you like, and Dickie took heart. He did not want to leave his future wife alone for eight months when he traveled to India. But giving up this chance to cancel would not have been good for his career. Knowing that Lord Reading, the Viceroy of India, had been a close friend of Sir Ernest Cassel, he asked Edwina if she had ever received an invitation from him to visit him in India with her grandfather. When she replied in the affirmative, but said it had never happened, Dickie unceremoniously asked her to

accompany him on the trip.
Since we met them at *Renown* at the beginning of October, Louise and I met Edwina for the first time. Mama had prepared us for the meeting, but I have to admit that I was immediately taken with her. She was far from being pretentious despite her wealth, natural and very warm. My brother had received a promise from her that she would try to accompany him on the trip. Although she was to receive an annual allowance of around forty-five thousand English pounds from her grandfather's inheritance, she only received a small sum for her upkeep at the time because she was not yet twenty-one years old and not yet married. She was therefore unable to finance such a trip. She could not expect any financial help from her father, because although he was keen on such a trip, he did not want to give or lend her the money for it. Her stepmother, on the other hand, found the idea of having a step-son-in-law in the family who was related to the English royal family extremely attractive, as it would give her a better foothold in English society.
Edwina was to prove her love to Dickie by finding a lady to accompany her as a chaperone, as her father had requested, and she asked her aunt, her grandfather's sister, for money. An invitation from the Viceroy of India had meanwhile arrived for her through Dickie's engagement, so that on the twenty-sixth of October, in Portsmouth harbour, she first had to confess that she did not have the money, but then, having organized it, she followed him to India a little later. It was the best proof of love she could give him, and even though she could only stay there for six days, during which he was tied up with the Prince of Wales's many official engagements, they still spent time together. He finally asked Edwina for her hand in marriage. By means of a telegram, he asked King George for his consent and he, like all of us, was naturally in favor of their marriage. The viceroy made the news public and they celebrated.
After six days Edwina traveled happily back to England and my brother accompanied the prince on to Ceylon, Malaya, Hong Kong and Japan, where they were received by the Emperor.
The wedding date was set for the eighteenth of July 1922, as Dickie and the Prince would not be back from their trip and land in Plymouth until the end of June. With the wedding now planned and Edwina engaged, her inheritance was paid to her at the bank, with thousands of pounds sterling coming in. She immediately bought a wedding present for Dickie - a sporty gray Rolls Royce. Mama was happy because she could now throw herself into the wedding preparations, support Edwina, who had a lively correspondence with Dickie and always kept Mama up to date.
When I left England again in October 1921, her only concern was Louise, but she suppressed it because she was so happy for Dickie. And I was also of the

opinion that he couldn't have made a better match. It was just very sad that my father, who had been so fond of Edwina, didn't live to see it.

When I arrived in Corfu, Andrea was back on Mon Repos because he had been given leave. He told me about the alleged refusal to obey orders. He was very offended that his abilities were not accepted and that he was instead supposed to blindly follow orders, which, from his point of view, would lead to nothing but a complete military disaster. Nevertheless, he was cheered up by our little son, whom he could finally hold in his arms. He also mourned my father's death very much, as he had held him in high esteem, but he objected that he had now been *dumped* just as coldly. Dickie's impending marriage to Edwina also interested him very much, but I felt that it pained him more than anything to know that there would be a real slaughter in the war with the Turks because his objections were simply ignored. He had been promoted to lieutenant general, but this was of no use to him if the other officers cut him and plotted against him. He was sure of that. In Eskişehir, one of the largest cities and capital of the Anatolian province of the same name, he had led a successful attack, for which he had risen in rank, but he found it useless. He had the uneasy feeling that he was only tolerated in the Greek army, but not really accepted for his abilities. He had therefore asked to be discharged for a short time.

But things were to get even worse for my husband. Andrea, Crown Prince George and Nicholas had given an interview in the Italian newspaper *Giornale d`Italia* in which they clearly spoke out against Venizelos. I didn't think they could be *blamed* for this, because this man had driven our family into exile. But the Greek press picked up on it at the end of October and suddenly Andrea was seen as controversial. George and Nicholas were also publicly attacked, but most of the criticism was focused on Andrea, as people had also learned about his retirement from military service and the reasons behind it.

On October 20, 1921, France and the Turkish National Assembly under Kemal concluded the *Treaty of Ankara*. In December 1918, France had occupied Mesopotamia and Cilicia, which later became southern Turkey and northern Syria. On November 1, 1919, an incident occurred that would go down in history as the *Sütçü İmam incident.* Sütçü İmam had come to the aid of three women who had been harassed by Armenian soldiers, who were using the French as support, in the city of Maraş in Cilicia. He killed one of the soldiers and then had to go into hiding. However, this incident turned the Turkish population of the city so much against the French occupiers that an uprising broke out just two months later. On February 11, 1921, the French were forced to evacuate the city. The Armenian community fled for fear of revenge from the Turkish majority. Resistance fighters formed large groups to fight

the French soldiers in the surrounding towns. On February 9th, France had already signed a peace treaty with the Turkish National Assembly, but now, with the *Treaty of Ankara*, the French switched sides and supported Kemal with arms supplies. It can be said that enemies did not become friends, but allies. France vacated the occupied territories and gave them up. However, this also meant that Greece lost an ally in the fight against the Turks. This political move by the French baffled my husband and it annoyed him greatly, as it did Tino and the rest of the royal family, of course.
But it also encouraged Andrea all the more not to believe that our troops would win.
In December, Andrea had to take command again. He now commanded the Fifth Army Corps of Epirus and the Ionian Islands, which was stationed in Jannina.
I had my refuge on Mon Repos, but I wanted to be by my husband's side so that his despair didn't weigh him down completely. Before he could travel to Jannina, he had to get treatment in Athens because a very serious purulent infection had developed on his gums. I followed him to the capital, left my children in the care of the nanny and traveled with him to Jannina after the successful treatment. Within one night, I organized a house for him so that we had somewhere to stay.
As soon as he started his service, he immediately told me that he wondered when this would all end, because it was obvious how the Greek troops were outnumbered by the Turkish. He witnessed the whole tragedy at close quarters. It was a very difficult time, I missed my children, especially little Philip, but it also weighed heavily on me how it all gnawed at Andrea.
Mama and Louise wanted to pay us a surprise visit in Corfu on the nineteenth of March 1922. They brought some boxes of silver objects from the Heiligenberg as well as numerous baby things as presents for little Philip. But I was still in Jannina when I heard about their arrival by telegraph. So I asked them to wait for us until Andrea and I found a way to get to Mon Repos. Mama and Louise were only too happy to take care of the children.
Andrea and I only returned to Corfu on the fourth of April to celebrate her birthday with Mama on the fifth of April and then Easter with everyone.
Mama told me that Aunt Irene had visited the alleged Anastasia in the Dalldorf asylum in Berlin. The lady, who had become very dubiously famous under the name Anna Anderson and was in the asylum after she tried to end her life by jumping into the Spree, told me hair-raising things about her alleged rescue by a soldier from Yekaterinburg. She was of course in all the newspapers and on everyone's lips. Not only Aunt Irene, but also other aristocrats such as the Crown Princess of Prussia Cecilie visited the lady. My aunt had not seen Anastasia since before the war, but immediately decided

found shards of ancient vases, plates, other tableware, bronze nails, coins and human bones, among other things. They meticulously noted down every find and confessed to us that they had found the bones in an ancient cemetery. Their best find was an ancient pot that was almost undamaged. I sent some of these pieces to the school for handicrafts in Athens so that they could use the patterns, which were often still clearly present and had cultural significance.

Only Andrea remarked that it might not be a good idea to attract too much attention with the finds, lest hordes of archaeologists soon storm the island and disturb our peace and quiet on Mon Repos.

"They'll turn our beautiful garden into a crater-like field," he sighed, but I objected that I wasn't sending all the finds to Athens, and if you worked the earth in Greece with a shovel, starting somewhere, you would surely find much better and more historically significant pieces. Besides, there were already many excavation sites. My only concern here was the fact that the girls were so committed and were very happy that their finds were appreciated.

Mama, however, was anything but enthusiastic about the bones, because she thought it was unpleasant to disturb the peace of the dead, no matter how old the bones were, and since she remarked that it disturbed her to see them, because she was thinking of Aunt Alix and her family, I asked the children not to look for any more or even bring them with them. I understood my mother, and even though I had always regarded death as a natural part of life, nobody liked to have the bones of strangers lying around the house.

Mama and Louise left soon after, as there was still a lot to organize for Dickie and Edwina's upcoming wedding.

In May, I traveled back to Jannina with Andrea. There I gave some tea parties for the local authorities and on the sixteenth of May I went back to Corfu.

Tino's health had not been good since the fall of last year. He felt weak, the armed conflict with Turkey was wearing on his nerves and, at the age of fifty-four, he was beginning to look much older. He was still maintaining his extramarital affair, but this additional balancing act between family and lover was taking its toll. And then he came down with typhoid. He was in a very bad way for a while, but then he recovered. Nevertheless, it was clear that he could hardly bear his burden any longer.

The economic situation in Greece also deteriorated noticeably, so Andrea and I had to live with financial losses, interest rates on loans turned negative and we lost about a quarter of our income and credit. Nevertheless, we still had enough money to live a pretty good life and money wasn't everything for me. I had already learned that from my mother. There were other things in life that mattered more than a big bank account.

In June, we all traveled to England for Dickie and Edwina's wedding. We were able to stay at Spencer House again and the girls were so excited the days before that they didn't want to take off their dolphin blue dresses, which Edwina had chosen according to the color of her eyes.

Dickie had originally wanted to get married in Westminster Abbey, but then thought it was a place where only the really big fish should get married. The church at Buckingham Palace was too small, so they decided to have the ceremony at St. Margaret's in Westminster. It was obvious from the outset that this marriage would be an extremely pompous event for London. Edwina wanted a mixture of royal flair and high society, which was entirely appropriate.

On July 18th, 1922, the wedding took place in the presence of King George, Queen Mary and Aunt Alexandra. The presence of the royal family, numerous relatives from the royal family and English high society as well as members of the British Navy made the marriage an unforgettable event.

Our girls' dresses were tailored in the newfangled *flapper style.* The skirts were short, they had to keep tugging them up to cover their knees, and the silk stockings kept slipping down so that Tiny and Cäcilie mocked the fact that they always had to be careful not to get them around their ankles. Nevertheless, it was fashionable, modern, in the new style of the 1920s, because people actually danced the new dances like the *Charleston* in these dresses.

Philip was still too small to attend the wedding directly, but he was allowed to wave to us from afar on his nanny's arm as we left the church, and then remained in her care at Spencer House.

The British *Pathé*, a weekly news program that was broadcast in European cinemas before the main film, filmed the event to report on it later. It was called "*The Wedding of the Season*". Crowds of onlookers had gathered everywhere on the streets, so that the cars could barely get through, and the number of police officers who had to direct traffic was enormous. Twenty thousand Londoners stood alone cheering behind the barriers in Parliament Square to catch a glimpse of the distinguished guests who had arrived. It was a mass spectacle of almost unimaginable proportions.

Our girls in July 1922, from left to right
Tiny, Cäcilie, Dolla and Margarita

Royal Bridesmaids at the Mountbatten - Ashley Wedding.

My girls were even mentioned in the journals as bridesmaids

Edwina's sister was her maid of honor and officers from the British Navy had been specially assigned as *groomsmen* for my brother.

Dickie and Edwina in front of the church with Tiny, left, and Cäcilie, right, who were allowed to wear the train of the wedding dress, July 1922

One of the official wedding photos from left to right: Mary Ashley, Margarita, standing, Joan Pakenham, a friend of the bride, Sophie, seated, Dickie, Edwina, Edward, the Prince of Wales, Mary Ashley-Cooper, who was Edwina's stepmother, Dolla, standing, and Cecilia, July 1922

The bride and groom didn't let the stress show. Even before the wedding, numerous presents had arrived at Brook House, where Edwina lived with her grandfather's sister after his death. The bride had never owned much jewelry, but now she received the most precious pieces from jeweled rings, diamond tiaras, precious brooches to valuable necklaces, which were given to her by Aunt Alexandra and even the Aga Khan, among others. She confessed to us that she actually had very simple tastes when it came to jewelry, but these were gifts that she now had to wear. It was a sign of her naturalness that she initially shied away from putting on such ostentatious jewelry and showing it off in public.

The schedule before the wedding had been very tight, as Dickie had to be back from his trip first. Shortly after his return, he had visited and met Edwina's father and stepmother in Broadlands, then they had been invited to a large family dinner at Buckingham Palace, followed by numerous invitations from distinguished London personalities. Their next four weeks were already completely scheduled.

After the wedding ceremony, the guests gathered at Brook House and soon

the house was almost overflowing with guests. Dickie told me later that he must have shaken about five hundred hands that day, but missed at least three hundred. When the King and Queen left the festivities, the party was able to disperse.
With a smile on her lips, Edwina told Dickie out loud to change his clothes and then they would make their way to Broadlands, which Edwina's father had put at their disposal for the night. The wedding present for my brother, the Rolls Royce *Silver Ghost*, was parked near the house in Upper Brook Street. Dickie was overwhelmed by the gift and immediately took a seat in it. Together with his bride, he drove off, honking the horn several times.
The party had been very opulent. The wedding cake alone was a confectioner's masterpiece, decorated with lifeboats and lifebuoys. And one gift in particular delighted the couple: a large silver globe on which the Prince of Wales had engraved Dickie's travel route with him.
On the drive to Broadlands, an incident occurred that Dickie would later repeat over and over again. When they stopped the car briefly because an acquaintance of Dickie's came across them in his car, Dickie introduced Edwina to him as his fiancée, Miss Ashley. Edwina raised her hand in annoyance, showed the man her wedding ring and grimaced. He later laughed at his mistake, but his bride was probably very angry with him for some time.
They then stayed at Broadlands for a few days, only getting up at midday and enjoying the hours.
Dickie, who always planned everything exactly as he had learned in the navy, was sure that his bride must be delighted with his honeymoon, because he had planned everything in detail. They were going to travel through Europe, but he had worked out in minute detail which hotel they would stay in and when, when they would have tea and much more. That was too rigid for Edwina, she wanted to have more freedom to organize her honeymoon, and the departure had to be postponed because of the invitations and a forecast bad weather front with a storm warning.
My brother had been released from his service in the Navy for six months and managed well even on half pay, as his wife had enough money.
Edwina and he would first have to get used to each other, said Mama. But their subsequent honeymoon, which was to begin in Paris and then take them through Europe, including visits to relatives in Hesse and Spain, was not enough for either of them, so they also traveled to America by ship. From New York to Washington, the Grand Canyon, Chicago and Niagara Falls, they visited all the sights and even had lunch with the President. They didn't want to be back until December. Their honeymoon already bore witness to the pomp *and splendour* that they were to continue in their later lives.
Dickie would be given a new command on the *Dreadnought* in January 1923

and so the two were able to fully enjoy their time together.
My brother quickly discarded all his well-laid plans, booked them out of the elegant *Ritz Hotel* in Paris and they slept in the attic of a small guesthouse instead, which delighted his wife, as he wrote to us.
We were all very impressed by the world Dickie had now married into.
And soon all the newspapers were reporting on the luxurious honeymoon, as it is safe to say that Edwina and Dickie soon became the most sought-after couple in *high society*. Everyone wanted to invite them and surround themselves with them, and they even met Charlie Chaplin in the USA. They even made a short silent film with him in Hollywood, in which they played lovers and he directed. It was Chaplin's wedding present to the couple.
My brother was soon to regret his status as a celebrity, however, because when he returned to duty after his honeymoon, the latest issue of *Tatler*, a gossip magazine from the world of the rich and famous, was already in the officers' mess and he and Edwina had graced the cover more than once. From then on, he had a hard time among his comrades, who had nothing to do with his fame and celebrity. He was involved in the navy, but otherwise lived a completely different life. As a result, many people made him feel directly rejected, which made me feel very sorry for my brother.

After the wedding, we traveled to Scotland, where we all went on beautiful nature trips with Nada, Georgie and their children in wonderful weather. Louise accompanied us and was very happy to spend time with her nieces and little Philip. She had also enjoyed Dickie and Edwina's wedding very much, but was still wistful about her own life. She felt like an old maid who no man wanted to marry because she was well past her marriageable age. I consoled her with the old, perhaps antiquated saying that a lid has always been found for every pot. Of course, it didn't really help her, because she immediately said that she would end up like Aunt Beatrice.
Unfortunately, dark clouds loomed on our horizon, forcing us to return to Greece, and neither Andrea nor I had any idea what was in store for us when we set off on our return journey on September nineteenth.
Mama feared that the Asia Minor campaign could have a bad impact on our lives, and I didn't know at the time how right she would be.
Andrea had already left a little earlier as he had been summoned to Athens. There was a meeting at the palace, which Tino, Andrea and Nicholas attended. They received Georgeios Vlachos there. He had founded a newspaper publishing house in 1919, which published *the Kathemirini*, an Athenian morning *newspaper*. Vlachos was a conservative and during this conversation my husband openly expressed what many people were thinking. He asked Tino to resign and hand over the government to his son. He also thought it

would be best if Tino resigned and went abroad, partly because of his state of health. Nicholas was absolutely opposed to Tino losing his claim to power again. After all, he had only just returned from exile and, from Nicholas' point of view, nothing had been lost in the conflict with the Turks.
Tino himself remained silent, which really annoyed my husband because he didn't like the fact that his brother didn't want to take a stance. Vlachos was also very skeptical about how to get a grip on the conflict.
On September 9th, the so-called *Asia Minor Catastrophe* occurred. Mustafa Kemal and his troops conquered Smyrna, which later became Izmir. Shortly after the conquest, the Turks turned their hatred on the Greek and Armenian inhabitants of the city. They attacked the people in their neighborhoods, driving them out or killing them in the cruelest of ways. As houses were set on fire, large parts of the city soon resembled a sea of flames from which people fled into the sea. Countless people drowned in their panic.
The fires spread, raging through the city for days. Around forty thousand inhabitants lost their lives during these days. It was a genocide of inhumane proportions, which was also extended to the surrounding villages, which were completely razed to the ground. In the city of *Van*, the entire Armenian quarter was wiped out, and they did not shy away from destroying places of worship.
Some people in Izmir had fled from the siege by Kemal on English ships provided, but most had thrown all warnings to the wind when it was feared that the city could be conquered. They could not be blamed, as they did not want to leave their property and perhaps believed that the Greek troops would help them.
On the tenth of September, Tino issued a proclamation in which he took no position on the genocide, but assured the Greek people that although he recognized the failure of the Greek army, it had proven itself in the First World War and now he would do everything he could to restore peace in the country with the help of the constitution. He appealed to the patriotism of the people, but it was basically a more than helpless attempt at damage limitation. The war against the Ottomans was lost. This was all too obvious.
We were constantly receiving reports of people being expelled from Asia Minor or forcibly resettled simply because of their religion. Tens of thousands of people died on the refugee treks that followed. For two thousand five hundred years, Greeks had lived peacefully with Armenians and Turks in Asia Minor, but now this ancient history was swept away in one fell swoop. It had been the cradle of Greek culture, producing philosophers like Thales, poets like Iliad and Homer.
At the same time, the Turks also had to flee Greece as they were driven out by brute force. Here, too, tens of thousands died while fleeing.

Andrea had seen it coming, and now my husband was being vilified for leaving the country to attend a wedding and simply not carrying out his command in Epirus. While tragedy struck, he had been celebrating happily in the eyes of other members of the military.

Francis Lindley, a newly appointed English ambassador, and his advisor Charles Bentinck were two very capable diplomats, but they were not very friendly towards Tino either, as England's resentment towards Tino's reinstatement still persisted. And as he was now failing as supreme commander in the Greek-Turkish conflict, these seemed to be coming true. Moreover, England was watching Tino's every move with suspicion, for which Sir Eyre Crowe, Permanent Under-Secretary of State at the Foreign Office, was responsible. Lindley and Bentinck reported every piece of news to him in detail, and when Tino asked them both for a meeting to discuss Greece's foreign affairs, it was not very fruitful for him. He was literally made to feel the rejection and contempt.

Lindley did not fear a revolution in Greece, but saw Tino's popularity wane when the first defeated Greek troops returned to Greece in August. Tino had utterly failed militarily, a fact that Andrea constantly emphasized when he ordered a major attack against the Turkish troops on the twenty-second of August, which was seen as the last stand. On the western front near *Afyonkarahisar*, the Turks broke through the lines of this counter-offensive on the second day. On the thirtieth of August, at the battle of Dumlupinar, Kemal finally crushed our troops. The Greek troops had to withdraw from Anatolia, sealing the long series of Tino's military blunders. And the catastrophe in Asia Minor did the rest.

Shortly afterwards, on September 11th, a revolutionary committee was formed, initiated by two officers of the Greek military who also wanted to stand up for their comrades in order to take revenge for the defeat in the Greek-Turkish conflict. They felt betrayed by the government and, above all, the king. Colonel Nikolaos Plastiras had served under Andrea and Colonel Stylianos Gonatas joined Plastiras. They were the masterminds behind the revolutionary committee and soon had leaflets printed and dropped over Athens. They demanded Tino's immediate resignation.

These officers were supporters of Venizelos, who was still keeping a close eye on the situation in Athens from his exile.

Lindley now felt compelled to telegraph to London immediately so that the government could send soldiers to prevent bloodshed and protect the royal family if the worst came to the worst. The main concern was to protect Tino and his family. There were no fears for other members of the royal family, but as the king consistently refused to abdicate, the situation threatened to escalate.

Finally, on September twenty-seventh, Tino realized that he had lost his claim to power for the second time in his life and agreed to abdicate. Crown Prince George lived with his wife Elisabeth at his in-laws' in Romania. He was now summoned back to Athens, accepted the crown and took the oath. As King George II, he became the new King of Greece, with his wife Elizabeth as Queen at his side, but George still carried the stigma of having been trained in the German military. Moreover, he took office when the revolutionary committee was trying to establish itself alongside him. So we could all only hope that he would not rule as a mere puppet like his brother Alexander.
A Greek steamship, the *SS Patris*, was organized for the departure of Tino, his wife Sophie and their two daughters Irene and Katherine, on which they were to leave Greece on the evening of the thirtieth of September. Lindley hoped that Nicholas and his family as well as Andrea, our children and I would follow them. But Andrea flatly refused to leave his homeland, and he saw no danger for me and the children in remaining on Mon Repos. We were there away from Athens and would wait for things to happen, but not interfere. We both resented the thought of going back into exile, wherever that might be. Our children loved Mon Repos, the very tranquil life there. We didn't want to take them away from home again. And we had only just come out of exile and had settled in again. It was unthinkable for us to leave again, to move around restlessly and just wait in another place to finally be allowed to return home.
However, Andrea, Nikolaus and Tino asked their mother to go into exile too, and as Tino's health was not good, she also wanted to be a support for him and immediately agreed to leave the country.
Aspasia, Alexander's widow, and her young daughter Alexandra remained unaffected by the revolutionary committee's demand that they leave the country, as they were of no great importance to the government. Since, contrary to all fears, Aspasia had not given birth to a son with a claim to the throne, her status could be described as quite uninteresting.
Nicholas and his family traveled to Paris, where they had already lived quite well during their first exile, because Elena, as a born Russian Grand Duchess, still owned a lot of jewelry, which they were able to sell to finance their living expenses.
Tino, his family and his mother-in-law traveled all the way to Italy. As they were able to choose their own exile, it was decided that the climate there would be best for Tino to recuperate, so they moved to *Villa Hygeia* near Palermo.
The revolutionaries now hoped that the forced abdication of Tinos would win back the trust of the Allies, especially England. This was linked to the hope that Eastern Thrace could remain Greek, but this was dashed. On October

Gounaris, Interior Minister Nikolaos Stratos, War Minister Nikolaos Theotokis, Foreign Minister Georgeios Baltatzis, Minister Michael Goudas, the other former Prime Minister Petros Protopapadakis, former Prime Minister Nikolaos Kalogeropoulos, who was simply considered senile and therefore arrested, were arrested. General Georgeios Hatzianestis, commander of the troops in Asia Minor and Thrace, Xenophon Stratigos, Minister of Communications and Colonel Constantinopoulos, former administrator of the military district of Athens were also placed under arrest and then also arrested. It was like a real witch hunt. The revolutionary committee simply needed a scapegoat to justify the catastrophe in Asia Minor and the defeat of the Greek army. But they used several scapegoats at once, all of whom they wanted to put on trial.

Lindley made his displeasure at a planned trial publicly clear by warning that any executions of the detainees could be seen as a pure act of revenge and would ultimately divide the country.

General Pangalos, who essentially led the interrogations of the prisoners as spokesman, was a supporter of Venizelo and an absolute opponent of the monarchy. He was made a public prosecutor. Together with Plastiras, he now proclaimed the *Hellenic Republic*. Although this was a purely formal proclamation, as Greece still had a king, he was merely a pawn in the revolutionary committee's efforts to assert their own claims to power.

On October 12, the committee established a so-called *extraordinary military tribunal*.

In the meantime, I had even tried to write to the Pope so that he would help my husband, because it was now clear to me that these men were capable of anything.

The tribunal was convened for the first time on October thirty-first. In a two-week trial, Gounaris, Baltatzis, Stratos, Theotokis, Protopapadakis and Hatzianestis were charged with high treason before a military court, then found guilty.

They were all sentenced to death. Considering that most of these men were opposed to Venizelos, the death sentence spoke for itself. In addition, the trial of Plastiras, Gonatas and Pangalos was presided over by Alexandros Othonaios as the presiding military judge, also an ardent supporter of Venizelos, who was brought to Athens to attend the trial as an extraordinary deputy of the committee.

The death sentences were published on November fifteenth, but by then the defendants were already dead. They had been shot in *Goudi*, an eastern part of Athens at the foot of Mount *Hymettos*, immediately after the death sentences were announced in the early morning of November fifteenth.

Admiral Goudas and General Stratigos received life sentences. The latter was

later allowed to go into exile in Switzerland as part of an amnesty.
News of the executions spread quickly throughout Europe. In Paris, unfortunately, there were also reports expressing displeasure that Tino, Nicholas and Andrea had not shared the same fate as the main culprits.

At the beginning of November, I still had vague hopes that my husband might be released. Georgie had spoken to the King in London and asked him to intervene. Lord Curzon had already made representations to the King about the situation in Greece, but as this had not been fruitful, Georgie now appealed to family connections. And King George agreed to help, saying he wouldn't mind if Andrea and we went into exile in England. But the days passed and nothing happened.
By now I understood my Aunt Alix, who had feared that Uncle Nicky would be put on trial in Moscow after his abdication. And the king had let her and her family down by refusing them exile in England. In a way, he had made himself guilty, which Mama still felt the same way, and now he wouldn't help again. My despair grew as I had already made plans with the girls about what we would do if their father was released. I wanted to send Dolla and Margarita to Mimi and George in Paris. The three younger children were to stay with me in Mon Repos.
Christo came to visit us on Corfu from London in mid-November. He was very shocked to discover that we were still under police surveillance. He sensed my inner excitement and anxiety, but he was also very worried about his brother.
He immediately decided to travel on to Athens and asked to be allowed to visit Andrea, but was firmly refused. Christo, although a member of the royal family, was safe because he had a check for a large sum of money with him, which his rich wife Anastasia had given him. This sum was to go to the Greek Red Cross. He was therefore allowed to enter the house where Andrea was being held prisoner, where a servant was allowed to go from time to time to bring him food, among other things. There, with the help of the servant, Christo managed to smuggle a message in a packet of cigarettes to my husband in the rooms. In an embroidered handkerchief, which Christo was supposed to deliver to me, he received a very disturbing message from Andrea. After my husband accepted his fate and expressed this to General Pangalos, the latter asked him how many children he had, but did not wait for an answer. Instead, he regretted that they would soon all be half-orphans.
Christo made his way to Tatoi and spoke to the new king, but he quickly realized that he too was in an awkward position, as he immediately revealed to him that he was also just like a prisoner in this country, afraid of the committee and the Greek people.

Before Christo left in a hurry, as he was unable to help, he demanded the cheque back, as he saw no point in supporting anything, anyone or any organization in Greece. He also demanded that Ellen, Nicholas' wife, return the awards she had received as part of her charitable activities, her collection of jewels still in the palace and her Persian cat. Everything was handed over to him and he was allowed to leave unmolested. He made a stopover off Corfu, but was not allowed to disembark. A policeman informed me of this and I went to the harbor, where he tried to tell me what he had learned and experienced in Athens. I gave him a letter for Mama so that she knew how we were doing and how my husband was doing. It was a great gesture on Christo's part not to omit or even gloss over anything in front of me, even though I now felt completely helpless.

In Turkey, too, the National Assembly under Kemal called for the end of the monarchy, and on the first of November it was decided to separate the caliphate from the sultanate, which was abolished at the same time. The rule of the House of Osman thus ended after 622 years. Sultan Mehmed VI was forced to leave the country and traveled into exile to Malta on the British warship *HMS Malaya* on the seventeenth of November, then on to San Remo on the Italian Riviera, where King Victor Emmanuel III provided him with a villa. The Sultan's cousin became the new Caliph of Turkey as Abdülmecid II. However, he too was more of a puppet under Kemal and the National Assembly.

On November twenty-second, King George met with the diplomat at the British Foreign Office, Sir Eyre Crowe, to discuss the situation in Greece and Andrea's situation. My mother had by now also spoken to the King, who finally admitted to her that he had followed the advice of his minister, Lloyd George, in refusing to offer Aunt Alix's family exile in England. He had been weak at a single Mamaent when he should have shown strength, and spoke openly to my mother that he did not want another cousin's blood on his hands. For the first and only time in his reign, he invoked his royal prerogative to make a decision.
Shortly afterwards, Lindley informed me that Crowe had telegraphed him from England with the news that the King was very concerned about Andrea's fate. He asked to be kept informed by Lindley at all times and complained about the criminal nonsense the Greek government was using to achieve its extreme political aims. Lindley should make every suggestion to the King as to the best way to help Andrea, and he should also leave no stone unturned to convince the Greek authorities of the absurdity of accusing Andrea. The most important goal now was to free my husband. The Greek government should

allow him to leave the country with his family.
This was a ray of hope, but at the same time we received the news that Andrea was to be tried at the end of November. Although the committee argued that the ministers who had already been executed bore the greatest guilt, Andrea was also to face the charges before the military court.
During this time, when I put on a brave front in front of my children, reassuring them that nothing would happen to their father, I sometimes didn't believe my own reassurances, and I also realized that Dolla and Margarita, because of their age, naturally understood the situation in its entirety and could share my worries more than the two younger sisters. I couldn't pretend anything to the two older ones. They gave me support and also hoped for help from the King of England.
When Cäcilie and Tiny, aged eleven and eight, asked about their father, or little Philip, it almost broke my heart.
How bad it must have been for my Russian cousins in exile, little Alexei, constantly monitored by the soldiers in a house under arrest ... and Aunt Ella - now I could empathize. We were never physically harassed by the police, but the mere presence was hard to bear. I constantly admonished the two younger girls not to say a word about their father when they were playing outside, not to say anything out loud about what we were discussing in the house.
And my husband was all alone. What kind of longing did he have for all of us?
There were nights when I could barely sleep, crying into my pillow, praying that this heavy burden would finally be lifted from us and that salvation would come.

Lindley was certain that Andrea would not be executed, but would be punished with exile, i.e. banishment from Greece. From his point of view, a trial against my husband would only serve to show that a revolution made no distinction between people, whether they were of royal blood or officers, ministers. He told me that he would only really worry about Andrea if there was a political upheaval. But these were all just assumptions, which now confirmed to me that it had been a mistake to stay in Greece. I assumed that I shared Andrea's opinion. In his predicament, he certainly regretted it far more than I did.
In the meantime, the Foreign Office in London had received a report via H. G. Mayes, which he addressed to the Junior Naval and Military Club, in which he described the course of the first trial in detail. He warned the Foreign Office that they were simply standing by instead of intervening, thus opening the doors to a very far-reaching justice system. Diplomatic relations

between England and Greece had now been destroyed. Maye's warnings were not taken seriously because the Foreign Office simply ignored the report. The Prime Minister knew nothing more about Mayes than that he had been the organizer of the Olympic Games in Greece.
On November twenty-fifth, the old government had to resign, General Gonatas formed a new one and the new Minister of War became General Pangalos. According to Lindley, he was one of the most violent soldiers he had ever heard of. Andrea's trial was set to begin on the thirtieth of November.
I could no longer sit idly by on Corfu and traveled to Athens immediately, because I simply had to be near Andrea.
From Athens, I tried once again to get help from the Pope, Ena's husband, the King in Spain and my two brothers, and then I learned that Dickie had already made representations to King George in England. Dickie even went to see the Prime Minister, Bonar Law.
Lord Curzon now intervened on Andrea's behalf, as he contacted Commander Gerald Talbot in Switzerland. He was employed by the British Foreign Service at the time and had also been accompanying the British naval envoy in Athens for some time. Curzon asked him to make sure that Andrea could leave Greece unharmed with us as his family.
With forged papers, Talbot set off immediately and reached Athens on the twenty-eighth of November. He arrived a few days before the trial. If Talbot had intended to kidnap Andrea, he decided against such a secret and perhaps dangerous method after speaking to Pangalos. On November thirtieth, the British Embassy in Athens sent an early morning telegram to the Foreign Office in London. In it, Talbot confirmed that the Minister of War and Colonel Plastiras had both assured him that Andrea would not be executed, but that he would be allowed to leave the country under Talbot's protectorate. However, this was subject to conditions, which were that my husband would appear at the start of the trial on the following Saturday and take part in the entire trial and take a stand. A conviction on his part would result in hard labor or the death penalty. But Plastiras would then pardon Andrea and hand him over to Talbot so that he could leave the country immediately with me and the family on a British warship bound for Brindisi. Or a route to England should be chosen via another port. The revolutionary committee demanded that a British warship be ready in the port of Phaleron exactly at noon on the third of December. The captain could receive an order from the British embassy about the route, but everything had to be done in secret. This meant that the captain was not to be informed about who was going on board or the reason for the journey.
The committee claimed to have made this concession with the greatest of efforts and that they had to adhere to the guidelines in order to save Andrea's

life. The agreement was to be considered secret; neither Andrea nor I were allowed to know anything about it beforehand, otherwise they would, to put it succinctly, reconsider everything. Any infringement would therefore be detrimental to Talbot's efforts, which were based on the fact that he invoked the King in England. But to Pangalos, it didn't matter if the King of England or anyone else of our kin insisted on anything, as he told Talbot, because it was the committee's decision alone.
King George had already called the English Admiralty a few days earlier, making it clear that he insisted on sending a ship to Athens to rescue his cousin. He emphasized that immediate action should be taken to keep Andrea alive. This royal exercise of power led to the immediate dispatch of *HMS Calypso*, a cruiser fully equipped with weapons, which set off for Piraeus. The cruiser was due to arrive on time, but when the ship positioned itself in the harbor of Phaleron, a supporter of the revolutionary committee immediately made his way to Athens, informing Pangalos that a British warship was in the harbor and that its cannons were pointed at the city. Of course, this was not true, but the cruiser was nevertheless something of a memorial, a silent threat to Pangalos.
The HMS Malaya was also in the harbor, waiting there at the request of the British embassy in Athens in case the king and his wife had to be taken out of the country. King George in England was informed of this and informed Tino and his family in Palermo so that they would not worry about their son and daughter-in-law. Tino's daughter Helen was skeptical, however, because she feared that an intervention concerning her brother would lead to an act of violence against him by the revolutionary committee, and my mother-in-law Olga, who was currently in Paris, wrote to the king that she hoped he would ensure the protection of her grandson and his wife.
On the first of December, Talbot obtained a promise from General Pangalos that no more political prisoners would be executed. He also interceded on behalf of the senile minister Nikolaos Kalogeropoulos. He was not sentenced to death as a result, but was released due to his physical and mental condition - he was already seventy-two years old. The old man posed no danger to the committee, so Talbot found his release absolutely justified. The minister was no longer in a position to actively follow a trial.
On the third of December, Andrea was taken to the parliament building where the trial took place. During the trial, Colonel Kalogeras accused him of refusing to carry out the orders of the commander-in-chief, General Papoulas, on the third of August 1921, thus evading confrontation with the enemy. Andrea testified that the orders meant for the *Third Army Corps* to defend, while the *First* and *Second Army Corps* were to attack. He added that in his *Third Corps* they kept an eye on the other two as the Turkish troops attacked. Colonel

Sariyannis, who had been summoned as a witness and was a former sub-chief of staff in Ionia, stated on the record that the colonel's orders had been ignored, had they been carried out, the battle at the Sakarya River would have been won.

Andrea was accused of disobeying orders and charged with simply abandoning his post, even though they were facing the enemy. Furthermore, my husband was accused of complete incompetence in commanding a large force, for which he was stripped of all military ranks, demoted and banned from Greece for life.

Although it was true that Andrea refused to obey orders, he took the initiative in battle and was very capable of commanding a larger force. He simply foresaw defeat. It therefore didn't matter whether it was claimed that they could have been victorious if Andrea had acted according to orders. The trial was a pure farce to make my husband a scapegoat for the incompetence of all the accused Greek politicians and generals.

Andrea, sitting on the far right, during the trial, December 1922

Talbot had been able to inform me in secret about some things that had been agreed with the committee. Frank Lindley had left Athens in the meantime, but Charles Bentinck was still present. When Talbot asked the Prime Minister and Colonel Plastiras for a meeting, Bentinck was also present. The meeting was about the committee assuring Talbot of the king's safety. Plastiras

assured him and Bentinck that the king had been appointed and that he would remain on the throne. There was no danger to him or to the civilian population in Greece. The political situation was to remain as it was at the Mamaent.
I have to say that I can only speak highly of Talbot as he has been a great help to my husband and our family.
In the shadows of the night, the evening after the trial, I was allowed to join my husband with Talbot. General Pangalos accompanied us. It was an indescribable feeling to finally be able to hold Andrea in my arms again. We both cried. When I met my husband for the first time in London during the coronation celebrations for Uncle Bertie, I immediately fell in love with him. In English they call it *dotty*. I was instantly crazy about him and at that Mamaent, there in those two rooms, reunited, that feeling came over me again. I loved Andrea to death and would have done anything in the world to see him alive again. I didn't care if we had to leave Greece, if we were never allowed to return. At that Mamaent, none of that mattered, we just wanted to get away.
We got into a car provided and were driven by General Pangalos to the harbor where the British cruiser was waiting for us. There, accompanied by Talbot, we boarded the ship, which was now bound for Corfu. Our girls and the nanny had already been informed. They came to the harbor with the luggage, but I was also allowed to pack up some things and enter the house one last time. Andrea hugged his children overjoyed. Together with a lady-in-waiting, the girls' governess and the nanny, Miss Roose, we left Greece and took one last look at Mon Repos. There was also a touch of melancholy in our departure, as we assumed we would never see this place again in our lives. There were so many happy memories of the girls' childhood, of Philip's birth, that we also cried because it was our home.
We reached the port of Brindisi on the fifth of December. During the journey, Andrea had talked a lot with the captain, who now thought the world of my husband but couldn't understand how anyone could seriously want to execute such a man, who was also the father of a family. Tiny quickly became the captain's favorite because she was always up for a joke and made us forget the fear of the last few weeks for a few Mamaents. And the sailors had converted an orange crate into a crib for Philip because there was no crib available. One of the sailors said it was Philip's introduction to the customs of the British navy, which we all accepted with a laugh, because it was very cute how the little one accepted his crib straight away.
We traveled on from Brindisi to Rome. Talbot made his way to London on his own. Naturally, we thanked him for his help. He first went to see the King, who sent him on to Mama to tell her about the events in Greece and our departure. I had already mentioned several times that my mother was a very

talkative woman who usually found it difficult to let other people have their say. So Talbot went to her now. Louise was also eagerly awaiting news and Dickie was also present, as he was visiting Mama and my sister.
Before Talbot could begin to report back to Mama, she immediately seized the conversation. She said she knew that the king had used his influence to persuade Talbot to help save her son-in-law from possible execution and that a cruiser had been sent to Greece. My mother suspected that Talbot had traveled to Athens and thus fulfilled part of his mission.
The poor man started again, took a breath, but she kept talking. He had certainly been chosen because he knew Greece well and therefore also General Pangalos. It was obvious to her that Talbot had met him, but it had probably not been fruitful.
It's worth mentioning how slowly the news from Greece spread. Mama hadn't read anything in the paper yet, so she wasn't aware of Andrea's rescue, and so she kept talking, making her own remarks about what had gone wrong and, to Talbot's astonishment, barely catching her breath. You could say that she spoke to him very warmly, calmly, but still without a dot or a comma.
When she finally fell silent and Dickie took the floor, he smiled at Talbot, sighed and said to Mama that now that she had explained her view of things to Talbot in minute detail, she should finally give him the chance to tell him what had really happened.
My mother immediately apologized and listened attentively as Talbot confirmed how difficult it had been to talk to the General, but he had been successful. Then he rose to leave, but Mama was so stunned, not grasping the situation as quickly as Dickie and Louise. She immediately invited Talbot to lunch.

When we arrived in Rome, we were stranded there because we had no passports and unfortunately had to realize that, contrary to all promises, no money had been provided for us. As our accounts in Greece were frozen and we couldn't get access to our assets, we were more or less penniless. Andrea had been able to take a little money with her, but that would never be enough to support us. And he wouldn't receive a pension from his service in the Greek army either.
The British ambassador, Sir Ronald Graham, intervened on our behalf. He sent us fourteen thousand lira and arranged for us to travel on to Paris. We were accommodated in the French embassy there on December 8th and were only supposed to spend one night there before traveling on to England the next day. Talbot had promised the Greek government that he would bring Andrea and our family directly to London. However, this suddenly turned out to be more difficult than expected.

King George in England had been worried about my husband and had organized help, but he was still nervous about whether it was a good idea to let Andrea into the country as someone who had been accused and banished by a revolutionary committee. The British Prime Minister agreed with him that they should avoid allowing a member of the Greek royal family to enter England, as it could well damage the King's reputation.
And then in the *House of Commons*, the lower house of the British parliament, Commander Kenworthy asked the quite justified question as to why a British cruiser had been sent to Greece to rescue a Greek prince and his family. A Greek ship could have been used instead. This question made its way to the Foreign Office, where Miles Lampson, the advisor there, commented on it by defending the rescue, but then asked whether it would not be better if we went to Palermo to live with Tino and his family.
At that time, the king had already sent a message to Mama in which he made it clear that it would not be advantageous for us to come to England. It was simply inconvenient to take us in at that Mamaent so as not to break off diplomatic relations with Greece completely.
Parliament was convened, discussed and it was agreed that we should not be allowed to enter England.
This was not very pleasant for my mother. She was more than annoyed at the way we were being treated. She telegraphed to me in Paris that she wanted us to come to England, expressing it as her personal wish, not that of the King. She immediately contacted Lord Stamfordham, the King's private secretary, and vented her anger. She pointed out that we had lost our home, that I was her daughter and that we had no money. We were left more or less destitute with the children. Mama knew that Christo and his wife would of course support us if we asked, but she said she would take money from their accounts to help us.
You could say that Mama put all her eggs in one basket because, as she told me later, her tone was not very polite, but rather that of a resolute mother-in-law, mother and grandmother at that Mamaent. She also insinuated that rich Greeks in London had informed the government that we should not be allowed to enter the country. Of course, this was pure conjecture on her part, but she believed that the king was being influenced by people other than his ministers or members of parliament. My mother was a woman who followed her heart, especially when she thought someone was being wronged.
Lord Hardinge, the British diplomat in Paris, received a telegram from the Prime Minister in which he made it clear on behalf of the King that at the Mamaent it was considered absolutely undesirable for us to enter England. Hardinge was to do everything in his power to dissuade us and thus prevent us from doing so.

Lord Stamfordham went to see Mama and said that she underestimated the poor relationship with the Greek royal family. They had been firmly against reinstating King Constantine, but this was due to the political problems and diplomatic tensions during the First World War. As soon as parliament adjourned, which should be around the fourteenth of December, nothing would stand in the way of a possible entry.

The King was aware of his help for Andrea and had offered it without hesitation, but they were still caught in a power structure based on the *Labor Party* and the poor diplomatic relations with the Greek royal family.

A telegram had arrived from Greece in which King George II of Greece thanked the King for his help, as this might have been for him too. He asked that we be allowed to enter the country, albeit perhaps with a delay, but it had all been very painful for me and Andrea recently.

Now Talbot interceded with Hardinge in Paris, but he would not issue visas unless the Foreign Office in England agreed. Talbot was sure that the committee would take revenge on other high-ranking people in Greece if he didn't bring us to England, because this was his job and he had made this promise to General Pangalos. He was worried about the king and his wife in Tatoi, who would literally have to *pay for* any failure on his part.

So he turned to Lord Curzon. He thought the whole thing was ridiculous and said there was no reason not to let us enter the country.

Talbot made his way to Crowe in London with this statement and met him on December eleventh. He had no reservations either and Talbot began to wonder why they were playing this game with us.

We were in constant contact and it was a very difficult situation for us. We were stuck in Paris, had been promised permission to enter England and then they had to discuss whether we were wanted or not. It was very stressful to be stuck without money, without passports and I couldn't thank Talbot enough for the effort he made for us.

At last we received a promise from the King that we would be allowed to enter England on Sunday, December seventeenth, or the day after. Parliament had then adjourned on Friday and we were to be treated like any other travelers in Dover. We were to be issued with Danish passports and we would also pass through customs so as not to cause a stir.

That Sunday, Talbot was summoned to the King, who knighted him and awarded him the title and distinction of *Knight Commander of the Royal Victorian Order*, the second highest order of the British Household Order. In my opinion, Talbot was well deserving of this, and when he went to see Mama to tell her that we would soon be arriving, he felt that the award was all too justified because, as she said, he had saved a life and this could not be appreciated enough. She told him how grateful she was for everything. He once again confirmed his assessment that Andrea had only been the scapegoat for King Constantine's bad decisions.

On the seventeenth of December, we finally set foot on English soil, traveled to London and were accommodated at *the Stafford Hotel*, a five-star hotel in St. James. We arrived without causing much of a stir. Andrea took the opportunity to appear before the King himself on the nineteenth of December to thank him for his help and commitment.

When we visited Louise and Mama at Kensington Palace, the joy was of course indescribable. However, my sister immediately noticed how changed I looked. You could clearly see the strain of the last few weeks. She said I looked very tired and not as relaxed as I had been at Dickie's wedding in the summer. She knew the reasons for this, but she was still shocked to see me like this.

On the occasion of Dickie's wedding, I had another session with the artist de László to have a new portrait made. It was almost finished and Louise had already seen it. So she compared it with the way I looked now. She was sorry for what had happened to us, but we wanted to put it behind us.

Andrea and I also agreed that we didn't want to stay in London. We left Dolla and Margarita with Mama and Louise and traveled to Paris with our younger children. Mimi, the wife of Andrea's brother George, had invited us to live in a house on her spacious property in *St. Cloud*, about ten kilometers west of Paris. It was located at 5, Rue de Mont-Valérien. A gamekeeper had once lived there.

Her first offer had been rooms in her palace in Paris, but there were so many servants there and the palace was close to the exclusive Bois de Boulogne. Andrea would never have been able to support the servants there. At the same time, we would have owed Mimi a lot of rent for the rooms in the upmarket area, so we decided against it and preferred what my husband called the *shoe-size house* on Mimi's property.

Mimi, who had a so-called open marriage with George, was very wealthy, as her father was wealthy, and she cultivated a very exclusive lifestyle. She did not shy away from flirting with other men, including making eyes at George's uncle Valdemar in Denmark and turning his head, then sending his eldest son Prince Aage into a frenzy of love. I have already mentioned her affair with the French Prime Minister Aristide Briand, which she only ended in 1919.

The only bizarre thing about her was her penchant for psychoanalysis, which she practiced on herself and others as a loyal follower and friend of Freud. Mimi considered herself frigid, felt she was incapable of ever achieving sexual fulfillment, and began to publish well-known publications on the subject. She had read a study that measured the distance between the clitoris and vagina in two hundred and forty-three women and published her analysis, which stated that this distance played a role in achieving orgasm. A short distance meant that you reached orgasm quickly, two centimeters or more distance was bad. These women found it difficult to climax. The most bizarre thing, however, was an operation she had performed on herself, in which her clitoris was moved closer to her vagina. Dr. Josef Halban performed this operation on her after she had to talk him into it for a long time, and she also published this method. However, it was hardly successful in her case, so she had the operation repeated.

She also posed as a nude model for the Romanian artist Constantin Brâncuşi. His stone sculptures were often very daring. The one of Mimi, in which she called herself *Princess X*, caused a great public scandal in 1919, as this sculpture showed her as a giant bronze phallus. The artist said that it was a woman bending down, representing femininity and vanity, but the sculpture was nevertheless removed from a well-known museum because the viewer saw it as a phallus.

It was an open secret in the family that Mimi's husband was very sensitive and often shed a tear or two when he felt offended, which also happened in public. Andrea was always amused to discover that their marriage was quite interesting.

Mimi and George had two children, Peter was now fourteen years old, Eugénie twelve. They had everything a child could dream of and their mother showered them with love. George, who spent most of his time in Denmark, also loved his children very much, but he was rarely with them. Perhaps, we in the family suspected, he was ashamed of his wife, but was too attached to the beautiful Mimi to leave her.

Even though Mimi was eccentric, she never hesitated to help others and so we gladly accepted her offer to move into the house. Our two older daughters were soon to come to St. Cloud too.

My husband had also aged considerably during his imprisonment and due to the psychological strain. The uncertainty during his detention had left clear marks on his face.

I didn't want to confront him directly with questions about the last few weeks and waited to see if he wanted to talk about it himself. But he only told me once that he didn't want to say another word about it. He would get over it in time and was grateful that he could be with us again. It was a very bitter memory for him that he didn't want to keep bringing up. I understood him and so we didn't say another word about it.

I've always believed that you should always pour your heart out when you're troubled, worried or anything else, but there were certain things that you could only deal with yourself. And it was certainly difficult for Andrea to burden me or possibly the two older girls with the details. He knew how much we had worried about him.

On New Year's Eve, Andrea and I decided to travel to New York with Christo and Anastasia, who were in Paris. The children understood that their parents needed a little break and the trip was to last two months. Christo and his wife invited us and we didn't have to think twice, as we were delighted to be able to take some time out. Anastasia was getting visibly worse due to her cancer, but of course she was still hoping for the expensive doctors and their help. She didn't miss out on any treatment and tried everything to get well again. For her and Christo, the trip with us was therefore a welcome distraction from Anastasia's suffering and her worries about the future…

Epilogue

As I have been studying the members of the last Russian tsarist family around Tsar Nicholas II of Russia and his wife Tsarina Alexandra for many years, in fact since I read a book about the false Anastasia at the age of fourteen, I quickly became very familiar with the family's relatives in Hesse and England. In recent years, I have deepened my knowledge, came across Princess Alice of Greece and studied her in more detail. Not much is known about the mother of Philip, the Duke of Edinburgh, and unfortunately history usually treats her very neglected. During my research for this biography, I realized that she was unjustly overshadowed by history, as she was a truly impressive personality and now, after completing the manuscript, I could only say one thing: Thank you, Princess Alice, it was a real honour and pleasure to get to know you better!

I always prefer to let my historical personalities speak for themselves when it comes to their lives, as this is the only way to get a more intimate and deeper relationship with the person in question. They should come back to life for the duration of the reading and take you on a journey through all their experiences, negative and positive included. You should be able to empathize with what the person went through or what they enjoyed. Of course, I hope that I have succeeded in doing this, because in the case of Princess Alice in particular, it is important to be able to share certain aspects of her very long life with her in a deeper way.

Most of the photographs used in this biography were very well dated, but there were a few discrepancies and I have tried to date them correctly. If I have made a mistake of one or two years, I apologize, but sometimes it was not possible to date a photograph exactly, even after several weeks of effort and research. This applies above all to photographs from the last years of the Princess's life.

To list all the books I have read in German, English and French about the last Russian tsarist family in the attached bibliography would unfortunately go beyond the scope of this article. I have therefore listed the titles that I explicitly used for this biography, as I am familiar with many of the historical facts from years of dealing with this subject.

I would like to take this opportunity to provide some final information:

With regard to the value of the English currency and for a better understanding, I would like to add the information that one hundred English pounds around 1910 would have an equivalent value of around eleven thousand pounds in 2019. The value of twenty pounds sterling in the 1920s would be equivalent to around one thousand pounds sterling today.

In 1925, the average wage of a worker in England was around five pounds sterling. However, it is also worth noting that some salaries were paid weekly. This is to better illustrate the value of money when amounts of money are mentioned in Alice's comments.

The stolen Hessian crown jewels were worth around 2.5 million US dollars in 1946, which refers to all the jewelry. Today, this would be comparable to around 30 million US dollars.

On February 17, 1970, in the so-called *Anastasia decision*, the Federal Court of Justice ruled in the last instance that the previous judgment of the Hanseatic Higher Regional Court of Hamburg, according to which Anna Anderson had not proven that she was identical to Grand Duchess Anastasia Nikolaevna of Russia, was not objectionable on legal grounds. On October 5, 1994, it was announced that a DNA test had clearly established that Anna Anderson-Manahan could not be a descendant of the Tsarina. This was also based on the discovery of the remains of the last Tsar's family and their servants who were killed with them, although the remains of Marie and Alexei were only found a few years later. Today it is clearly proven that Tsar Nicholas II of Russia and his family were all murdered in Ekaterinburg.

Bibliography

Richard Hough (ed.), Advice to my Grand-daughter, Letters from Queen Victoria to Princess Victoria of Hesse, Simon & Schuster, New York, 1975

Barbara Hauck, Capriolen, The male friendships of the last Hessian Grand Duke Ernst Ludwig, Booy-Verlag, Beatrix van Ooyen, Bad Nauheim, 2017

Julia Gelardi, Born to rule, Granddaughters of Victoria, Queens of Europe, Headline Publishing Group, London, 2006

Katrin Boeckh, Von den Balkankriegen zum Ersten Weltkrieg, Kleinstaatenpolitik und ethnische Selbstbestimmung am Balkan, Oldenbourg Wissenschaftsverlag, Munich, 1996

Edward J. Erickson, Defeat in Detail: The Ottoman Army in the Balkans, 1912-1913, Praeger Publishers, Greenwood Publishing Group, Inc., USA, 2003

Helen Azar, In the steps of the Romanovs, Final two years of the Russian Imperial family 1916-1918, CreateSpace Independent Publishing Platform, UK, 2018

Richard C. Hall, Balkan Wars 1912-1913, Prelude to the First World War, Routledge, London, 2000

Gunnar Hering, Die politischen Parteien in Griechenland 1821-1936, Oldenbourg Wissenschaftsverlag, Munich, 1992

Marie Fürstin zu Erbach-Schönberg, Prinzessin von Battenberg, Memoiren, 1852-1923, Geschichtsblätter für den Kreis Bergstrasse, Sonderband 13, Bensheim, Verlag Laurissa, 1991, published by the Interessengemeinschaft Schönberger Vereine and the Museumsverein Bensheim in conjunction with the Arbeitsgemeinschaft der Geschichts- und Heimatvereine im Kreis Bergstrasse, third, improved edition

Deborah Cadbury, Queen Victoria`s Matchmaking, The royal marriages that shaped Europe, PublicAffairs, Hachette Book Group, NewYork, 2017
Marilyn Pfeifer Swezey, The Romanovs under house arrest, From the 1917 diary of a palace priest, The Diary of Archpriest Afanasy I. Belyaev, Holy

Trinity Publications, The Printshop of St. Job of Pochaev, Holy Trinity Monastery, Jordanville, New York, 2018

Manfred Knodt, Ernst Ludwig, Grand Duke of Hesse and by Rhine, His Life and Times, Schlapp, H. L., Darmstadt, 1978

Walter A. Büchi, Karl August Lingner, Das große Leben des Odolkönigs (1861-1916), Eine Rekonstruktion, Edition Sächsische Zeitung, Dresden, 2006

Christopher Warwick, Ella, Princess, Saint & Martyr, John Wiley & Sons, Ltd, The Atrium, England, 2006

Timothy Knatchbull, From a clear blue sky, Surviving the Mountbatten Bomb, The Random House Group Limited, London, 2009

Frances Welch, The Imperial Tea Party, Family, Politics and Betrayal: The Ill-Fated British and Russian Royal Alliance, Short Books, London, 2018

Die Vertreibung des Königs Konstantin von Griechenland, dargestellt auf Grund amtlicher Urkunden, Deutsch-Griechische Gesellschaft (ed.), J. F. Lehmanns Verlag, Munich, 1918

Ernst von Falkenhausen, Major in the Great General Staff and former military attaché at the Imperial German Legation in Athens, Die Erdrosselung Griechenlands, Ullstein-Kriegsbücher, Verlag Ullstein & Co. Berlin, Vienna, 1918

Antony Lambton, The Mountbattens, The Battenbergs and young Mountbatten, Constable and Company Limited, London, 1989

Royal romances, love that made history, booklet number 20, Lord Louis Mountbatten and Lady Edwina, Marshall Cavendish International Ltd, Hamburg, 1991

Garabed Hatscherian and Dora Sakayan, Smyrna 1922, The Diary of Garabed Hatscherian, Kitab, Klagenfurt, Vienna, 2006

Heinz A. Richter, The Greek-Turkish War 1919-1922, Peleus, Volume 72, Studies on the Archaeology and History of Greece and Cyprus, Verlag Franz Philipp Rutzen, Harrassowitz, 2016

Christopher Clark and Norbert Juraschitz, Die Schlafwandler, Wie Europa in den Ersten Weltkrieg zog, Deutsche Verlags-Anstalt, Munich, 2013

Holger Afflerbach, On a knife's edge: How the German Reich lost the First World War, C. H. Beck-Verlag, Munich, 2018

Prince Andrew of Greece, Towards Disaster, The Greek Army in Asia Minor in 1921, John Murray Publishers, London, 1930

Pavlos Tzermias, Eleftherios Venizelos' historical achievement, The path of a "white mountain man" to world fame, Sedones 13, Verlag Dr. Thomas Balistier, Moravia, 2010

Célia Bertin, The Last Bonaparte, Freud's Princess, A Life, Kore, Verlag Traute Hensch, Freiburg, 1989

In memory of the passing of H. HRH the Grand Duchess Eleonore, the Hereditary Grand Duke Georg Donatus, the Hereditary Grand Duchess Cäcilie, Prince Ludwig, Prince Alexander von Hessen, Baron Joachim Riedesel zu Eisenbach, Sister Lina Hahn, Crashed in an airplane on November 16, 1937, 3.45 p.m., near Ostend, memorial sheet, L. C. Wittich Verlag, Darmstadt, 1937

Rena Molho, The Holocaust of the Greek Jews, Studies in History and Memory,
Publisher J. H. W. Dietz Nachf., GmbH, Bonn, 2016

Christoph U. Schminck-Gustavus, Winter in Greece, War, Occupation, Shoah, 1940-1944, second edition, Wallstein Verlag, Göttingen, 2010

Martin Gilbert, The Righteous, The unsung heroes of the Holocaust, Transworld Publishers, The Random House Group Ltd, London, 2002

Mark Mazower, Greece under Hitler, Life during the German Occupation 1941-1944, S. Fischer Verlag GmbH, Frankfurt am Main, 2016
Martin Gilbert, Endlösung, Die Vertreibung und Vernichtung der Juden, Ein Atlas, revised new edition, Rowohlt Taschenbuch Verlag, Reinbek bei Hamburg, 1995

Richard Hough, Louis & Victoria, The Family History of the Mountbattens, second edition, George Weidenfeld & Nicholson Limited, London, 1984

Douglas Liversidge, The Mountbattens, From Battenberg to Windsor, Arthur Barker Limited, London, 1978

Philip Eade, Young Prince Philip, His turbulent early life, Harper Collins Publishers, London, 2012

Queen Friederike of the Hellenes, Experiences, Rainer Wunderlich Verlag, Herrmann Leins, Tübingen and Stuttgart, 1971

Janet Morgan, Edwina Mountbatten, A life of her own, Harper Collins Publishers, London, 1992

E. H. Cookridge, From Battenberg to Mountbatten, Arthur Barker Limited, London, 1966

Alden Hatch, The Mountbattens, The last royal success story, Random House, New York, 1965

Louis Wulff, M.V.O., Elizabeth and Philip, Our heiress and her consort, An authentic sketch of H.R.H. the Princess Elizabeth and Lieutenant Philip Mountbatten, R.N., Sampson Low, Marston & Co. Ltd, London, 1947

Margit Fjellman, Louise Mountbatten, Queen of Sweden, George Allen and Unwin Ltd, London, 1968

Hugo Vickers, Alice, Princess Andrew of Greece, Penguin Group, Hamish Hamilton Ltd, London, 2000

Royal Romances, Love that Made History, Issue 2, Queen Elizabeth II and Prince Philip, Marshall Cavendish International Ltd, Hamburg, 1991

George Rainbird Ltd, London (ed.), Mountbatten, Eighty years in pictures, MacMillan London Ltd, London and Basingstoke, 1979
Richard Hough, Mountbatten, An Extraordinary Life, Paul Neff Verlag, Vienna, 1980

Royal Romances, Love that Made History, Issue 20, Lord Louis Mountbatten and Lady Edwina, Marshall Cavendish Ltd, Hamburg, 1991

Brian Connell, Manifest Destiny, A study in five profiles of the rise and influence of the Mountbatten family, Prince Louis of Battenberg, Sir Ernest

Cassel, Countess Mountbatten of Burma, Earl Mountbatten of Burma, H.R.H. The Duke of Edinburgh, Cassell and Company Ltd, London, 1953

Lady Pamela Hicks, Daughter of Empire, My life as a Mountbatten, Simon & Schuster, New York, 2012

Rainer von Hessen (ed.), Joachim Horn, Alexander Jehn, Hans Sarkowicz, The Battenbergs, A European Family, Waldemar Kramer in the Verlagshaus Römerverlag GmbH, Wiesbaden, 2019

Kathy Kacer, The brave Princess and me, inspired by a true story, Second Story Press, Ontario, Canada, 2019

Movies

Eleni, by Peter Yates, 2004

The Star of India, by Gurinder Chadha, 2017

Princesse Marie, by Benoit Jaquot, 2004

The Crown, seasons 1 and 2, by Stephen Daldry, 2017 and 2018

Picture credits

The images in this books are made up of antique postcards from my own collection and press material that I have collected over the last years. Some photographs and articles were kindly made available to me by collectors, but only Marylene Marsh from New York wishes to be named.

Acknowledgments

First of all, I would like to thank the Hessian State Archives in Darmstadt, Hesse, for permission to use archive material. My special thanks goes to Dr. Rainer Maaß, who was also very helpful with some questions about the Grand Ducal Family of Hesse and by Rhine, and to Ms. Eva Haberkorn, graduate archivist and official at the Hessian State Archives.
Also to my mother Angela, who always makes herself available as the first reader and harshest critic.
I would also like to thank the historically interested collectors who talked to me about the House of Battenberg, the Grand Ducal House in Hesse and the English royal family and were also able to help me with their knowledge.

Read more historical articles by Silke Ellenbeck at DeBehr

Read the sequel volume 2 - the years 1923 to 1969

Silke Ellenbeck

In der Stille die Freiheit

Das bewegte Leben der Prinzessin Alice von Griechenland, Prinzessin von Battenberg, Mutter von Prinz Philip, Duke of Edinburgh, 1885- 1969

Band 2

Historische Romanbiografie

DeBehr

532 pages paperback, 14.95€, ISBN: 9783957537157

Australia in the middle of the 19th century. The two convicts Henry and Hagen escape from captivity on the red continent. They are soon united by their tragic fate in the Australian wilderness. A deep friendship develops. Driven by the hope of a new beginning, the two men travel through the vast, almost untouched land. Along the way, they meet other lost people whose fates are often no less tragic. But soon the cohesion of the two men is to be put to the test when a young girl enters their lives ...
Vast land and red earth - in the British colony at the end of the world, two escaped convicts fight for their fortune. A magnificent work of longing, love and hope under the endless Australian sky.

474 pages paperback, ISBN: 9783944028705

"

When I was still a little girl, I often sat on the lap of my father, Tsar Nicholas II, and told him about my dream. When I grew up, I would get married - it would have to be to a soldier - and I wanted to have lots of children, preferably twenty of them. " But that would never happen... In 1899, a third daughter was born to the Russian ruler Nicholas II. Maria, as she is called, grows up in an anachronistic court, torn between her father's autocratic policies and the people thirsting for reform. Her childhood and youth turn into an interplay of family gatherings, extensive travel, sorrow and joy, illness and what is soon to be a bourgeois family life - but it becomes apparent that this balancing act cannot last forever under the pressure of the population and the political unrest. The threat to the sheltered life behind the palace walls, the familiar security, is soon overshadowed by the impending upheavals in the country... A moving, historically based biographical novel with numerous family portraits of the time, written from the perspective of the tsar's daughter Maria.

678 pages paperback, 14.95€, ISBN: 9783957532206

A hen Princess Caroline Reuß zu Greiz walks down the aisle in Bückeburg on April 30, 1903, she is heartbroken. The marriage was more of an imperial command than a loving union. Her fiancé Grand Duke Wilhelm Ernst, like herself, frequently asked to be released from the marriage vows in the run-up to the ceremony. The young marriage between the choleric militarist Wilhelm Ernst and the artistic free thinker Caroline is correspondingly fragile. This book provides deep and honest insights into a life that is only allowed to know caritas, status and duty, into a system that relentlessly sifts out those who want to be more than just a man's wife. Her all-too-short life becomes more and more of a farce in the restrictive court and drives her into melancholy... A moving biography based on historical facts. Ellenbeck's moving biography is based on historical facts and offers a multifaceted and complex impression of Princess Caroline Reuß zu Greiz in her era. Accompanied by numerous family pictures of the time.

354 pages paperback, 12.95€, ISBN: 9783957534378

Printed in Dunstable, United Kingdom

70882955R00198